FROM SEED TO HARVEST

FROM SEED TO HARVEST

The Growth of the
Research Triangle Park

ALBERT N. LINK

PUBLISHED BY
THE RESEARCH TRIANGLE
FOUNDATION OF NORTH CAROLINA

ISBN: 0-9648051-1-1
Library of Congress Control Number: 2002101623

CONTENTS

ILLUSTRATIONS

TABLES

ACKNOWLEDGMENTS

For more than a decade I have had the privilege to be involved with the leadership of Research Triangle Park. My research on *A Generosity of Spirit: The Early History of the Research Triangle Park* began in 1990 and has culminated with this second volume. Over the years, I have come to appreciate the unselfish commitment that many have made to ensure that Research Triangle Park would be the success that it has been. These are remarkable individuals who never lost sight of the fact that they were working for the good of North Carolina. I thank them for having the confidence in me to chronicle their remarkable story.

Many individuals have been helpful in the research and preparation of this volume, but three have been exceptional. First, there is Elizabeth Aycock, whose dedication and ambassadorship to the Park for more than forty years has inspired me to persevere through archival file after archival file to make sure that this wonderful story be told completely and with passion. Second, there is Bill Little, whose involvement and leadership in Park affairs for many decades has impressed upon me how fortunate North Carolina has been to have such unselfishly committed citizens.

And there is also my wonderful wife, Carol. Her patience, support, and love over these years in seeing this project evolve, and now culminate, has been an inspiration. Carol is my friend and my companion in life, and for that and all that she has done I am forever grateful.

FOREWORD

Research Triangle Park is North Carolina's finest example of successful civic entrepreneurship. It was accomplished through more than four decades of sustained effort by a dedicated corps of the state's civic, educational, and governmental leaders. And it was accomplished without the kind of involvement of public funds that normally would have characterized such a venture begun in recent decades. While strongly supported by governors and other state officials, the Park has always been a nonprofit, nongovernmental venture.

Professor Albert N. Link recounted the origin and development of Research Triangle Park from its inception in the mid-1950s to its takeoff in 1965 in *A Generosity of Spirit: The Early History of the Research Triangle Park*. Here he continues that interesting account to the close of the twentieth century, a period of achievement for the Park in physical growth, business success, economic benefit to the state, and international reputation that would have pleased—and astounded—its founders. He measures the Park's success and identifies the reasons for it, including careful targeting of selected research-intensive industries for pursuit as prospective tenants. The individuals who established and nurtured the Park during its formative period, when success was unsure, are credited with their respective contributions. And he recounts the successful institutionalization of Park management as Luther Hodges, Archie Davis, and other early leaders (who largely managed the Park as volunteers) passed from the active scene and were followed by professional administrators.

The large commercial tenants of the Park capture chief public awareness, but Link points out that the Park is not just for large multinational companies. Among the more than one hundred current tenants, most are smaller organizations: half of the tenants have twenty or fewer employees. He also notes that more than 70 percent of the organizations in RTP are start-ups or spin-offs. RTP, with the Triangle universities, has been a platform from which the region has become one of the nation's "hot spots" for high-technology entrepreneurialism. More than a thousand technology-based start-up and spin-off companies have emerged in the Triangle area since 1970. Employment in these new companies has been estimated to exceed the number of employees in the Park.

Moreover, the establishment in or relocation to the Park of several nonprofit research and related organizations of national and international stature has been of major benefit to the Park's three sponsoring universities and also to its business tenants. Link describes each of these entities and the ways in which the Research Triangle Foundation of North Carolina (the Park's developer) has through financial and other assistance to them employed the resources gained through successful development of the Park to aid in the intellectual and cultural upbuilding of the region and the nation.

Graphs and tables show Park land acquisitions and sales by the Research Triangle Foundation and growth in the number of tenants, square footage of developed space, and Park employees. Maps illustrate the careful physical planning that has characterized the Park. A collection of sales and promotional brochures records the early concepts of the Park and approaches to tenant recruitment.

Professor Link's ably written account reminds us again of our debt to a generation of North Carolinians, now mostly gone, who wrought faithfully and fruitfully for the good of their fellow citizens in many ways—and none more valuably than in their creation of Research Triangle Park.

JOHN L. SANDERS
Member, Board of Directors,
Research Triangle Foundation of North Carolina, 1984–2001,
and professor of Public Law and Government Emeritus,
the University of North Carolina at Chapel Hill

CHAPTER 1

PLANTING THE SEEDS

Begin at the beginning . . . and go till you come to the end: then stop.
—LEWIS CARROLL

At a luncheon at the Carolina Hotel in Raleigh on September 25, 1956, North Carolina's Governor Luther H. Hodges and Robert M. Hanes, president of Wachovia Bank and Trust Company, announced to forty-five prominent business leaders in the state that the Research Triangle Committee, Inc., had been established. While most in attendance knew about the Triangle, at least in the most general of terms, this luncheon signaled to these men, and, in fact, to the citizenry of North Carolina, that it was time for the leadership of the state and universities to step forward and begin to build a foundation for the future economic growth of North Carolina.

At noon, just before the luncheon, Governor Hodges, Hanes, and Brandon P. Hodges, treasurer of North Carolina and no relation of the governor, signed the Certificate of Incorporation of Research Triangle Committee, Inc. Therein it was stated:

> The objects and purposes for which the corporation is formed are to encourage and promote the establishment of industrial research laboratories and other facilities in North Carolina primarily in, but not limited to, that geographical area or triangle formed by the Uni-

1

versity of North Carolina at Chapel Hill, North Carolina State College of Agriculture and Engineering of the University of North Carolina at Raleigh,[1] and Duke University at Durham. It is the intent and purpose of the corporation to promote the use of the research facilities of the three above-named institutions through cooperation [among][2] the three institutions and cooperation between the institutions and industrial research agencies, to bring to the attention of industry throughout the country the unique and undeveloped advantages of this State and thereby attract industrial research laboratories and other facilities to this State. It is the purpose through such activity not only to attract industrial research laboratories and facilities but to attract the establishment of industries and thereby to increase opportunities of citizens of this State for employment, and to increase the per capita income of the citizens of the State.

Few, if any, of those at the luncheon would have envisioned Research Triangle Park as it is today. With more than one hundred organizations (owners and tenants) occupying more than 17 million square feet of developed facilities and employing more than 45,000 individuals, Research Triangle Park has in forty-five years grown from a concept to a reality that is the envy of the world. Research Triangle Park today is "where the minds of the world meet,"[3] and no other park can plausibly make, much less substantiate, such a claim.

As documented in *A Generosity of Spirit: The Early History of the Research Triangle Park*, the pre-1965 growth of the Park—from concept to reality—was the result of many factors, particularly the nearby location of three preeminent research institutions and their commitment to the Park's success, the dedication and energies of corporate and state leaders, a favorable geographic location on the eastern seaboard between Atlanta and Boston, as well as good timing and good luck. Not one of these ingredients is more important than any other. The combination of these ingredients may explain the growth and prominence of Research Triangle Park among science parks in the world.

The organizational events that transpired after the September 25, 1956, luncheon are chronicled in detail in *A Generosity of Spirit*, but they are briefly summarized here so as to set the stage for the history of the growth of the Park that is told in this volume.

- In October 1956, George L. Simpson, then a professor of sociology at the University of North Carolina at Chapel Hill, assumed responsibilities as director of the Research Triangle Committee, Inc. His secretary, "partner," and friend in the development of the Park was Elizabeth J. Aycock (Simpson 1988, p. 7). Simpson and Aycock worked with leaders from the private sector, the government, and the universities to advertise the Research Triangle to research companies throughout the United States.
- A for-profit company called Pinelands was formed on September 30, 1957. It was independent of the work of the Research Triangle Committee, Inc., but had the knowledge and encouragement of the committee and the governor. Pinelands purchased or optioned more than 4,200 acres of land within what would eventually become Research Triangle Park.
- In August 1958, Governor Hodges and Robert Hanes, president of the Research Triangle Committee, asked Archibald ("Archie") K. Davis, also of Wachovia Bank and Trust, to help attract North Carolina investors for the Pinelands Company. Davis recognized that the Research Triangle had the potential to be extremely important for the future economic direction of the state, and he realized that if the Triangle was designed for public service rather than for private gain it would be much easier to raise money from corporations, institutions, and the like that were interested in serving the state of North Carolina. Thus he agreed to raise contributions (rather than solicit financial investments) upon the condition that the pledged funds would be used to acquire the Pinelands Company and pay its debt ($415,000), to finance a research institute ($500,000 est.), and to hire staff and build a main building ($250,000 est.). Figure 1 shows the portrait of Davis that hangs prominently in the Hanes Building in the Park, the home of the Research Triangle Foundation of North Carolina.
- On January 9, 1959, Governor Hodges announced at a luncheon at the Sir Walter Hotel in Raleigh that Archie Davis, on his own, had collected pledges totaling $1.425 million from across the state.[4] These funds would be used, as the contributors were promised, for two general purposes: to acquire the land assembled by the Pinelands Company and to pass control of this enterprise to the re-

Figure 1. *Archibald ("Archie") K. Davis, 1988.*

cently constituted nonprofit Research Triangle Foundation of North Carolina;[5] and to establish as a centerpiece for the Park the Research Triangle Institute for the purpose of doing contract research for business, industry, and government, as well as to construct a building to house the Foundation and Institute in the center of the Research Triangle area.[6] Governor Hodges and Robert Hanes are pictured at the January 9 luncheon in Figure 2. They are holding one of the first maps of the Triangle area.

- Chemstrand Corporation announced four months later, on May 25, 1959, its decision to locate in the Triangle, making it the Park's first major industrial tenant.[7]
- The Park slowly moved forward between 1959 and 1965. During those years, George Simpson, Elizabeth Aycock, Archie Davis, along with William C. Friday, president of the University of North Carolina, dedicated university faculty members such as William F. Little, and others, worked together to advertise the Park to industrial research corporations throughout the country and to attract their future laboratory expansion to North Carolina. (Five advertising brochures from that time are reproduced in the back of this book, starting on page 121. They include pharmaceuticals [Appendix A] chemistry [Appendix B], electronics [Appendix C], engineering [Appendix D], and forestry and forest products [Appendix E]).
- The turning point for the Park came in 1965. On January 6, Governor Terry Sanford, on his last day in office, announced that the U.S. Department of Health, Education, and Welfare had selected Research Triangle Park for its $70 million National Environmental Health Sciences Center.[8] And on April 14, Governor Dan Moore announced that IBM would locate a 600,000-square-foot research facility on four hundred acres in the Park.

The early history of Research Triangle Park, as told in *A Generosity of Spirit*, may be defined as the period from the conceptualization of the park idea in the early 1950s to the realization of that idea in 1965 when the Park became a viable organization. The early history reflects the generosity of spirit of many individuals dedicated to the Research Triangle because it was for the common good of North Carolina.

The years were not always rosy during the decade leading up to

Figure 2. *Robert M. Hanes (left) and Governor Luther H. Hodges holding one of the first maps of the Triangle area at the January 9, 1959, luncheon at the Sir Walter Hotel in Raleigh.*

1965, and indeed they were sobering at times. But the Foundation's leadership never doubted that the venture was going to be a success. As Bill Friday (1993) expressed the mood of those times: "We were saying to ourselves, well, we've made this investment, we've built this structure, we've got this property, and we've got to make this work, so where are we not doing what we need to be doing? [The early years were] a reassessment time to be sure . . . [but] there was never a time when we lost faith in the project."

When Archie Davis (1992) was asked to reflect on the early years of the Park in light of both the visible growth of the Park since 1965 and the reputation that it enjoys as the premier science park in the world, and on why it took so long for the Park idea to gel and for the Park to begin to grow, he said, "As Elizabeth [Aycock] used to remind us all, 'it's a long time from seed to harvest.' "

The seeds of the Park were described in *A Generosity of Spirit*; the following chapters document the harvest—the history of the growth of Research Triangle Park.

CHAPTER 2

PLANNING FOR GROWTH

Not a having and a resting, but a growing and a becoming
is the character of perfection ...
—MATTHEW ARNOLD

Research Triangle Park has grown beyond the expectations of those involved when the Park was envisioned and being formed. Most expected the Park to grow and to be beneficial to the state, and the Foundation planned accordingly. However, no one expected the Park to grow as dramatically as it has over the past four and a half decades.

Elizabeth Aycock recalled that she and George Simpson were in their temporary office on the upper floor at 118 West Edenton Street in downtown Raleigh (Fig. 3) late one summer afternoon in 1958. "George was in a contemplative mood," Aycock (1991) remembered: "[He] was looking out of the window and I said, 'George, how long do you think it would take [the Park] to reach . . . a population of 50,000 or 60,000?' And he said, 'fifty years . . . a hundred years.' There were no employees in the Park in 1958, but in 1999 there were about 42,000 as well as about 10,000 independent contractors."

When Bill Friday (2000) was asked about his early expectations for how the Park would grow once the concept was firmly in

Figure 3. *118 West Edenton Street, Raleigh. The first office* (upper floor) *of what would become known as the Research Triangle Foundation.*

place, he said "I don't think anyone, even in their wildest imagination, thought the Park would become what it is today. Institutions were feeling their way along day by day."

Asked how he had expected the Park to grow after the momentous events of 1965, Friday (2000) said, "We realized how important IBM was. We were committed to a research park and not a manufacturing park. IBM was a polar star, and it marked a new era of growth for North Carolina."

ACQUIRING LAND

The Pinelands Company purchased the first tract of land for the Park on September 17, 1957. This Rigsbee tract totaled 998.97 acres and was bought for $104,000. This tract was more than twice as large as any other purchased by Pinelands or by the Foundation to date.

Figure 4 shows the 7,233 acres identified by the Pinelands Company in early 1958 as potentially defining Research Triangle Park. The Rigsbee tract, in the northern portion of the Park, is labeled as tract No. 2. In 1958, Pinelands owned or had optioned 3,917 acres, and it considered, as also noted on Figure 4, another 3,316 acres as being "very desirable." Today, there are nearly 7,000 acres within the Park's eight-mile by two-mile boundaries.

Figure 5 shows the growth in the acquisition of Park land from 1957 through 2000.[1] In 1957, 1,333 acres were acquired, and another 2,651 acres were added to the Park in 1958. By the end of that year the Park owned more than half of its present 6,971 acres.

Figure 6, which is based on Figure 5, illustrates the cumulative number of acres acquired.[2] The cumulative number of acres increased noticeably in 1957 and 1958 but was relatively flat during the 1960s and 1970s. Then in the early 1980s more than 1,000 acres of land were acquired. Since that time, the size (in acres) of the Park has been relatively stable.

Figure 7 shows both the cumulative number of acres acquired (Fig. 6) and the cumulative number of acres sold or donated for development.[3] The events of 1965, as summarized in Chapter 1 and detailed in A Generosity of Spirit, are clearly reflected by the steep

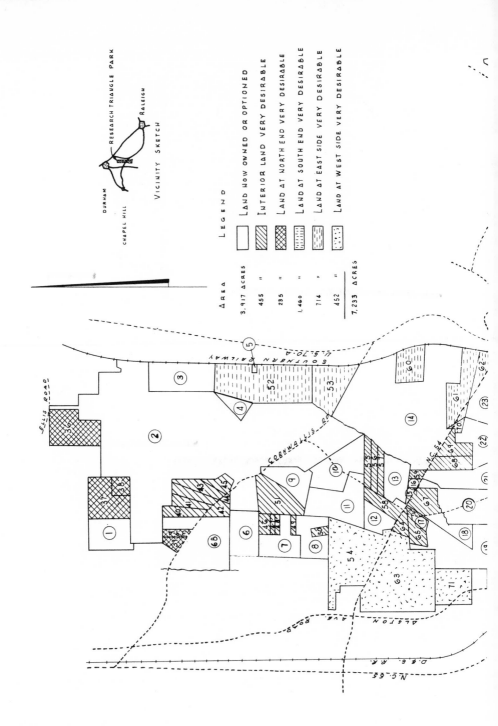

LEGEND

		AREA
Land now owned or optioned		3,917 ACRES
Interior land very desirable		455 "
Land at north end very desirable		235 "
Land at south end very desirable		1,460 "
Land at east side very desirable		714 "
Land at west side very desirable		452 "
		7,233 ACRES

VICINITY SKETCH

DURHAM
RESEARCH TRIANGLE PARK
CHAPEL HILL
RALEIGH

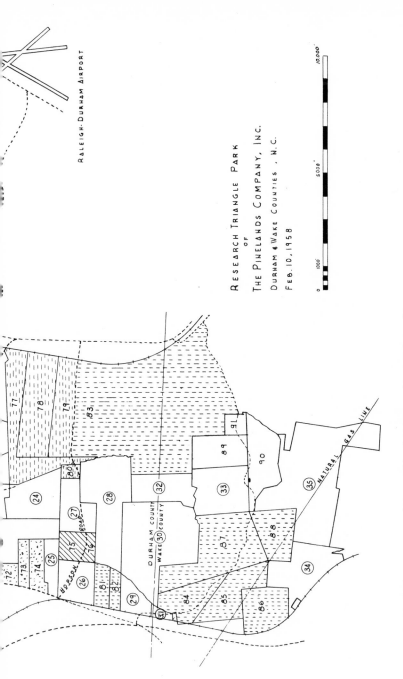

RESEARCH TRIANGLE PARK
OF
THE PINELANDS COMPANY, INC.
DURHAM & WAKE COUNTIES, N.C.
FEB. 10, 1958

RALEIGH-DURHAM AIRPORT

NATURAL GAS LINE

DURHAM COUNTY
WAKE COUNTY

Figure 4. *Detailed planning map of tracts of land in Research Triangle Park, 1958.*

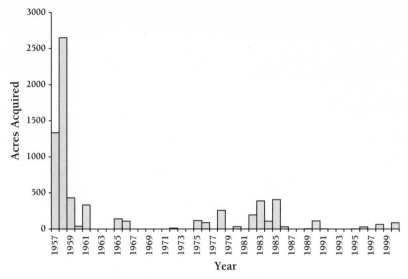

Figure 5. *Acres acquired by the Research Triangle Foundation, 1957–2000.* Source: *Research Triangle Foundation.*

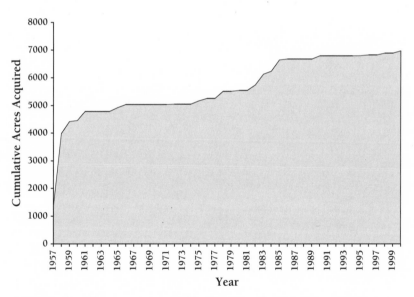

Figure 6. *Cumulative acres acquired by the Research Triangle Foundation, 1957–2000.* Source: *Research Triangle Foundation.*

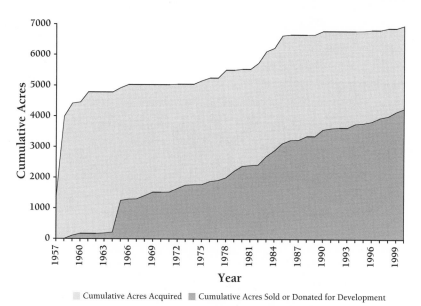

Figure 7. *Cumulative acres acquired and sold or donated for development by the Research Triangle Foundation, 1957–2000. Source: Research Triangle Foundation.*

increase on the graph. In 1965, for example, IBM purchased 401 acres, Beaunit Corporation purchased 100 acres, and the Foundation donated 509 acres for the National Environmental Health Sciences Center. In 1965 alone, 1,035 acres, or 21 percent of the Park's then 4,927 acres, were either sold or donated for development.

The Research Triangle Foundation's first map of the Park area, produced and distributed in 1965, is reproduced as Figure 8. Clearly labeled on the map (reading north to south) are the Chemstrand Research Center, International Business Machine Corporation (IBM), Beaunit, and the National Environmental Health Sciences Center. In the center of the Park is the Research Triangle Institute, occupying almost a third of the 128 acres reserved by the Foundation for the Institute. The legend on the figure notes the Forestry Sciences Laboratory being on twenty-seven acres of donated land, the American Association of Textile Chemists and Colorists on ten acres, and the North Carolina Board of Science and Technology on nine acres.

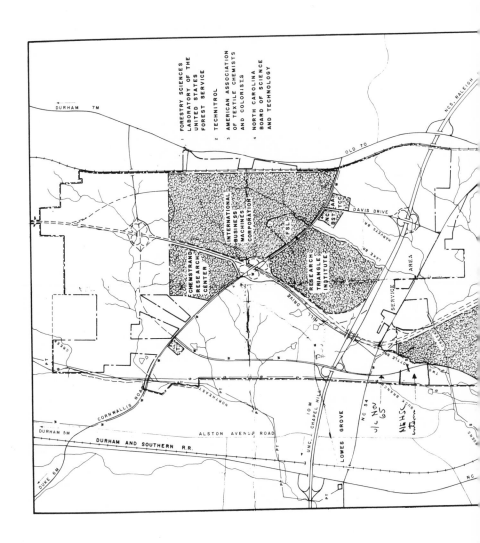

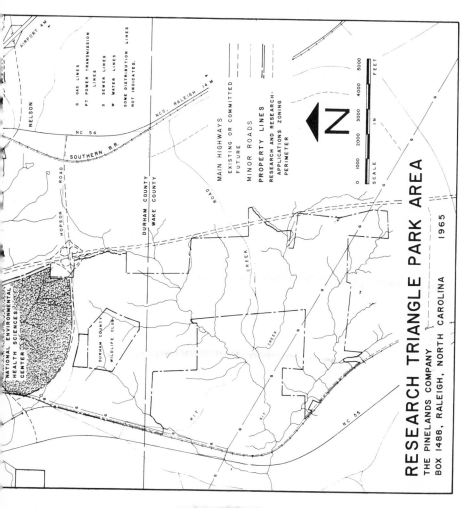

Figure 8. *First map of the Research Triangle Park area, 1965.*

The acreage growth illustrated in the preceding section, and discussed in more detail in the following chapter, came about as a result of diligent planning by the Foundation's leaders and took place within carefully constructed bounds. Pearson H. Stewart, a professional planner, was hired by the Research Triangle Committee on January 18, 1958, to be the assistant director to George Simpson. Stewart prepared the first planning map of the Park (Fig. 9), and other planning materials necessary for orderly growth. The contents of the early planning documents, such as covenants and restrictions and zoning restrictions, are discussed in *A Generosity of Spirit*. Several documents that are not in that volume, yet are historically important, are discussed below.

The Research Triangle Regional Planning Commission was created by an Act of the General Assembly of North Carolina in 1959.[4] Section 1 of that Act states: "There is hereby created the Research Triangle Regional Planning Commission.[5] The Commission shall have the duty of studying total development in counties surrounding the Research Triangle Park, to prepare, in collaboration with counties and municipalities in the area, plans which will promote the orderly and economical development of the area, to submit such plans to county, municipal, state and federal agencies having jurisdiction in the area, and to encourage the execution of such plans." The "area" referred to in Section 1 is the tri-county region of Durham, Orange, and Wake counties, and commissioners are appointed from Chapel Hill, Durham, and Raleigh.

The planning commission is not a part of the Research Triangle organization, but Stewart and the Foundation realized early on that the future growth and success of the Park would depend in large measure on the geographical, economic, and social attractiveness of the surrounding countryside, including the nearby cities. And with the expectation that the Park would grow, sound regional planning would be needed if the attendant problems of urban expansion were to be handled.

Stewart prepared two booklets with this in mind. The first, *Maps, Data: The Research Triangle, North Carolina* (see Appendix G), was

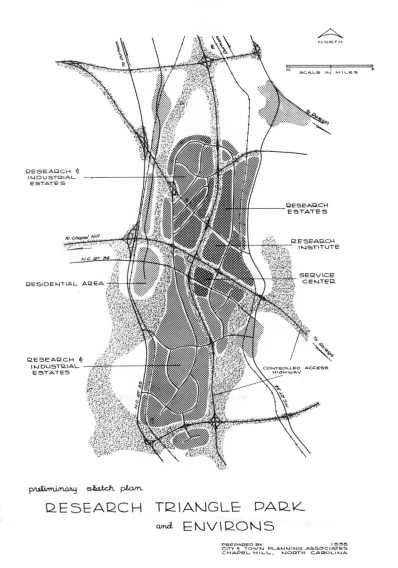

Figure 9. *First planning map of the Research Triangle Park, 1958. Courtesy of Robert N. Anderson, Jr., City Planning & Architects Associates.*

Figure 10. *Ground breaking of the Chemstrand Research Center, 1960.*
Left to right: *James P. Shea (Research Triangle Foundation), William Crabtree,
Earl Harrison, L. C. Gattett, Berg Newhouse, and Walter Smith (Chemstrand).*

published in 1959. The purpose of this publicity was to define the
Triangle region—especially important for those companies located
outside of North Carolina—to highlight the three universities, and to
provide demographic comparisons of the Triangle region to the rest
of the nation.

In September 1960, with the assistance of the Department of
City and Regional Planning of the University of North Carolina at
Chapel Hill, *Guides for the Research Triangle of North Carolina* (see
Appendix H) was published and distributed. At the time that this
second booklet was prepared, several Park buildings were under
construction: the Research Triangle Foundation building, to be dedicated as the Robert M. Hanes Memorial Building on December 16,
1960 (a copy of the dedication brochure is in Appendix I), and the
Chemstrand Research Center (Fig. 10).

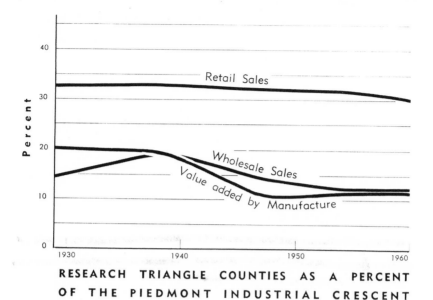

RESEARCH TRIANGLE COUNTIES AS A PERCENT
OF THE PIEDMONT INDUSTRIAL CRESCENT

Figure 11. *Relative historical growth of the three Research Triangle counties.*
Source: Guides for the Research Triangle of North Carolina *(1960), page 6.*

Simpson and Stewart displayed exceptional foresight in this particular planning exercise. *Guides for the Research Triangle of North Carolina* sets forth a general view of the requirements that will be generated by the future urban development of the Triangle area, given the anticipated growth of the Park, and alternative possibilities for meeting these requirements.

While much of the planning material in *Guides for the Research Triangle of North Carolina* will be of selected interest, one aspect of the booklet is immensely important to the historical understanding of why the Park was started. As stated in *Guides* (p. 5):

> One of the ways of measuring the economic health of a region is to compare its economy with that of a larger region within which it is contained. [Fig. 11] shows the relationship between the three-county Research Triangle Region and the Piedmont Industrial Crescent [which includes Greensboro and Charlotte, among other areas southwest of the Triangle]. Three economic indices, value added by manufacture, retail sales, and wholesale sales, have been

used for comparative purposes. As can be seen, the relationship of economic activity in the Triangle to that in the Piedmont Crescent differs somewhat for each index. All three indices show a decline in the region's position in relation to the Crescent from 1929 until 1947. The Triangle Region's relative position began to improve with respect to value added by manufacture in 1947, and with respect to wholesale sales in 1954 [and it has continued to improve].

Given these within-state trends, as well as the more pervasive post–World War II decline in the state's traditional industries of furniture, textiles, and tobacco, it is understandable why the state's leaders were anxious to find ways to improve the economic condition of North Carolina and to build an economy suitable for the employment of the talented graduates from the three sister institutions.

Shortly after the publication of *Guides for the Research Triangle of North Carolina*, Stewart prepared (in July 1961) a report entitled "Research Triangle Region Population Estimates 1970–1980" for the Research Triangle Regional Planning Commission. It is of planning interest to understand how conscientious the Foundation was in its formative years in anticipating the growth of the Park and the growth of the surrounding areas; it is of historical interest to note that the growth of the Park and its spillover growth to the broader Triangle area was forecast in 1961, in some dimensions quite accurately. In other dimensions growth has surpassed all expectations.

Stewart wrote in his 1961 report (pp. 10, 13–14):

> Since the Research Triangle Park became a reality the question of its influence upon the population of the region has been raised many times. The logical course is to turn to Park officials and ask how many people the Park will employ by, say, 1980.
>
> A logical answer must recognize [that there are] several unknown factors. . . .
>
> It is useful to consider Park capacity, however, since it is a partial measure of eventual expectations of the area. The Park and the Triangle effort are continuing enterprises, not to be disbanded at an arbitrary year of, say, 1980.
>
> Park capacity can be estimated as follows:

Total area, Research Triangle Park	5,000 acres
Less 12.3% for rights-of-way and 14.43% of area now developed or committed for service areas, etc.	1,337 acres
Owned area to be developed	3,663 acres
Maximum amount of development area (10%) that may be devoted to floor space[6]	366.3 acres or 15,956,028 sq. ft.
Maximum number of employees at average of 200 sq. ft. per employee	79,780
Average number of employees per acre of floor space	218

Each research worker will represent—on the average—about 4.25 other individuals (members of their families, and workers attracted by the creation of new jobs). It follows that the total number of people added to the region would be approximately 339,065.

In 2000 the Park was still not at full capacity. As shown in Figure 7, by the end of 2000, 4,262 acres had been sold or donated for development out of a total of 6,971 acres.[7] Two hundred and seventy-five acres had been sold or donated for infrastructure and another 113 acres set aside for natural area preserves. The Park's development has been clearly greater than the 5,000 acres forecast by Stewart and others. However, the point to emphasize is not the accuracy of the forecast but rather that the Foundation was perceptive in its vision to plan and artful in its effort to anticipate potential future problems and then to insulate the future of the Park against them.

ENSURING GROWTH

During the 1980s, the City of Durham was extraordinarily aggressive in its annexation strategy in an effort to increase its tax base. Anticipating the possibility of annexation,[8] Archie Davis worked with Representative Casper Holroyd of Raleigh and Senator Bill Staton of Sanford and others to introduce on May 13, 1985, House Bill 926, "An Act to Authorize Counties to Establish Research and Production Service Districts." Therein is the definition of a research and production service district:

> The [B]oard of [C]ommissioners may by resolution establish a research and production service district for any area of the county that, at the time the resolution is adopted, meets the following standards:
>
> (1) All real property in the district is being used for or is subject to covenants that limit its use to research or scientifically oriented production or for associated commercial or institutional purposes.
>
> (2) The district contains at least 4,000 acres.
>
> (3) The district includes research and production facilities that in combination employ at least 5,000 persons.
>
> (4) All real property located in the district was at one time or is currently owned by a nonprofit corporation, which developed or is developing the property as a research and production park.
>
> (5) A petition requesting creation of the district signed by at least fifty percent (50%) of the owners of real property in the district who own at least fifty percent (50%) of total area of the real property in the district has been presented to the board of commissioners.

The bill also states that "No municipality may annex any or all of the following described territory in Durham or Wake Counties," and the metes and bounds of Research Triangle Park are described clearly and explicitly. The bill's final reading was on June 10, 1985, and it was then ratified on June 24.[9]

This effort by Davis ensured that the Park, and the Park alone, would have full control over its economic future.

CHAPTER 3

MEASURING THE PARK'S GROWTH

The Park will never be more crowded than it is today . . .
—GOVERNOR LUTHER H. HODGES (OCTOBER 1969)

The growth of Research Triangle Park can be measured in different ways. In the previous chapter, growth was dimensioned in terms of acres acquired and then acres sold or donated for development. However, there are other measures that chronicle the history of the Park's growth.

BRICKS AND MORTAR

Consider facilities. Figure 12 illustrates the total square footage of construction in the Park.[1] Of course, the visible upward trend in square footage is due to at least three factors: more organizations entering the Park over time, the Park increasing its acreage to accommodate growth, and existing Park organizations expanding. Figure 13 shows the ground breaking for the American Association of Textile Chemists and Colorists in 1964, Figure 14 shows the ground breaking of the original IBM facility in 1966, and Figure 15 shows the dedication of Burroughs Wellcome in 1972. Clearly, the Park has grown.

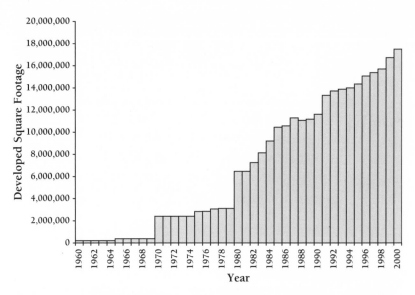

Figure 12. *Developed square footage by Research Triangle Park tenants by year,* *1960–2000.* Source: *Research Triangle Foundation.* Note: *Data were collected by* *the Foundation in 1960, 1965, 1970, 1975, 1980, and annually beginning in* *1982. Developed square footage is assumed to have remained constant during the* *initial five-year intervals. No data were collected by the Foundation in 1981; de-* *veloped square footage in that year is assumed to have been the same as in 1980.*

More complete statistical information is available on the number of organizations in the Park, by year, than on developed square footage. The organizations in the Park can be broadly segmented into research organizations and service organizations. The growth in each is illustrated in Figure 16.

The first service organization in the Park was the Triangle Service Center, Inc., a for-profit subsidiary of the Research Triangle Foundation created to develop commercial and leased facilities (discussed in Chapter 5). Clearly from Figure 16, the growth of research organizations and service organizations has been positive, although the rate of growth in each was relatively greater during the 1970s and early 1980s compared to the 1990s (recalling that there were fewer acres sold for development in the 1990s than in the earlier years, as was illustrated in Figure 7 in Chapter 2).

Figure 13. *Ground breaking for the American Association of Textile Chemists and Colorists, 1964. Archie K. Davis is at the podium.*

Figure 14. *Ground breaking of the original IBM facility, 1966.* Left to right: *Governor Luther H. Hodges, Karl W. Knapland (IBM), and George Watts Hill.*

PARK EMPLOYMENT

Figure 17 illustrates the growth in the number of Park employees since 1959. As would be expected, that growth lags the growth in the number of new organizations in the Park each year. Whereas the number of new organizations increased most rapidly in the 1970s and early 1980s, employee growth was most rapid during the late 1970s and late 1980s.[2]

By the end of 2000, 67 percent of the Park's land was "in use."[3] Of the total 6,971 acres within the Park, 4,262 had been sold for

Figure 15. *Dedication of Burroughs Wellcome, 1972.*

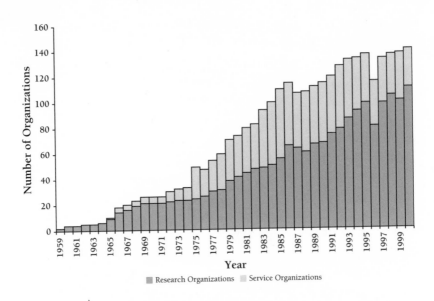

Figure 16. *Number of research organizations* (lower darker bars) *and service organizations* (upper lighter bars) in *Research Triangle Park by Year, 1995–2000.* Source: *Research Triangle Foundation.*

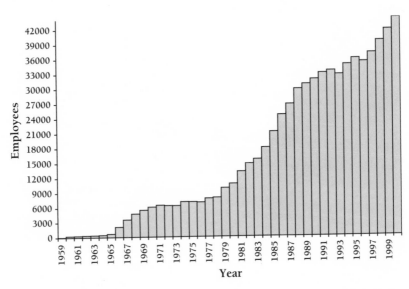

Figure 17. *Number of employees in Research Triangle Park by year, 1959–2000.* Source: *Research Triangle Foundation.*

development, 275 had been sold or donated for infrastructure, and 113 had been set aside for natural area preserves. Based on this percentage and the number of employees in the Park at the end of 2000 (44,000 employees), the Park may likely have close to 66,000 employees when it is completely occupied.[4]

CHAPTER 4

HAS THE PARK BEEN A SUCCESS?

Success depends on three things: who says it, what he says, how he says it.
—JOHN, VISCOUNT MORLEY OF BLACKBURN

Has Research Triangle Park been a success? Based on the growth patterns illustrated and discussed in Chapters 2 and 3, this question may appear rhetorical. How could one possibly reflect on the previous growth trends and reach any conclusion other than that Research Triangle Park has been an overwhelming success?

WHAT PEOPLE HAVE SAID

Many notable individuals in government, industry, and academia throughout the state have been saying for a long time that Research Triangle Park has been an unprecedented success. Governor James B. Hunt, Jr., speaking on March 3, 1999, at the Archie K. Davis Awards Luncheon to celebrate the fortieth anniversary of Research Triangle Park,[1] recalled that before the Park's beginnings North Carolina had been a very poor state. In fact, although Governor Hunt did not delve into the related statistics, data from the U.S. Department of Commerce show that in 1950 only five states in the nation had a per capita income level lower than North Carolina's, and by 1952 only two states did—Arkansas and Mississippi. The most recent data available from the Department of Commerce rank North Carolina thirty-first among the fifty states in personal income per capita. According to Governor Hunt: "Since this Research Triangle Park was created, primarily because of it, we have gone up . . . among the states in per capita income. . . . The success of this Park, and the way we have worked on it together, has emboldened us in North Carolina. We now believe we can do big things."

Bill Friday (2000), reflecting on his many years of involvement with the Park both in his capacity as former president of the University of North Carolina and as an active and involved citizen of the state, responded when asked if the Park had been successful: "The Park has been a phenomenal success. It has raised the level of involvement of the corporate, political, and academic communities to work together as brothers to build something great. Research Triangle Park is the most significant economic and political manifestation of will in the state in the last century."

Marcus E. Hobbs, former provost, dean of the graduate school, professor of chemistry at Duke University, and one of several individuals instrumental in Duke's active involvement in the Park concept as early as 1954, said in a speech delivered at Florida State University in 1982 (Hobbs 1982),[2] "[T]he Triangle concept . . . of a great industrial research center in North Carolina . . . is now duly justified and finally established and the Research Triangle Park by any reasonable standard is a resounding success." Bill Little, a former professor of chemistry at the University of North Carolina at Chapel Hill and perhaps the one faculty member from all of the three sister universities who has been most intimately involved in the leadership of the Park over the past forty-five years, addressed the International Congress of Pacific Basin [Chemistry] Societies (Little 1989) in 1989: "While there has been no economic study of the impact of the Research Triangle on the overall economy of the State, there is anecdotal as well as some hard evidence that it has brought economic diversification, added science-based industries, and . . . expanded employment opportunities."

Figure 18 shows Little and Hobbs with George Herbert, former president of the Research Triangle Institute, at an RTI function in 1979.

Figure 18. Left to right: *William F. Little (University of North Carolina at Chapel Hill), George Herbert (Research Triangle Institute), and Marcus E. Hobbs (Duke University) at an RTI function, 1979.*

Figure 19. Left to right: *Members of the Research Triangle Institute board. Ferebee Taylor (University of North Carolina at Chapel Hill), Vivian Stannett (North Carolina State University), Louis C. Stephens, Jr. (Pilot Life Insurance Company), and Joab L. Thomas (North Carolina State University) at a Research Triangle Institute board meeting, 1976.*

Louis C. Stephens, Jr. (2000), former chairman of the Research Triangle Foundation's board (Fig.19), said that "the Park has been a tremendous success. It opened a new dimension for the state of North Carolina by sponsoring interested businesses and employment opportunities."

In 1986, *The Leader*, a publication dedicated to Park activities, published several special issues on the early history of the Park. The issues contained the reflections of key individuals who envisioned and guided the Park through its formative years. For example, in response to an interview question, "Has the Park become what the early leaders . . . thought it could become?" Elizabeth Aycock acknowledged that it had (*The Leader* 1986): "I believe it has achieved that goal. I think it has probably been reached more quickly than they thought possible. George Simpson said this [Park] was not meant to be an overnight success."

CRITERIA FOR MEASURING SUCCESS

The impressions and opinions noted above clearly indicate that these active and influential leaders in the Park's growth believe that the Park has indeed been a success. But to reach a definite conclusion on such an important issue one must reflect not only on measured growth in terms of acres and employees but also on the goals and purposes for founding the Park. By so doing, success can then be defined systematically in terms of whether those original goals and purposes have been met.

The goals and purposes of the Park—as manifested in the Certificate of Incorporation of Research Triangle Committee, Inc., in 1956, which became, by charter amendment, the Certificate of Incorporation of the Research Triangle Foundation of North Carolina on December 28, 1958—through cooperation among the three sister universities and between the universities and industrial research agencies, are to

- "attract industrial research laboratories and facilities" to North Carolina,

- "increase opportunities of citizens [of North Carolina] for employment," and
- "increase the per capita income of the citizens of the State."

Figure 16 in Chapter 3 illustrates that "industrial research laboratories and facilities" have over time been attracted to the state. Before 1959 there were no major industrial research laboratories in North Carolina. And, in fact, the majority of the tenants in the Park are new. According to Little (2000a), more than 70 percent of the tenants listed in the Park's *Owners and Tenants Directory* are start-ups. Figure 17 in Chapter 3 illustrates the employment growth that is associated with all such organizations.

However, as to the second purpose of the Park, one might reasonably ask, Has the growth in the Park also been associated with an increase in the standard of living throughout the state?

Governor Hunt's comments at the fortieth anniversary of Research Triangle Park make explicit his belief that the Park has been directly responsible for the improved economic conditions of the citizens of North Carolina. As well, James O. Roberson, president of the Research Triangle Foundation since 1988, noted in a recent television documentary about the Park (Research Triangle Park 1999) that "nearly every county in the state has someone contributing products or services to the companies in the Park."   *area Served.*

Little (2000a) has documented more than 1,000 technology-based start-up companies in the Triangle counties since 1970 (those still in existence), more than 150 of which are directly traceable to Park companies and nearly one hundred traceable to the Triangle universities. Employment in these start-ups exceeds employment within the Park. These start-ups not only provide immediate employment opportunities for North Carolinians but also have demonstrated the potential to influence the state's economic growth in the future as they grow and possibly act as magnets for related organizations to move into the area.

It is well known that technological change is the most important economic factor that causes economic growth and improved

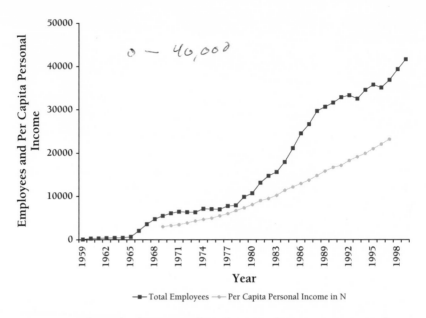

0 — 40,000

Figure 20. *Relationship between Park employees and per capita income in the state, 1969–1997.* Source: *State Bureau of Economic Analysis.*

standards of living. This is true not only at the national level but also at the regional level. Since the mid-1950s the technology base of the state's economy has increased, but that of the Triangle region has soared. As documented by Hammer, Siler, George Associates (1999), the percentage of workers in technology-based industries in North Carolina grew greater than the national average between 1956 and 1995: 179 percent compared to 56 percent. And the percentage of workers in the Triangle increased 215 percent over those years.

Certainly the Park has affected the growth of the state, and in turn that growth has acted as a stimulus for even greater growth in the Park.

Regarding the third purpose of the Park, increased per capita income, Figure 20 suggests a definite relationship between Park growth and "the per capita income of the citizens of the State." Per capita income in the state increased steadily from 1969 through 1997.[3] Growth over time in per capita income mirrors closely the growth in the number of total Park employees; in the post-1980 pe-

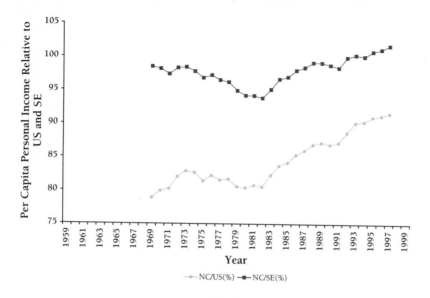

Figure 21. Relative per capita personal income in North Carolina, 1969–1997. Source: State Bureau of Economic Analysis.

riod the number of employees in the Park increased more rapidly than per capita income in the state,[4] but still the relationship between the two trends remains visually evident and, in the view of Governor Hunt, causal. In other words, as the Park grows so does the state. This symbiosis is due to the fact that many industries have been established throughout the state to support the activities of the Park companies, and as those companies do well, so does the supporting cast.

Figure 21 illustrates how well the North Carolina economy has done relative to the rest of the United States in terms of personal income per capita, and in particular how well it has done relative to the southeastern states. Since 1981, the standard of living of North Carolinians has increased dramatically relative to that of citizens in other southeastern states and especially relative to the rest of the nation. With reference again to Figure 20, the total number of employees in the Park also began to increase rapidly in the post-1980 period, thus reinforcing Governor Hunt's contentions.

As Bill Friday recalled, this two-way relationship is precisely what Archie Davis had envisioned. He saw the Research Triangle

Park enterprise as "the economic force that was going to make North Carolina change" (Research Triangle Park 1999).

Therefore, if one considers whether Research Triangle Park has been a success from the perspective of fulfilling its stated purposes, the answer is obviously yes. New industrial research laboratories and facilities have entered the state, and with them has come increased employment opportunities not only in the Triangle but also, as Jim Roberson pointed out, throughout the state. And the standard of living enjoyed by the citizens of North Carolina has increased in both absolute terms (Fig. 20) and in relative terms (Fig. 21). Finally, inter-institutional cooperation through TUCASI (see Chapter 7) is yet another measure of the Park's success.

It is important to emphasize the *statewide* scope of the three purposes to which the Park was started: to diversify the state's industrial economic base thereby increasing employment opportunities and raising overall standards of living. Not by coincidence, those individuals and organizations that in December 1958 pledged their contributions to Archie Davis in support of the Park idea because it was important for North Carolina represented the state as a whole. More than 25 percent of the $1.425 million initially raised by Davis came from Winston-Salem, nearly 12 percent came from Charlotte, 11 percent from Raleigh, nearly 9 percent from Durham, almost 5 percent from Greensboro, and many other sizeable donations came from as far west as Canton and as far east as Elizabeth City (Foundation archives). The citizenry of North Carolina came forth to invest in the future of their state.

Given that the Park has been successful by so many measures, the next logical question to ask is, Why?

CHAPTER 5

WHY HAS THE PARK BEEN
A SUCCESS? A FIRST LOOK

The secret of success is constancy to purpose.
—BENJAMIN DISRAELI

There are several reasons Research Triangle Park has been successful. Three are immediately obvious—dedicated people, three outstanding universities, and a world-class research institute—but people and universities are two important, yet somewhat incomplete, explanations for why the Park has grown as it has and, more important, for explaining what makes the Park unique. A third answer to the question, Why has the Park been a success?, is discussed in Chapter 6.

DEDICATED PEOPLE

People, and the generosity of spirit they exhibited for the good of the state, are important reasons the Park concept became a reality with the early location of the Research Triangle Institute (RTI) and Chemstrand Corporation—the Park's "anchors" (Little 1993) —in 1959, and then with IBM and the National Institute of Environmental Health Sciences in 1965.

Table 1 Chairmen of the Research Triangle Foundation Board

Chairman	Tenure
Robert M. Hanes	1959
Gordon M. Gray	1959–1965
Luther B. Hodges	1965–1972
Milton E. Harrington	1972–1973
Hugh G. Chatham	1974–1978
Archibald K. Davis	1978–1987
Louis C. Stephens, Jr.	1988–1992
John F. McNair, III	1993–2000
David L. Ward, Jr.	2001–present

Table 2 Presidents of the Research Triangle Foundation

President	Tenure
Archibald K. Davis	1959–1981
Fred A. Coe, Jr.	1982–1984
Robert Leak	1984–1988
John T. Caldwell (interim)	1988
James O. Roberson	1988–present

It is logical to look toward people, meaning both the public-sector and private-sector leadership in the Park in the post-1965 period, for a similar explanation of why the Park prospered. Consider the leadership of the Research Triangle Foundation as selectively noted in Tables 1 and 2. Louis Stephens (2000) was asked to reflect on how leadership contributed to the ongoing growth and development of the Park: "The Park is the realization of the dreams of its founders. [Subsequent leaders] continued to cooperate effectively with the universities. The Park [and its leaders] made people stretch. The people of North Carolina had a greater vision than without the Park."

Governor Hunt (Research Triangle Foundation 1999) emphasized the importance of people to the success of the Park, but in his perceptive view the body of contributing individuals is, indeed, broader than those in a visible leadership position on the Research

Triangle Foundation's board, although the board consists of university and public sector representatives. According to Governor Hunt, "The secret [of the Park's success] is the relationships between those people who teach, those people who do research, and the public and the private sector and those of us in government."

The Triangle Service Center

In the early 1960s—well before the defining events of 1965, described in detail in *A Generosity of Spirit*, when the U.S. Department of Health, Education, and Welfare selected the Park for its National Environmental Health Services Center (in January 1965) and when IBM decided to locate a research facility on 400 acres within the Park (in April 1965)—Archie Davis realized the importance of the "Foundation having income in perpetuity when all of the land is sold" (Aycock 1999). As this idea jelled, he along with Pearson Stewart and Ned E. Huffman, the Foundation's executive vice president, envisioned a service center within the Park that would be a wholly owned, for-profit subsidiary of the Foundation.

It was fortunate that Davis, Stewart, and Huffman were as forward looking on this matter as they were because their vision greatly assisted the transition into the Park of the National Environmental Health Sciences Center, known today as the National Institute of Environmental Health Sciences. The minutes from the Foundation's semiannual meeting of its directors on May 18, 1965, record that G. Akers Moore, Jr., Foundation vice president and president of the service center, stated to the group that "it seemed advisable to organize a wholly owned subsidiary corporation to be incorporated as the 'Triangle Service Center, Inc.' to develop the appropriate 100-acre service area that had long been programmed for the Triangle Park." He commented that " . . . the land might be leased to some developer who would build a motel, bank building, post office, shops, etc. on the property, the ground rent to be income to the Research Triangle Foundation."

On June 16, 1965, the Triangle Service Center, Inc., was incorporated by Thomas W. Alexander, treasurer of the Foundation, G. Akers Moore, and Archie Davis. As written in the Articles of Incorporation, the purposes for which the corporation was organized were: "to own, lease, rent, sell, mortgage, encumber and develop real estate; to build, construct, own and lease buildings of all kinds; and to engage in the general business of developing, owning and maintaining shopping centers and service centers in the Research Triangle Park."

At the November 10, 1965, board meeting, Luther Hodges announced that the Foundation would deed approximately ninety-two acres for development into a service center.[1] Interim buildings to lease to the National Environmental Health Sciences Center would be built on another fifty-two acres. The board expected to borrow about $1.3 million to construct these buildings.[2] Then, on December 30, 1965, the Foundation transferred by gift 509.2 acres of land to the U.S. government for the National Environmental Health Sciences Center.[3]

Regarding the development of the service center, the board agreed to enter into an agreement with Nello L. Teer Company to develop the center under a long-term land lease.[4] A U.S. post office and the Governors Inn were opened in 1972. The Governors Inn was the first hotel to be constructed between Chapel Hill, Durham, and Raleigh.

Roads and Rails

While the above example of the Triangle Service Center well illustrates the forward-looking leadership in the Park and the ability of that leadership to follow through quickly and effectively on ideas, not all future needs of the Park were met with such efficiency. Consider the matter of roads.

At the time of the January 1959 luncheon at the Sir Walter Hotel in Raleigh, when the Research Triangle Foundation was announced (see Chapter 1), N.C. Highway 54 and Cornwallis Road (not shown in Figure 22) were the only roads within the Park; both were two lanes. As shown on the planning map in Figure 22, N.C. Highway 54 and the nearby N.C. 55 and old U.S. Highway 70 were also two-lane roads. The North-South Freeway was being planned at that time, as was the East-West Freeway, known today as I-40 (Fig. 23).

Stewart demonstrated time and time again during his tenure as the Foundation's vice president his ability to anticipate the needs of

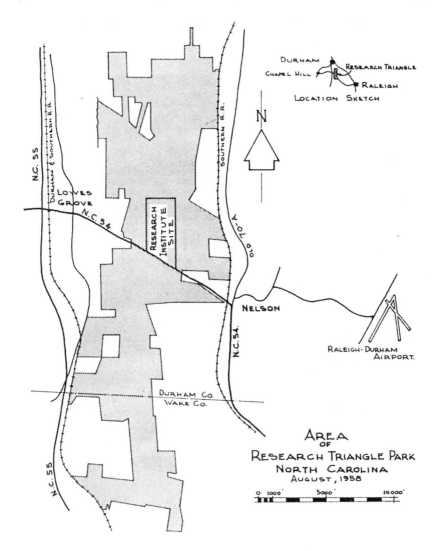

Figure 22. *Planning map of the Research Triangle Park area, 1958.*

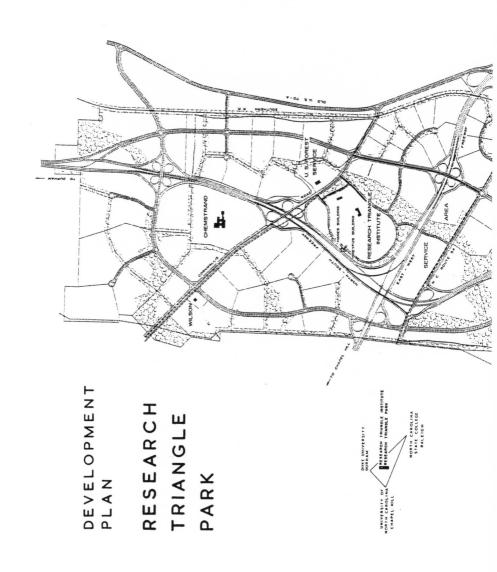

DEVELOPMENT
PLAN

RESEARCH
TRIANGLE
PARK

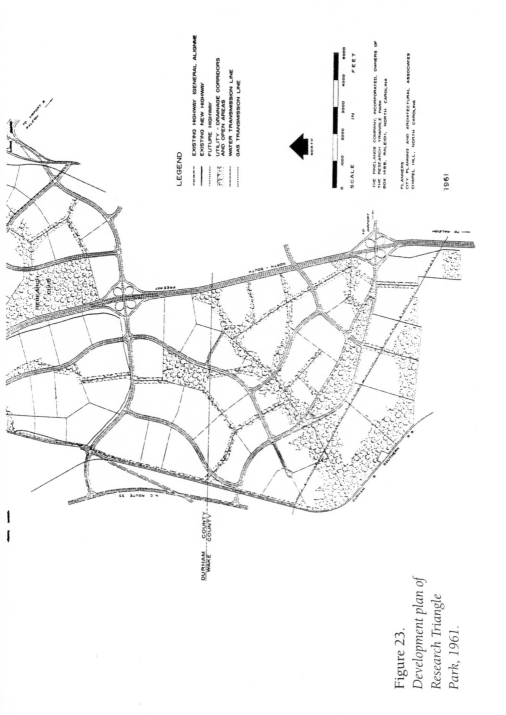

Figure 23.
Development plan of
Research Triangle
Park, 1961.

Figure 24. *Robert Leak (left) and Pearson Stewart at the Research Triangle Foundation, 1986.*

the Park and to set in motion plans to meet those needs (Fig. 24). According to Stewart (2000), "Although we planned ahead and had the full and generous support of the state, we recognized that we were always playing catch up in [road] construction."

At the April 22, 1967, dedication of IBM's research facility, Governor Dan Moore, in a good spirited way, acknowledged that even from the beginning there were transportation problems in the Park (*The Leader* April 26, 1967, p. 3): "Ladies and gentleman and all you friends of Highway 54. It is still on schedule. I've never appeared at any dedication where there was not a highway [a]waiting completion." Related discussions on that day were also reported as (*The Leader* April 26, 1967, p. 4): "There was a bit of good-natured joshing back and forth during the ceremony about the expansion of Highway 54 which goes through Research Triangle Park from Raleigh to Chapel Hill." Although the state had promised IBM a new road before it selected Research Triangle Park, Thomas J. Watson, Jr., chairman of the board of IBM, "took the high road," so to speak, and remarked during his press conference about the decision to locate in the Park (*The Leader* April 26, 1967, p. 4): "All I know is the country was beautiful between here and the airport. . . . The dogwood was beautiful." Although the Foundation's leadership, as well as the state's, were running behind on their commitments to Park transportation, sometimes they were ahead of the curve. Luther Hodges recalled his involvement with an IBM representative who came to the Park early on to investigate it as a possible location (*The Leader* April 26, 1967, p. 4): "'We may need a railroad siding,'" the IBM man said. And I asked if 30 minutes would be too long for an answer. He didn't know I had foreseen the question."

From then until now, transportation has been a point of contention. A *Leader* article appearing on May 31, 1967, (p. 1), quoted Huffman as saying, "The roads are way behind. . . . We didn't prespend the money on roads . . . but now we desperately need them." In 1967, about 25 percent of the Park's land had been sold or donated for development. The state's Department of Transportation was behind then and has remained so ever since.

Later that year, on October 11, 1967, the *The Leader* ran a headline, "Traffic Nears Peak in RTP." While the Park has certainly changed over the thirty plus years from this understatement of what is now known to be the case, the problems associated with congestion have not. This is not to disparage the important role people had in planning for the Park's transportation infrastructure but rather to emphasize that the traffic situation has never kept pace with the ever-changing RTP.

Governor Hunt, reflecting on the history of congestion in the Park at its fortieth anniversary luncheon, coined a perceptive maxim: "We can't simply pave our way out of congestion." Much in the tradition of the bold thinkers who have long been associated with the Park, he described as a possible solution to the congestion problem a Triangle transit system that relies on light commuter rail transportation.

The men described in this chapter, and those with whom they worked both as members of the Research Triangle Foundation's board and as contributors to the public sector, are one important explanation of why the Park has been such a success. Without such leadership, and the cooperation that leadership brings in solving problems, the Park would certainly not have prospered as it has.

THREE OUTSTANDING UNIVERSITIES

The three sister universities,[5] Duke University, North Carolina State University at Raleigh, and the University of North Carolina at Chapel Hill frame the Research Triangle, and collectively they have been a magnet not only for attracting research organizations to the Park but also for keeping them there.

Governor Hunt reminded the audience at the fortieth anniversary luncheon that the success of Research Triangle Park has been based generally on the people of North Carolina and specifically on "the strengths of our [three] great universities." This is not a new theme. Governor Hodges emphasized the importance of the three sister institutions more than thirty years ago in an interview with the The Leader (July 3, 1968): "If the Research Triangle has a secret weapon, it is these universities. . . . Neither the idea for the Research Triangle nor the Triangle as it exists today would have been possible without the universities and their interest, involvement, continued cooperation and support."

Governor Hunt is not the only person to single out the role of the universities in attracting research companies to the Park. Drawing upon information collected during an interview with Bill Little, the Triangle Business Journal reported in January 1999:

> Research-oriented businesses move to the area to take advantage of cutting-edge academic research and a large pool of highly skilled technicians coming from universities.
>
> As a result, more top research faculty are attracted to the universities because they want to be where the research is. The schools and businesses identify mutual needs and work to support them.
>
> Top industry scientists strengthen university departments in unusual specialties by becoming adjunct professors. And university professors bolster scientific corporations' knowledge through consulting. And the companies send their employees to get

M.B.A.s at the universities to help prepare the business leaders of tomorrow.

The cycle has created a complex relationship between corporate residents of Research Triangle Park and Duke University, North Carolina State University and the University of North Carolina at Chapel Hill.

Little, along with Governor Hunt and others addressing those attending the fortieth anniversary luncheon, was specific about the explicit contributions the universities have made to Park tenants. Of primary importance to the tenants are the students who graduate from the three sister institutions. In 1998, nearly one fourth of the professionals hired by Park tenants came from one of the three Triangle universities, and the majority of those professionals held undergraduate degrees. Of secondary importance to Park tenants is the availability of the Triangle universities to train their employees.

Of course, the universities also benefit from being juxtaposed to the research companies in the Park. Between 1994 and 1998, Park tenants sponsored nearly $130 million in research at the three universities. And in 1998, more than 350 Park scientists held adjunct appointments at one or another of the institutions.

Over the years, the universities and the Park tenants have become partners in growth in several dimensions. Not only have the Park tenants looked to the universities for bright scientists, but also they have shared research relationships (Fig. 25). To illustrate by example, Charles Putman, senior vice president of Duke University, noted (Research Triangle Foundation 1999) that "the Glaxo and Duke relationship with Alzheimer's, I think, is a classic model of where the ideas and concepts that were developed at Duke are now being converted into products, both diagnostic and therapeutic, that are going to make an impact on the disease."

Molly Corbett Broad, president of the University of North Carolina, also described a similar symbiotic relationship between the University of North Carolina and the Duke medical schools and pharmaceutical companies in the Park (Research Triangle Foundation 1999): "As managed health care begins to impact the ability of the schools of medicine to generate revenues from patient services, it is possible for some of that skill to be directed to perform clinical

Figure 25. Left to right: *Gene Addesso (IBM), Allen Eberhardt (IMSEI), Richard Daugherty (IBM), Larry Monteith (North Carolina State University), Leon Henderson (IBM). IBM developed a robotic system and donated it to the Integrated Manufacturing Systems Engineering Institute (IMSEI) at North Carolina State University in 1986 (Daugherty 2000).*

Figure 26. *Paul M. Gross (left) and William F. Little at a Research Triangle Institute board meeting, 1975.*

trials [for Park companies] and to generate the kinds of revenue to be reinvested back into the laboratories and instrumentation in the schools of medicine." President Broad went on to say that the Park still remains "an area of enormous potential."

A WORLD-CLASS RESEARCH INSTITUTE

As documented in Charles X. Larrabee's *Many Missions* (1992), Paul M. Gross, vice president of Duke University during the initial stages of the Park's planning, fathered the idea for a research institute in the Park (Fig. 26). Gross's thinking was that an institute was needed in the Park's planning in the early years (late 1950s and early 1960s) to keep faculty interested in the general concept. And according to Elizabeth Aycock (1991), an institute was important because it was a visible and tangible sign to corporate leaders that *the Research Triangle planners had enough faith in the concept to establish first their own facility* [author's emphasis].

The Research Triangle Institute was incorporated as a nonprofit organization on December 29, 1958, and on January 9, 1959, the members of its board elected George Watts Hill as chairman (Table 3). George R. Herbert was hired as president in December 1958 and remained president until 1989 (Table 4).

Table 3 Chairmen of the Research Triangle Institute Board

Chairman	Tenure
George Watts Hill	1959–1993
Earl Johnson, Jr.	1993–present

Table 4 Presidents of the Research Triangle Institute

President	Tenure
George R. Herbert	1958–1989
F. Thomas Wooten	1989–1998
Alvin M. Cruze (interim)	1998–1999
Victoria Franchetti Haynes	1999–present

In 2000, RTI, with more than 1,800 employees, performed more than $200 million dollars in contracted research, and it continues to interact with faculty from the three sister institutions on numerous research projects. This start-up organization is the fifth largest organization in the Park.

CHAPTER 6

WHY HAS THE PARK BEEN A SUCCESS? A SECOND LOOK

The greatness of art is not to find what is common but what is unique.
—ISAAC BASHEVIS SINGER

Research Triangle Park is a success, but has it been an unparalleled success? Or has the Park's record of growth been much like that of all the other science parks in the United States?

If it is the case that the record of growth of the Park is similar to the record of growth of other research and science parks, that is very impressive and important to document since one of the explicit purposes of the Park was economic growth.

In 1998, the Research Triangle Foundation commissioned an assessment of the impact of Research Triangle Park on the region and the state. The study concluded convincingly that the Park has indeed had a measurable economic impact on both. In particular (Hammer, Siler, George Associates 1999):

- It is estimated that more than $87.1 million is spent each year in Park vicinity businesses by Park employees on work trips. These expenditures generate annual sales taxes of $5.2 million.
- It is estimated that the real and personal property located in the Park is nearly $2 billion with a tax yield of more than $17 million.

- The positive impact of the Park in the state outside of the Triangle counties has also been very important as evidenced by manufacturing facility development directly related to the research activity of Park tenants.
- Park entities and their employees have strengthened the community fabric and quality of life. Companies have adopted public schools, donated computers and other equipment, contributed generously to major civic projects, supported educational initiatives, and encouraged their employees to become involved in their communities and the central city problems.
- The image of the state has been substantially improved because of the Research Triangle Park experience.

COMPARING RESEARCH TRIANGLE PARK
TO OTHER U.S. SCIENCE PARKS

In 1998, the Association of University Related Research Parks (AURRP) published its *Worldwide Research & Science Park Directory 1998*. The directory contains information about every member research and science park in the United States, including relevant information for approximating the rate of growth of those parks. Specifically, the directory reports the year that each park was founded, its present acreage, its number of employees, and its number of buildings.

The directory is careful to note (AURRP 1998, p. 2):

> The definition of a research or science park differs almost as widely as the individual parks themselves. However, the research and science park concept generally includes three components:
> - real estate development
> - organizational program of activities for technology transfer
> - partnership between academic institutions, government and the private sector.

For purposes of the illustrations in this chapter, AURRP's definition of a research or science park is not questioned, and thus the characteristics of parks throughout the United States are assumed to be comparable.

AURRP collected information on 137 research and science

Table 5 Oldest Research and Science Parks

Park	City	State	Year Established
Stanford Research Park	Stanford	Calif.	1951
Cornell Business & Technology Park	Ithaca	N.Y.	1952
University Research Park (originally Swearingen Research Park)	Norman	Okla.	1957
Research Triangle Park	**Research Triangle**	N.C.	1959
Purdue Research Park	West Lafayette	Ind.	1960

parks in the United States in 1998. Parks that were begun in 1990 or more recently are not considered for comparison to Research Triangle Park. Excluding the newer parks for this comparative analysis is not without logic. The topic investigated in this chapter using the AURRP's data relates to the prominence of Research Triangle Park among all research and science parks in this country. One hallmark of the Park is that it has survived the test of time. Because parks come and go, a ten-year survival window was used, although one might reasonably argue that a longer time period would be more appropriate. The oldest five U.S. parks are listed in Table 5.

Tables 6 through 8 list the largest five parks in the United States, where size is defined in three ways: by acreage, employees, and buildings.[1] Each of these size measures is a meaningful characterization of a park's absolute size. In terms of acreage and employees, Research Triangle Park dominantly ranks first (Tables 6 and 7), and it ranks second to Stanford Research Park in terms of number of buildings (Table 8). Collectively these size measures indicate the prominence of Research Triangle Park among its sister research and science locations.

Because parks differ in terms of their age, meaning the number of years since being formed, Tables 6 through 8 are not appropriate by themselves for comparing the growth of parks over time, and growth is one indicator of the success of a park. Table 9 lists the

Table 6 Largest Research and Science Parks,
by 1998 Acquired Acres (rounded)

Park	City	State	Year Established	Acquired Acres
Research Triangle Park	**Research Triangle**	N.C.	**1959**	**6,800**
Cummings Research Park	Huntsville	Ala.	1962	3,800
University Research Park	Charlotte	N.C.	1968	3,200
Princeton Forrestal Center	Princeton	N.J.	1974	2,150
The Woodlands Research Forest	The Woodlands	Tex.	1984	2,000

Table 7 Largest Research and Science Parks,
by 1998 Employees (rounded)

Park	City	State	Year Established	Employees
Research Triangle Park	**Research Triangle**	N.C.	**1959**	**37,000**
Cummings Research Park	Huntsville	Ala.	1962	26,000
Stanford Research Park	Stanford	Calif.	1951	26,000
MetroTech	Brooklyn	N.Y.	1986	18,000
University Research Park	Charlotte	N.C.	1968	18,000

Table 8 Largest Research and Science Parks, by 1998 Buildings

Park	City	State	Year Established	Buildings
Stanford Research Park	Stanford	Calif.	1951	165
Research Triangle Park	**Research Triangle**	N.C.	**1959**	**102**
Cummings Research Park	Huntsville	Ala.	1962	95
University of Pittsburgh Applied Research Center	Pittsburgh	Pa.	1986	55
Princeton Forrestal Center	Princeton	N.J.	1974	40

Table 9 Largest Research and Science Parks,
by 1998 Acres Acquired per Year

Park	City	State	Year Established	Acres Acquired per Year
Research Triangle Park	**Research Triangle**	N.C.	1959	174.36
The Woodlands Research Forest	The Woodlands	Tex.	1984	142.86
Oakland Technology Park	Auburn Hills	Mich.	1983	120.00
Texas Research Park	San Antonio	Tex.	1987	112.36
University Research Park	Charlotte	N.C.	1968	106.67

Table 10 Largest Research and Science Parks,
by 1998 Employees per Year

Park	City	State	Year Established	Employees per Year
MetroTech	Brooklyn	N.Y.	1986	1,500.00
Research Triangle Park	**Research Triangle**	N.C.	1959	948.72
Cummings ResearchPark	Huntsville	Ala.	1962	722.22
University Research Park	Charlotte	N.C.	1968	600.00
Stanford Research Park	Stanford	Calif.	1951	553.19

five largest parks in terms of their relative size, as measured in acres per year in operation. Research Triangle Park ranks first. In terms of employees per year, as shown in Table 10, Research Triangle Park ranks second. In terms of buildings per year, the Park ranks fourth (Table 11).

However—and this is the point of emphasis—Research Triangle Park is the *only* research or science park that ranks among the largest and most successfully growing parks in the nation, if not the world, in terms of *all* the growth measures considered. No other park is present in *every* one of the tables.

Table 11 Largest Research and Science Parks,
by 1998 Buildings per Year

Park	City	State	Year Established	Buildings per Year
University of Pittsburgh Applied Research Center	Pittsburgh	Pa.	1986	4.58
Stanford Research Park	Stanford	Calif.	1951	3.51
Cummings Research Park	Huntsville	Ala.	1962	2.64
Research Triangle Park	Research Triangle	N.C.	1959	2.62
OREAD WEST Corporate & Research Park	Lawrence	Kans.	1987	1.73

THE PROMINENCE OF RESEARCH TRIANGLE PARK

What accounts for the prominence of Research Triangle Park? Dedicated people? Certainly there are numerous examples over the years of a generosity of spirit shown by the state's leaders. However, it could be interpreted as presumptuous to posit that the private-sector, public-sector, and university leaders in North Carolina, as accomplished as they are, are unrivaled by leaders in any other state. When the Park was formed, North Carolina ranked unfavorably among states in terms of per capita income, so it may be the case that North Carolina's leaders were more motivated than the leaders in other states in their efforts to ensure a diversified and growing economy. However, such a proposition, while intuitive, cannot easily be proven. However, to emphasize that intuitiveness, it should be noted that North Carolina was the first state to form a state symphony (in the 1930s) and a state art museum (in the 1950s). In addition, North Carolina's leadership established the nation's first school of performing arts, the first residential school in science and mathematics, and a Board of Science and Technology (to build a science and technology infrastructure in the state) (Aycock 2000, Little 2000a).

The other prominent parks listed in the tables, such as Stanford Research Park, Cummings Research Park, and the Forrestal Center at Princeton, are juxtaposed to eminent universities such as Stanford University and Princeton University, as well as to such significant research institutes as the NASA research laboratories in Huntsville, Alabama, and the David Sarnoff Research Center in Princeton. In this regard, these parks, as well as most of the parks in the tables, have a research infrastructure to draw upon—just as the Research Triangle Park does through its three universities and the Research Triangle Institute—for complementary research resources to attract and retain companies.

According to Richard Daugherty (1998), former vice president of worldwide manufacturing and senior state executive at IBM, "IBM gets its core competencies from the universities. N.C. State is the largest single provider of students to IBM."

As the epigram at the beginning of this chapter reminds us, the measurable "greatness" of Research Triangle Park lies not in "what is common but what is unique." And there is one unique aspect of the infrastructure of the Park unrivaled by any park in this country, and that is TUCASI.[2]

CHAPTER 7

TUCASI: A "PARK" WITHIN A PARK

An empty bag cannot stand upright.
—BENJAMIN FRANKLIN

As written in the September 25, 1956, Certificate of Incorporation of Research Triangle Committee, Inc.: "It is the intent and purpose of the corporation to promote the use of the research facilities of the [University of North Carolina at Chapel Hill, North Carolina State College of Agriculture and Engineering of the University of North Carolina at Raleigh, and Duke University at Durham] . . . through cooperation [among][1] the three institutions and cooperation between the institutions and industrial research agencies . . . "

Also written in the Certificate about the Committee: "The corporation is a non-profit, benevolent, charitable, and educational corporation and has no capital stock. Upon the dissolution of this corporation, all assets of the corporation shall be divided equally among the University of North Carolina at Chapel Hill, North Carolina State College of Agriculture and Engineering of the University of North Carolina at Raleigh, and Duke University at Durham, to be used by such institutions for the purposes for which said institutions were founded."

In a charter amendment dated December 23, 1958, the name of the corporation was changed from the Research Triangle Committee,

Inc., to the Research Triangle Foundation of North Carolina, Inc. On May 18, 1960, again by charter amendment, there were minor changes to the wording of the statement of purpose. However, there has never been a change in the statement regarding the distribution of assets upon the dissolution of the corporation, and this fact underscores the intended and observed strength of the relationship between the Park and the three sister institutions. In addition, the by-laws of the Foundation, initially approved on January 2, 1959, are explicit about university representation on the Foundation's board. The universities are represented by eight individuals:

president of the Consolidated University of North Carolina
president of Duke University
two trustees of the Consolidated University of North Carolina
two trustees of Duke University
one other appointee of the president of the Consolidated University of North Carolina
one other appointee of the president of Duke University

A HOME FOR THE UNIVERSITIES

In early 1974, Archie Davis, in his role as president of the Foundation, charged the leadership of the University of North Carolina and Duke University—President William Friday and President Terry Sanford, respectively—to ensure the presence of the three Triangle universities in the Park. As Davis explained (Caldwell 1982, p. 2):[2] "One of these days the Research Triangle Park will have liquidated all of its land holdings. It would be a shame . . . for the principal beneficiaries of the Park—the universities—not to have some land in the Park for their own use. . . . [I]f the Foundation should make available a hundred acres or so to the universities jointly, what would you do with it? Think about it [speaking to President Friday and President Sanford] and see what you can propose to the Board of Directors of the Foundation."

Friday and Sanford, in response to this charge and with respect to the wisdom and foresightedness of Davis, solicited suggestions from each of their campuses first through the formation of an informal study group and then through a more formal committee.[3] Based on the recommendation of Davis, this study group/committee would have three representatives from each of the three campuses, three representatives from the Foundation, and President Friday serving as chairman.[4] The group was informally known as the Committee of 13.

What emerged from this study committee was the suggestion to use the offered Park land to house one or more research centers. The committee presented a report entitled "A Proposal to the Research Triangle Foundation" to the board of directors of the Foundation on May 13, 1975. Six possible centers, or joint ventures as the report so referred, were proposed, some of which had been previously developed by one campus or another.[5] Each of the proposals is interesting from an academic perspective and all are listed below. It is also interesting from an historical planning perspective how the university-dominated committee put into a broad context its charge (Committee of 13 1975, pp. 4–5):

> Success creates its own problems. Among people who recognize the importance of the Park, there is some concern about problems they see on the horizon. These problems are a result of the success of the Park itself and its continued and projected rapid development. It appears now that the Park has reached a point in its development where new laboratories and other installations are likely to be constructed in the Park at an accelerated rate, and the remaining land in the Park may be fully committed at a date considerably earlier than might have been dreamed when the Park first became a reality.[6] There could be an increasing problem from this point in controlling the quantity and quality of this expansion.
>
> It is apparent, with the growth of the Park and the creation of new and expanded industrial structures, that the influence and central role of the universities is diminishing relative to the magnitude of what is happening in the Park. To the extent that this is true, the universities may not be able to take advantage of opportunities that have been afforded in the past for interaction with Park organizations, and Park organizations will be deprived of the level of interaction with the universities that was previously enjoyed. Something could also be lost in the level of interinstitutional cooperation among the universities. *Increased university*

presence in the Park will be required if the character of the whole Research Triangle concept is to be preserved [emphasis added].

The Committee of 13 proposed the following six centers:

1) *Center for the Study of Transnational Problems* This center was motivated by the following premise:

> In brief, we live today in a complex and interdependent world, and the economic and social well being of North Carolina is linked to intelligent and informed responses of its citizens to an intricate mosaic of transnational and trans-disciplinary relationships. The State of North Carolina can make an important contribution to its future generations if it will begin now to mobilize the rich intellectual resources available to it to attack the major problem areas and to educate and train North Carolinians to function effectively in this new milieu.

2 *Triangle East Asian Center* This center was patterned after a proposal previously submitted to the Office of Education by the three sister institutions for training the state's public school teachers who are involved in teaching non-Western studies:

> It would be of great service to the citizens of the state if serious study were made of alternative strategies that might be followed in our state in coping with or taking advantage of some of the transnational issues. New approaches, new ways of thinking about our interaction with the rest of the world, imaginative and useful strategies can surely emerge from a center dedicated to focusing our combined efforts on these matters.

It was proposed that this cooperative venture become a focal point of the Triangle Universities Center for Advanced Studies (see below).

3 *National Humanities Center* The proposal for this center was relatively more focused than the two above:

> The project we are planning and working on is called the National Humanities Center. We think of it as an autonomous institution, although it will have to be located near a major university and

will have to make arrangements to have some of that university's resources available to it. The Center itself will consist of forty to fifty Fellows invited each for one year. There will also be a small administration and supporting staff.

The major purpose of the Center is to act as a focus for clarifying the functions, improving the quality, and influencing the direction of humanistic studies in America today. One important means of achieving these ends is to break down the boundaries that artificially separate the various humanistic disciplines and perpetuate the extreme fragmentation, specialization, and trivialization that characterize so large a part of the academic world today. The humanities must be brought out of the isolation in which they currently exist. That isolation is a double one. The various humanistic disciplines remain largely isolated from one another. And the humanistic disciplines as a whole remain generally isolated from the social and natural sciences.

The National Humanities Center will aim to demonstrate that such isolation is both unnecessary for and harmful to the pursuit of intellectual inquiry into important issues of human affairs.

Center for Productivity Enhancement This center was previously proposed in January 1975 to the administration at North Carolina State University by the faculty of the Department of Industrial Engineering and the Industrial Extension Service. Like the proposed National Humanities Center, this center proposal was very well focused. The proposed productivity center follows from the perspective that:

> . . . productivity is a matter of national concern. . . . There is a substantial need to stimulate productivity growth through new methods and technology. . . . Committee hearings have been conducted and federal legislation is pending on the creation of a National Productivity Center. Such a center would encourage (a) adoption of new technology, (b) dissemination of information, and (c) improvement of methods, techniques, systems, equipment, and devices. It is proposed that NCSU embark on a path leading toward formation of a North Carolina Productivity Center to perform similar functions at the state level.

6. *A Specialized Triangle Universities Optical Center*   The premise of this center is that the construction of a facility for electron microscope installations would:

> ... create an almost unique capability for a large number of scientists in many fields in all three universities to achieve leadership in discoveries in medical and biological sciences, solid state physics, energy research, textile science, the study of surfaces and the study of the molecular basis for failure of materials.

At this time there were only six such facilities in the country.

7. *National Academy for Science and Technology Applications*   The proposed center was based on the proposition that there is a need for a new discipline or expertise.

> This discipline [of science and technology applications] would concentrate on integrating the knowledge that is being generated by existing disciplines so that the broad aggregate problems of society can be attacked. ... [There would be] three basic program areas very closely related. These would include:
> (1) distinguished scholar's program
> (2) team research program
> (3) interaction of science and society program
> These three program elements should be viewed as a loosely coordinated continuum leading from basic research to decision-making.

Also stated in the report of the Committee of 13 (p. 9):

> In the face of the rapid allocation of land in the Research Triangle Park to existing and new research organizations and with a recognition, based on experience, that multi-university joint undertakings will be increasingly important to the Triangle Universities in the future, it is critically important to preserve the option of the Triangle Universities to develop in the Park programs of mutual value to the universities and to the overall Park development. The basic need at this time is to provide for this option in terms of land resources.
>   It is proposed that 100 or more acres of land be set aside by the Research Triangle Foundation and dedicated to future use by

the three Triangle Universities for cooperative programs. While the present economic climate for the three universities is not appropriate for instituting immediately any one of the above listed projects, the time is at hand when land could be conveyed to the three universities, and a significant effort could be devoted to planning for its use.

Inevitably, such an acreage reserved for use by the three universities would accommodate a number of buildings and centers that would constitute a "*campus*" [emphasis added], possibly to be known as the Triangle Universities Center for Advanced Studies. The first step the universities should take would be the development of a rational plan for the implementation of this concept. This would include a plan for land and facilities development as well as governance of the overall program. A planning body made up of representatives of the three Triangle Universities should be established as soon as the land is acquired.

The proposal stated that the planning committee would submit a report to "the administrative officials of the three universities and of the Research Triangle Park" by June 1976. In that plan would be, among other planning and organizational recommendations, a structure for a "Center for Advanced Studies." In particular, the components of the forthcoming report would include the following:

1. physical and/or land use plans
2. organizational structure for the Center for Advanced Studies
3. draft of a charter
4. set of by-laws
5. research agenda
6. program staffing
7. facility requirements
8. a detailed strategy for securing funds for the capital and operating costs of the Center
9. plans for affiliated programs

TRIANGLE UNIVERSITIES CENTER FOR ADVANCED STUDIES, INC.

During the Executive Committee meeting of the Foundation on May 14, 1975, Archie Davis moved, in response to the planning committee's proposal for this, that the Foundation authorize $25,000 for a committee to study and plan for a Center for Advanced Studies, and that it authorize an additional $25,000 when needed and when the committee's report was received. He also moved that land in the Park be set aside. The amount of land later transferred was 120 acres.

In response, as requested by Davis, President Friday submitted a letter dated May 22, 1975, to the Research Triangle Foundation: "Please regard this letter as a formal request for $50,000 to further develop plans for the Center as described in the proposal. Special attention will be given to plans for the utilization of a parcel of land of 100 or more acres in support of the Center."

This letter was signed by President Friday and President Sanford, Chancellor N. Ferebee Taylor of the University of North Carolina at Chapel Hill, and Chancellor John T. Caldwell of North Carolina State University at Raleigh.[7]

Independent of the specific work of the planning committee, although faculty on all campuses knew about the committee's agenda, C. Hugh Holman of the Department of English at the University of North Carolina at Chapel Hill brought to President Friday's attention the possibility of having the proposed National Institute for the Humanities locate in Research Triangle Park.[8] Holman was aware that the American Academy of Arts and Sciences in Boston was in the process of seeking a location for a National Humanities Center.[9] Holman brought this to the attention of Friday, who informed Davis. The September 4, 1975, minutes of the Executive Committee of the Research Triangle Foundation record that Davis reported that "an 'Institute for Humanities' might be persuaded to locate in the Triangle Park, that 15 acres . . . might be made available as a site, that the University of Texas had offered land and $5 million but had been turned down, that Pennsylvania and Michigan were trying to get the Institute with its proposed $13 million of funding."

Davis suggested that the Institute would "be a fantastic resource, a positive identification and within the broader context of a major institute." In a letter to President Friday dated September 30, 1975, Holman emphasized the broad-based potential of a humanities center within the Park:

I would like to describe to you, if I may, the benefits which will accrue to higher education in North Carolina and, in particular, to departments of English, History, Modern Languages, Classics, Philosophy, and the Fine Arts in our colleges and universities, if we are fortunate enough to have the proposed National Institute for the Humanities located in Research Triangle Park.

As you know, the idea for a National Institute for the Humanities originated with a group of humanists who are members of the American Academy of Arts and Sciences and who have been fellows at the Center for Advanced Study in the Behavioral Sciences at Palo Alto, California. Among the people in this planning group are Professor Morton Bloomfield, of the Department of English at Harvard University, Professor Steven Marcus, of the Department of English at Columbia University, Professor Henry Nash Smith, of the American Studies Program at the University of California at Berkeley, Professor Meyer H. Abrams, of the Department of English of Cornell University, and a number of other distinguished scholars in various fields of the humanities. These people believe that the humanities are not being taught or advanced at an appropriate level in American colleges and universities; and they believe further that humanists are failing to relate the essential qualities and important truths of their disciplines to the problems which confront the world. Their idea is to create an institute with pleasant surroundings to which annually some forty to fifty of the most brilliant and most promising scholars in the various humanistic disciplines can come together to pursue their own research and at the same time to be associated on an informal basis with a group of other humanists of true distinction. The productivity that has been generated by the Center for Advanced Studies at Palo Alto and by the Institute for Advanced Studies at Princeton indicates that assembling outstanding scholars to pursue their own interests free of other responsibilities and in an environment bringing them in informal contact with many of the outstanding scholars in the humanities does, indeed, produce great results. . . .

One of the immeasurable but very real benefits to be gained by all educational institutions, as well as the State itself, from the location of the National Institute for the Humanities in the Research Triangle Park would be the great distinction which it would bring to the State and to the region. . . .

I am sure that you join me in hoping that we can succeed in persuading the people selecting a site for the National Institute for the Humanities to recognize in the Research Triangle Park an ideal setting for the type of institution which they wish to create.

The October 1, 1975, minutes of the Executive Committee of the foundation record that Davis referred to the possibility of the National Humanities Center locating in Research Triangle Park as a "golden opportunity to help the universities." It was noted by Davis that the cost to acquire the center would be at least $2.75 million, and that the American Academy of Arts and Sciences would make its site selection on November 1 of that year. The committee moved and seconded that "the Research Triangle Foundation of North Carolina provide a total of $250,000 [for a building] to be given to the corporation to be chartered as the Triangle [Universities] Center for Advanced Studies—this pledge to the center to be used for the establishment of a National Humanities Center if decision is made to locate said Humanities Center in the Research Triangle Park." The minutes record that President Friday said "you will be proud of your action today."

Efforts continued to finalize the planning for the Triangle Universities Center for Advanced Studies. On November 21, 1975, independent of the pending decision of the American Academy of Arts and Sciences, the Articles of Incorporation of the Triangle Universities Center for Advanced Studies, Inc., A Non-Profit Corporation, were signed. The incorporators were Archie Davis; Jackson Rigney, acting chancellor of North Carolina State University; President Sanford; and Chancellor Ferebee Taylor. The articles stated both the general and the specific purposes of the corporation:

> The general purpose of this corporation shall be to assist in and facilitate the planning and execution of nonprofit research and educational programs that utilize and enhance the productivity of the intellectual and physical resources of the University of North Carolina at Chapel Hill, Duke University, and North Carolina State University at Raleigh. . . . The specific purposes shall include, but not be limited, to the following:
> (a) Planning, design, and management to insure continuity and coherence in development and physical design.

(b) Working cooperatively with the universities named herein above in the planning and design of research and educational programs which enhance their ability to carry out their educational missions.

(c) Assisting in obtaining and managing funds in support of concepts and projects which are determined to be desirable and feasible.

(d) Conducting, sponsoring, or facilitating, as appropriate, programs whereby scholars and other persons of appropriate expertise are enabled to perform research or undertake educational missions consistent with the general purpose.

(e) Sponsoring or facilitating conferences, workshops, seminars, lectures, or gatherings in furtherance of the general purpose.

(f) Acquisition, maintenance, utilization, and disposition of books, equipment, materials, libraries, information storage and retrieval apparatus, and other learning resources in furtherance of the general purpose.

The minutes of the November 26, 1975, organizational meeting of the board of trustees record that Archie Davis was elected chairman of the board of trustees, John Caldwell was elected president of the corporation, and L. Felix Joyner was elected the corporation's secretary-treasurer. On December 10, at the first meeting of the board, Fred A. Coe, Jr., succeeded Archie Davis as chairman, and, by consensus, the acronym TUCASI was agreed upon for the corporation. Following that meeting, a news conference statement was released, and therein it was stated:

A unique undertaking, TUCASI, represents the nation's first three-university corporation designed to plan and develop joint research and educational activities in a major research park whose creation was based on the existence of nearby universities.

The center also is seen as the beginning of a new concept in the overall development of the Research Triangle. . . .

One of the first projects of TUCASI has been to invite the new National Humanities Center to locate in the center. . . .

Dr. John Caldwell, former chancellor of N.C. State University and president of the new corporation, said, "The establishment of the Triangle Universities Center for Advanced Studies has far-reaching implications for the programs at these three universities, and will create new ways for the vast talents at these institutions to be extended for the benefit of mankind.[10]

Certainly this kind of undertaking will also make the Research Triangle Park *unique among research parks in the nation* [emphasis added]"

IN QUEST OF A VISION

In late 1975, the American Academy of Arts and Sciences finalized its decision to locate the National Humanities Center on the TUCASI campus. The next few years were devoted to designing and building the Archie K. Davis Building to house the center, and to undertaking commitments and agreements for the Microelectronics Center of North Carolina to be the second tenant on the TUCASI campus.

As well, according to Caldwell (1982), the TUCASI Board reviewed the following; however, none of these ever came into being:

1. the International Industrialization Institute proposed by the Agency for International Development and the National Academy of Engineering;
2. the Mathematical Sciences Research Institute proposed to the National Science Foundation;
3. the possibility of the Roper Center relocating from Williams College in Massachusetts;
4. the Institute of Natural Philosophy proposed by Ashly Montague of Princeton;
5. the possible relocation of the Babbage Institute, which instead moved to the University of Minnesota;
6. a world affairs center, proposed by faculty at the University of North Carolina at Chapel Hill; and
7. a center for the study of productivity, which had been previously considered by the Committee of 13.

The relationship between TUCASI and the three sister institutions was enhanced by the Research Triangle Foundation in 1978. On December 18, President Friday presented to the TUCASI board of trustees the following proposal, which was unanimously endorsed (Caldwell 1979):

a. that TUCASI become the recipient of funds awarded by the Research Triangle Foundation in lieu of direct transfer of assets from the Foundation to each of the three Universities. In effect, thereby, the Universities and the Foundation would adopt support of the purposes and programs of TUCASI as fulfilling the beneficial relationship between the three Universities and the Foundation.

b. that on the basis of an estimate of funding requirements TUCASI should submit to the Foundation annually a request for budgetary support for (1) capital projects and (2) operating expenses.

In December 1980, Davis informed TUCASI that the Foundation had approved an "endowment" grant of $250,000 for property and operating expenses.

At the June 1981 meeting of the TUCASI board, Craufurd Goodwin of Duke University, Lyle Jones of the University of North Carolina at Chapel Hill, and Claude McKinney and Robert Tilman, both of North Carolina State University, were asked to prepare a report for the board outlining the future roles of TUCASI. On December 3, 1981, the *ad hoc* committee submitted its report, "TUCASI: In Quest of a Vision." The report contained conceptual ideas, such as the development of a leadership center for university faculty. Perhaps more important than these generalities was the final section of the report in which the committee concluded that it was:

> . . . convinced that TUCASI contains the seed of an idea capable of almost limitless development redounding to the benefit of all—the three constituent universities, the Park, the Triangle, the state, and the nation. The committee is also convinced that this is a propitious moment to move forward boldly in the development of TUCASI. The existing intellectual resources of the area are of heroic proportions, but it is our view that TUCASI, acting as a leavening agent, can create in the Triangle *an intellectual and scholarly environment greater than the sum of its parts* [emphasis added].

Since that time, five institutions have located on or are planning to locate on the TUCASI campus in addition to the National Humanities Center.[11]

The organizations sponsored by the TUCASI organizations are:

- National Humanities Center
- Microelectronics Center of North Carolina (now MCNC)
- North Carolina Research and Education Network (operated by MCNC)[12]
- North Carolina Supercomputing Center (operated by MCNC)[13]
- North Carolina Biotechnology Center
- Sigma Xi, The Scientific Research Society
- National Institute of Statistical Sciences
- Burroughs Wellcome Fund

CHAPTER 8

A PRESENCE IN THE PARK

*The open society, the unrestricted access to knowledge, the un-
planned and uninhibited association of men for its furtherance—
these are what may make a vast, complex, ever growing, ever
changing, ever more specialized and expert technological world,
nevertheless a world of human community.*

—J. ROBERT OPPENHEIMER

Jim Roberson (1999) is correct in his opinion that no other park in
the world has within its boundaries an assemblage of organizations
like those on the TUCASI campus: "With regard to TUCASI, I believe it is truly unique. I know of nothing comparable at any other
park anywhere." However, simply because TUCASI is unique to
the Research Triangle Park is not a sufficient explanation for why
Research Triangle Park has been unrivaled in its growth and ar-
guably therefore the most successful research park in the nation.
What does TUCASI bring to the Park that is so special?

Archie Davis was instrumental in guiding Research Triangle
Park from a concept to a reality. As he traveled the state in the fall
of 1958 raising money for a nonprofit research park for the good of
North Carolina and its citizenry, Davis (1992) reminded contributors that when the Park flourishes, "and it will flourish," it will in

turn enrich the three universities that form its boundaries. "People in North Carolina are loyal to their universities," he said. Davis envisioned that the Park, with its institute and research organizations, would one day be intertwined with each of the three universities, both complementing their research mission as well as providing a location for graduates to be employed and thus to remain in the state.

In a sense, then, TUCASI is the universities' home within Research Triangle Park. The TUCASI campus is an ever-present symbol that the universities are the heart of the Park's mission and therefore at the heart of its success. According to Bill Little (2000a), "The major reason for companies coming to the Park has been the three universities. They have been a source of employees and consultants, as well as intellectual climate. As the Park grew, the universities needed an additional presence and TUCASI provided just that." As Elizabeth Aycock (1998) often explained, "TUCASI is like a park within a Park."

TUCASI is a visible reminder of the importance of industry/university cooperation, an idea that goes to the essence of the Park concept. According to Richard Daugherty (1998): "TUCASI is the manifestation of university cooperation toward a common end. It is a valuable intangible asset."

Daugherty (1998) explained that over the years IBM has relied on TUCASI tenants for various important functions. It used the resources at the National Humanities Center for educational programs for its employees and still relies heavily on the computer network at the Microelectronics Center of North Carolina (MCNC).

TUCASI's resources have also served other companies over the years. Margaret B. Dardess (1998), senior vice president of Corporate Affairs at GlaxoSmithKline, explained that GlaxoSmithKline has over the years relied indirectly on the North Carolina Biotechnology Center. The center encourages the growth of small biotechnology companies, and these companies in turn can and often perform some of the routine research needed by GlaxoSmithKline as well as license some of its products. The National Humanities Center has also been a valuable asset to GlaxoSmithKline but in a less pragmatic way than with IBM. According to Dardess (1998), "The National Humanities Center is an important bridge between science and the humanities. Having the Humanities Center in the Park assists in our recruiting scientists to the area because it provides a point of visual intellectualism."

Frank D. Hart (1998), former president of MCNC, echoed this theme and the importance of TUCASI to the Park's success. TUCASI brings university faculty to the Park on a daily basis, and this is an outward sign that the companies in the Park and the universities are in a sense partners in seeing the Park succeed. In particular, especially in the early 1990s, MCNC's supercomputer gave a "halo effect" to the Park that attracted the attention of industry leaders worldwide. In fact, Daugherty (1998) believes that: "TUCASI's presence in the Park was perhaps more influential in bringing CEOs to the area than in influencing scientists to come to North Carolina."

Indeed, Research Triangle Park is unique in the nation if not the world in that it houses a "university" campus. TUCASI is the Park home of the three universities—as reflected through the organizations on the TUCASI campus—and the universities are fundamental to the early history of the Park as well as to the history of the growth of the Park.

TUCASI has benefited from outstanding leadership in much the same way as the Park has through the Research Triangle Foundation's board chairman and presidents. Table 12 lists the former chairmen of the TUCASI board, and Table 13 lists its former presidents.

The organizations on or planning to be on the TUCASI campus are described in the following chapters. It may be the case that not one of these organizations has been instrumental in defining Research Triangle Park as the most prestigious and successful science

Table 12 Chairmen of the TUCASI Board

Chairman	Tenure
Fred A. Coe, Jr.	1975–1982
Louis C. Stephens, Jr.	1982–1988
Sherwood H. Smith, Jr.	1988–present

Table 13 Presidents of TUCASI

President	Tenure
John T. Caldwell	1975–1982
William F. Little	1982–1987
Jerry D. Campbell	1987–1995
Claude E. McKinney	1995–present

park in the nation; yet taken together, the TUCASI campus—the home of the three sister institutions—has been over the years an intangible asset that many believe makes the Park unique. Whether it is a *reason* for the success of the Park, it certainly is a *symptom* of the spirit that created it.

CHAPTER 9

NATIONAL HUMANITIES CENTER

The desire of knowledge, like the thirst of riches,
increases ever with the acquisition of it.

—LAURENCE STERNE

"[T]he humanities embody the historical, cultural, and intellectual contexts in which we live as individuals, communities, and nations. [If] we turn to the record of the past, the great achievements of literature and the arts, and the enduring insights of philosophical, moral, and religious thought [we will] attain a more profound understanding of the human condition." This statement of principle of the National Humanities Center exemplifies why Research Triangle Park is "where the minds of the world meet."[1] The Park is an internationally recognized hallmark of industry-university cooperation in research, and from research comes knowledge, and from knowledge comes advancement for mankind. The soul of the Park is TUCASI, the universities' home within the Park, and at the foundation of TUCASI is the National Humanities Center and its quest for an understanding of the human condition.

Meyer H. Abrams, Cornell University professor of English, Morton W. Bloomfield, Harvard University professor of English, and Gregory Vlastos, Princeton University professor of philosophy, were

Fellows at the Center for Advanced Study in the Behavioral Sciences at Stanford University in 1968. At that time they began to discuss the idea for a similar institute as a private retreat for scholarship devoted to the humanities (Mullikin 1998). In November 1972, Bloomfield approached John Voss of the American Academy of Arts and Sciences to discuss the possible role of the academy in planning such an institution.[2] According to Voss (1996), Harvey Brooks of Harvard University, president of the academy at that time, approved a $1,000 grant to explore the idea. Shortly thereafter, the Ella Lyman Cabot Trust provided $3,000 to support a planning meeting (Mullikin 1998).

The May 1973 planning meeting was held in New York City at the offices of the American Council of Learned Societies (ACLS).[3] Along with Abrams, Bloomfield, and Vlastos, the others included Robert Goheen of the Council on Foundations, Charles Frankel and Steven Marcus of Columbia University, Henry Nash Smith of the University of California at Berkeley, and Lawrence Stone of Princeton University. A committee was formed with Marcus as the coordinator. In January 1974, a planning office was opened on the Columbia University campus.[4]

In early 1975, the committee began looking at possible sites for an institute. It approached the University of North Carolina at Chapel Hill and Duke University, but neither was in a position to underwrite the necessary funding (Davis 1975). However, in early September, guided by the wisdom of President Friday, the possibility of attracting the academy's institute to the Park gained momentum.[5]

In early September, at the request of President Friday, representatives from the American Academy of Arts and Sciences visited the Park. President Friday and Archie Davis met at the Carolina Inn in Chapel Hill with Bloomfield, Marcus, and Voss. President Friday was impressed with the academy's vision, and the academy's representatives were impressed with the TUCASI campus and its proximity to the three universities (Connor 1998). But the academy was seriously considering other locations, including the University of Texas, the University of Pennsylvania, and the University of Michigan.

On September 11, 1975, President Friday approached Archie Davis, in his capacity as a spokesperson for both the universities and the Park, to help with this project. Davis quickly put together a list of fifteen friends of the universities, including some of the companies that were already in the Park, and he contacted them in an effort to raise $1.5 million. In the letter that he sent to each potential contributor he wrote, "What [the proposed institute] could mean to the tone and character of higher education in North Carolina, particularly in the field of the humanities, is in my judgment almost indescribable. Dr. William C. Friday feels that no stone should be left unturned to insure that North Carolina is named as the site for this development."

Davis also explained in his letter:

> Of the $2,750,000 North Carolina requirement, it is estimated that $1,500,000 will be required for the construction of the building embracing 30,000 to 40,000 square feet. The balance of $1,250,000 will be required for funding annual operating expenses of about $250,000 for a period of five years. It is believed that the three universities will underwrite the expense funding, so our problem is to raise $1,500,000 for the building. It is to this effort that the Research Triangle Foundation is committed to give the land and in addition, based upon my recommendation to the Board, $250,000 as a cash contribution.

In mid-October 1975, Davis sent to President Friday a list of twenty-five organizations that had pledged a total of $1,502,500.[6] The academy made its decision to locate on the TUCASI campus October 21, 1975, although the decision was made public at a later date. According to Frankel (1980), "There were many attractive proposals made to us [the academy], but by far the most attractive was the proposal made . . . by the Research Triangle Foundation and by the consortium of the Triangle Universities to create a National Humanities Center."

Throughout this process, faculty from the three universities were not only supportive but also encouraging of the administration's efforts to attract the academy's attention. For example, on September 30, 1975, C. Hugh Holman wrote to President Friday:[7]

> I would like to describe to you, if I may, the benefits which will accrue to higher education in North Carolina and, in particular,

to departments of English, History, Modern Languages, Classics, Philosophy, and the Fine Arts in our colleges and universities, if we are fortunate enough to have the proposed National Institute for the Humanities located in Research Triangle Park. . . .

One of the immeasurable but very real benefits to be gained by all educational institutions, as well as the State itself, from the location of the National Institute for the Humanities in the Research Triangle Park would be the great distinction which it would bring to the State and to the region. . . . The image of the State of North Carolina would be enriched in the national eyes by locating the formal center for advanced humanistic study in this state, and the entire State and all its educational institutions would benefit greatly.

Holman went on to say (and his thoughts underscore the uniqueness that the TUCASI campus brings to Research Triangle Park, to which testimony was noted in Chapter 8), "In another sense an immediate and very important beneficiary would be the Research Triangle Park itself. This experiment in research and industrial planning, which has been successful beyond the greatest hopes of its original founders and which has earned true distinction for the State as well as increasing substantially the resources of the State, would by the introduction of the National Institute become unique among research centers and parks, in that it would have the *broadest spectrum of interests in human knowledge concentrated at any place in the United States* [emphasis added]."

On February 17, 1976, a Memorandum of Understanding was signed by John Caldwell in his capacity as president of TUCASI and then countersigned by John Voss for the American Academy of Arts and Sciences on March 1. This memorandum set forth a mutual understanding regarding the establishment of the National Humanities Center in Research Triangle Park. Noted therein were the obligations stated to the academy by President Friday in his October 22 letter to Voss. Specifically, TUCASI would provide a building site of fifteen acres on its campus, it would construct 30,000 square feet of building(s) at an approximate cost of $1.5 million, and the three universities would each provide $75,000 annually for five years for an annual operating budget of $225,000.

In his February 23, 1976, statement about the academy's decision to locate in the Park, Governor James E. Holshouser, Jr., wrote, "To have been chosen the permanent home of the National Humanities Center is indeed a major national accomplishment in higher education. I salute the universities involved in the Triangle Universities Center for Advanced Studies for bringing about such outstanding international recognition of our State."

On February 24, Caldwell released his statement to the effect that the academy's decision to locate in the Park is "a compliment to the three North Carolina [u]niversities; an endorsement of the soundness of their new Center for Advanced Studies; a reward for the generosity and vision of the Research Triangle Foundation's leadership; and a fitting response to the brilliant efforts of William Friday and Archie Davis. It's one of those decisions that's slated to be a winner for all concerned. We must now make it so."

President Friday's statement on the following day noted the importance of the location of the National Humanities Center in the Park: "[The location of the Center] is a major development in higher education and a great tribute to the people of this State who over all these years have supported these institutions so that they could achieve the level of excellence that brought this decision about."

Finally, on February 27, Joab L. Thomas, chancellor of North Carolina State University, remarked that "the establishment of the National Humanities Center inaugurates a new and exceptional era in humanistic studies."

That same day, there was this announcement at an American Academy of Arts and Sciences luncheon at the Lotus Club in New York City:

> The National Humanities Center will occupy a site on the campus of the Triangle Universities Center for Advanced Studies [TUCASI]. This new Center chartered by the University of North Carolina at Chapel Hill, Duke University, and North Carolina State University is located in the beautifully planned and executed Research Triangle Park situated within a 12-mile radius of the three universities. . . . The 120-acre campus was made available to the three universities by the Research Triangle Foundation of North Carolina.

Each year, about fifty scholars from the various humanistic disciplines will become Fellows of the Center. They will study a wide range of subjects as they relate to broad cultural, social, and intellectual issues. Since these issues engage the intellectual community as a whole, the Center will also invite a number of distinguished scientists and people from public life—businessmen, government officials, journalists and writers—to serve as Fellows.

Groundbreaking will be in the Fall of 1976, and occupancy of the Center is projected for 1978.

The ground breaking in fact took place on April 16, 1977, as described by the program announcement in Figure 27. Figures 28 and 29 show various guests at the ground breaking. The National Humanities Center opened in September 1978, and the building was dedicated and named the Archie K. Davis Building on April 7, 1979. Figures 30 and 31, respectively, show President Friday and John Hope Franklin at the dedication.

Charles Frankel was the first director (1977–1979) of the National Humanities Center. After his untimely death, William J. Bennett served as director. He left the center in 1981 when President Reagan appointed him chairman of the National Endowment for the Humanities. He subsequently became secretary of education in the Reagan Administration. In 1983, Charles Blitzer, formerly assistant secretary of the Smithsonian Institution, became director, and then W. Robert Connor (Fig. 32) left Princeton University to succeed Blitzer in 1989.

By 1979, National Humanities Center seeds had been sown, but what about the harvest that followed? When asked about this, Conner (2000) noted:[8]

Since the Center opened its doors in 1978, more than 800 scholars have spent an academic year in residence at the Archie K. Davis building. [These individuals represent more than 40 academic fields, 182 American institutions, and 133 institutions in 33 nations outside of the United States.] Some of them, including William Leuchtenburg and John Hope Franklin, have been so impressed by their experience at the Center that they have moved to North Carolina, accepting professorships at Triangle universities,

```
                        PROGRAM
                GROUND-BREAKING EXERCISE
                NATIONAL HUMANITIES CENTER


                  Saturday, April 16, 1977
                        3:00 p.m.

Presiding  ........................John T. Caldwell, President
                                   Triangle Universities Center
                                     for Advanced Studies, Inc.

Welcome ................................James B. Hunt, Jr.
                                   Governor of North Carolina

Remarks .....................................Joseph Duffey
                                   Assistant Secretary of State
                              for Educational and Cultural Affairs

Remarks and Introduction of Dr. Boorstin .......Charles Frankel
                                   President and Director,
                                   National Humanities Center

Remarks ...................................Daniel Boorstin
                                   Librarian of Congress

Recognition of:  Morton Bloomfield  .........John T. Caldwell
                 John Voss

Presentation of Deed
       to the Three Universities  ........Archie K. Davis, President
                                   Research Triangle Foundation
                                       of North Carolina

Acceptance of the Deed ............Fred A. Coe, Jr., Chairman
                                   Triangle Universities Center
                                     for Advanced Studies, Inc.
          Terry Sanford, President, Duke University
          N. Ferebee Taylor, Chancellor, University of North
            Carolina at Chapel Hill
          Joab L. Thomas, Chancellor, North Carolina State
            University
          William C. Friday, President, The University of North
            Carolina

The Ground-Breaking

Reception - Burroughs Wellcome Co.
            3030 Cornwallis Road
```

Figure 27. *National Humanities Center ground-breaking exercise program.*

and enriching the intellectual life of the region. Collectively, the Fellows of the Center have written more than 700 books and countless articles, essays, and reviews. At least 50 of these books have won major prizes.

Figure 28. *Elizabeth Aycock* (left) *and Charles Frankel at the National Humanities Center's ground breaking, April 16, 1977.*

Figure 29. *Ground breaking of the National Humanities Center, April 16, 1977. Rear left: Archie K. Davis. Front left to right: Terry Sanford (president of Duke University), William C. Friday (president of the University of North Carolina), Morton W. Bloomfield (Harvard University), N. Ferebee Taylor (chancellor at the University of North Carolina at Chapel Hill), Joab L. Thomas (chancellor at North Carolina State University), Elizabeth Aycock, Isaac Shapiro.*

Figure 30. *William C. Friday (president of the University of North Carolina) speaking at the dedication of the Archie K. Davis Building, April 7, 1979.*

Figure 31. *John Hope Franklin (then professor of American History at the University of Chicago, now the James B. Duke Professor Emeritus of History at Duke University) speaking at the dedication of the Archie K. Davis Building, April 7, 1979.*

Figure 32. *Archie K. Davis* (left) *and W. Robert Connor, director of National Humanities Center, 1989.*

CHAPTER 10

MCNC

The imperatives of technology and organizations, not the images of
ideology, are what determine the shape of economic society.
—JOHN KENNETH GALBRAITH

NORTH CAROLINA BOARD OF SCIENCE AND TECHNOLOGY[1]

In 1963, Governor Terry Sanford appointed a scientific advisory committee to counsel him on how to better use the scientific talent of the state for industrial growth. The committee—which included such eminent scientists as Paul Gross and Marcus Hobbs of Duke University, "Buck" Menius of North Carolina State University, and Everett Palmatier, George Nicholson, and Bill Little of the University of North Carolina at Chapel Hill, among others—recommended the creation of a Board of Science and Technology to help build the state's science and engineering infrastructure. The General Assembly established such a board that same year "to encourage, promote, and support scientific, engineering, and industrial research applications in North Carolina."[2]

The board began to use its $2 million allocation from the General Assembly almost immediately. In 1964, it allocated approximately $150,000 as seed money to establish the Triangle Universities Computation Center (TUCC) to provide time-shared computer technology to the state, and another $150,000 as seed money for the three sister universities to acquire funding for a shared nuclear physics laboratory located at Duke University (Triangle Universities Nuclear Laboratory, TUNL).

Governor Hunt reorganized the board during his first term (1977–1981), making himself chairman and Quentin Lindsey, researcher at the Research Triangle Institute and former professor of agricultural economics at North Carolina State University, executive director. In addition, Hunt realized that the future economic development of the state would be tied more than ever to its scientific resource base and that strengthening those resources should be directly tied to public policy. Hence, Lindsey also became his science and public policy advisor.

During Hunt's administration, the board took on three important and related tasks. The first task was to create the North Carolina School of Science and Mathematics at Durham (noted in Chapter 6). The second task was to strengthen the state's technological infrastructure in microelectronics (discussed below), and the third task was to strengthen the state's biotechnology industry (discussed in Chapter 11).

MICROELECTRONICS IN NORTH CAROLINA

In early 1980, 40 percent of the Park's land had been sold for development, as described in Chapter 2. But the North Carolina economy was still growing slowly and seemingly not benefiting from the Park to the extent that the state's leaders had expected. It was well known that the semiconductor industry was booming. For example, in 1979 industry growth had created 40,000 to 50,000 new jobs in the Palo Alto area alone (*Electronic News* 1980). In contrast, in 1979 only 37,500 new jobs in all fields had been created throughout the entire state of North Carolina.

Governor Hunt charged the Board of Science and Technology in 1980 to visualize the frontiers of science, that is, to anticipate what would be the "key scientific areas of tomorrow" (Lindsey 2000). The board did this and reported to the governor that the state already had some strength in microelectronics and biotechnology; they recommended that the state build on these strengths, and the governor agreed.[3] Coincidentally, at about that same time the state's Department of Commerce learned that General Electric (GE) was interested in opening a facility in the Park, but they needed a microelectronics center to provide highly trained researchers. Governor Hunt, realizing first and foremost the long-run importance of an electronics industry to the state (and secondarily the political leverage that GE's immediate interest in the Park would have) asked the Council of State in early June to set aside $972,000 to start a center in microelectronics. On June 16, 1980, the Microelectronics Center of North Carolina (MCNC) was incorporated as a public-private nonprofit partnership, with Sherwood Smith as interim president and George Herbert as chairman of the interim board of directors.

MCNC's mission as stated in 1989 was encompassing (*Communications Update* 1989):

1. to build North Carolina's technical infrastructure for science-based economic development,
2. to keep North Carolina's universities at the forefront of research and education in communications, microelectronics, and supercomputing, and
3. to manage a statewide communications network, an advanced research and technology laboratory and program in microelectronics, and a supercomputing center that promotes research and education among North Carolina participating universities and industry.

More specifically (MCNC Annual Report 1985, p. 2), "MCNC incorporates universities which concentrate on basic research and education, a research institute conducting applied research, and the capability of a full manufacturing research laboratory. The MCNC program is dedicated to accelerating the transfer of research and technology to practical application in industry."

As reported in the Raleigh *News & Observer* on June 29, 1980, "Hunt has proposed making the Research Triangle a 'Silicon Valley East.' " (GE purchased 90.45 acres in August.)

In 1982, the North Carolina General Assembly committed

Figure 33. *Governor James B. Hunt, Jr.* (left) *and Sherwood Smith at MCNC ground breaking, 1983.*

$24.4 million for the construction of an 84,000-square-foot facility on thirty-six acres of the TUCASI campus that TUCASI was urged to lease to the Microelectronics Center (Fig. 33). At this time it was reported that (*Integrated Circuits* 1983, p. 2) "North Carolina leads all other states in being the first to make such a substantial commitment to the development of the modern electronics industry."

At the dedication of the facility on June 12, 1984, Christopher Fordham, chancellor at the University of North Carolina at Chapel Hill, said (*The Leader* 1984, p. 12) that "this is one more giant step in a North Carolina story which has attracted national and international interest. . . . [This] dedication cannot fail to evoke the memory of our predecessors—those who started RTP. This is an inspiring extension of leadership." As the scope of the activities of the center evolved, its name was officially changed to MCNC in 1997.

Communications

Alan Blatecky (2000), former vice president of information technology at MCNC, cited one important example of how the three sister universities have benefited directly from MCNC's research as well as how the companies in the Park have benefited from having MCNC on the TUCASI campus:

The three universities have benefited from, for example, activities involving next generation internet technologies. MCNC was the central focal point and catalyst to create the most advanced next generation networking testbed and infrastructure in the world. This activity, now called the North Carolina Networking Initiative, has created the fastest production internet network in the nation, one of the leading edge optical research networking centers in the nation, and an unrivaled national evaluation center for Internet2.[4] These activities not only have had and will continue to have a positive teaching and research impact on the three universities, but also they will have enhanced the research climate of the universities and the intellectual capital of faculty associated with MCNC.

Blatecky went on to note one of many examples of a Park company that has directly benefited from being juxtaposed to MCNC:

"The networking and telecommunication expertise at MCNC, coupled with its proximity to the three universities and their eminent faculty has proved to be of significant benefit to Cisco Systems. Not only have they expanded their facilities beyond their initial plans, but also they have increased the scope and depth of products centered in the Park."

Bill Little (2000a) singled out the important role of MCNC in the North Carolina Networking Initiative (NCNI). One of NCNI's goals is to exploit emerging technologies and their applications to the competitive advantage of both the universities (Duke University, North Carolina State University, and the University of North Carolina at Chapel Hill) and businesses (MCNC, Cisco Systems, IBM, Lucent Technologies, and Nortel Networks) involved in the initiative. The goal is to make the state an attractive home for technology-based organizations, with the spillover benefit of enhanced economic development.[5]

Supercomputing[6]

The three Triangle universities began to express a need for their faculties to have a supercomputer in the Triangle area. In December 1986, a task force was appointed by the chancellors of the state universities and the president of Duke University to study the issue. The task force included the chief computer officers from the three universities and from General Administration as well as George Worsley of North Carolina State University, in his capacity as chairman of TUCC, Richard Fair, in his capacity as vice president of MCNC, and Bill Little (chairman of the task force), in his capacity as president of TUCASI. In April 1987, the task force recommended the need for a local supercomputer for both academic and economic development purposes.

Thanks to the support of Durham Senator Kenneth Royall, a bill was introduced in the General Assembly and then passed in mid-1987 for an initial appropriation of $12.6 million over two years for capital equipment and $5.2 million over two years for a building and operating expenses. In 1989, the North Carolina Supercomputing Center (NCSC) opened on the TUCASI campus as a division of MCNC.[7]

According to Richard Daugherty (1998), the supercomputing center is a good example of why MCNC in particular and TUCASI in general are important to IBM: "IBM frequently went to MCNC for silicon and supercomputing needs because MCNC, because of its presence on the TUCASI campus, could easily bring together the talent in the three universities to interact with the company."

MCNC, like the National Humanities Center and the other TUCASI organizations, is indeed a critical factor for explaining the growth and prosperity of the Park over the past forty-five years, and it will be the cornerstone for the growth and prosperity of the Park over the next forty-five years.

CHAPTER 11

NORTH CAROLINA
BIOTECHNOLOGY CENTER

He who makes two blades of grass grow in place of one
renders a service to the state.

—VOLTAIRE

Biotechnology, a term first used in the early 1900s, is a collection of technologies that use living cells and/or biological molecules to solve problems and make useful products.[1] As noted in the previous chapter, the Board of Science and Technology identified, along with microelectronics, the state's strength in biotechnology and the importance of developing that strength for economic gains.

Most of the nation became aware of the potential of the biotechnology industry in the mid-1970s, when breakthrough research demonstrated that DNA from different sources could be recombined and then inserted into living organisms—recombinant DNA technology. The National Institutes of Health stepped forward as a standards-setting body to oversee genetic research, and in 1980 the U.S. Supreme Court ruled in *Diamond* vs. *Chakrabarty* that genetically engineered life forms could be patented.

Governor Hunt and scientists at the three universities—North Carolina State University in particular because of the agricultural, marine life, and animal applications of biotechnology—realized that biotechnology could be greatly beneficial to the state (Burke 1998):

> These same leaders also understood that North Carolina was ideally suited for biotechnology. The state's traditional industries—agriculture, forestry, pharmaceuticals, textiles, food processing, etc.—were the very ones that could benefit most from biotechnology. North Carolina also had the necessary resources to develop biotechnology, including a tradition of technological development, . . . large research parks, leading research universities, four medical schools, a progressive business climate, long-term governmental support, an extensive community college system, and abundant natural resources.[2]

In 1981, the North Carolina Biotechnology Center (NCBC) was created by the North Carolina General Assembly. It was the nation's first state-sponsored initiative to develop biotechnology, and as such this initiative gave "political verification" to the idea that the state could stimulate the birth of this industry (Burke 1998). The center was housed in the North Carolina Board of Science and Technology in Raleigh as part of state government, but to give it more flexibility and nonpartisan neutrality it was reconstituted as a nonprofit corporation on August 17, 1984, with an annual budget of $6.5 million.[3] Charles E. Hamner (1998), president of the North Carolina Biotechnology Center (Fig. 34), noted:[4] "This was a very large amount of money for an agency without a mission. The Center was given a charge to develop a strategic mission, unfortunately, there was little precedent to follow. The idea of an economic development agency being centered around science and technology was revolutionary. The traditional role was for science and technology centers to be housed in universities not as state-funded private non-profit organizations."

The center's mission is: "to provide long term economic benefit to North Carolina through support of biotechnology research, development and commercialization statewide."[5] And toward this mission of "catalyzing technology," the center's forty-member staff works in pursuit of five goals:[6]

Figure 34. *The North Carolina Biotechnology Center's Council on Competitiveness, 1990. Left to right: Jim Roberson (Research Triangle Foundation), Governor James G. Martin, Vice President Dan Quayle, Charles E. Hamner, unidentified member.*

- strengthen North Carolina's research capabilities in its academic and industrial institutions
- foster North Carolina's industrial development
- inform and educate the public about biotechnology
- develop mutually beneficial partnerships among all parties involved in moving biotechnology from research to commercialization
- establish for North Carolina a leadership role in biotechnology and its commercialization

It is important to note that these five goals involve industry, the universities, and the state in one way or another. According to Hamner (1998), "My objective, or one of my objectives, was to get industry, the universities, and the state to think beyond their traditional roles and to think as a team. Most efforts in other states in biotechnology have not been successful because centers are established in universities and therefore ignore other players."

The North Carolina Biotechnology Center's prominence on the TUCASI campus is obviously not an accident. Its location within the universities' home in Research Triangle Park is symbolic of the interplay between industry and academe that is necessary for the state to grow a biotechnology industry.

The center has been very successful in fulfilling its mission and goals. According to Steven Burke (1998), senior vice president for Corporate Affairs and External Relations, North Carolina companies are responsible for about 10 percent of the nation's $12 billion biotechnology industry: "In 1984 there were 6 North Carolina companies in biotechnology; in 1988 there were 15 to 20 with about $100 million in sales; in 1998 there were 80 companies with $1.2 billion in sales; and by 2003 there will be 100 companies with sales over $3 billion." And the reason for this success, according to Hamner (1998), is: "NCBC thinks holistically in terms of all players: scientists, businesses, and society."

The presence of the biotechnology center on the TUCASI campus has directly benefited the Park. NCBC was instrumental in attracting BASF, Biogen, and Covance Biotechnology to the Park, among others. According to Hamner, the center gained "instantaneous credibility when it moved on the TUCASI campus," and its presence there has been a visible sign to companies that university resources are available and that the state is actively supporting the growth of its biotechnology industry.

CHAPTER 12

SIGMA XI

> The scientist values research by the size of its contribu-
> tion to that huge, logically articulated structure of ideas
> which is already, though not yet half built, the most
> glorious accomplishment of mankind.
>
> —SIR PETER BRIAN MEDAWAR

Sigma Xi, The Scientific Research Society, is an international honor society for scientists and engineers. It was founded in 1886 at Cornell University by professor Frank Van Vleck and a group of engineering students.[1] The organization's purpose was not only to reward excellence in research but also to encourage collaborations among scientists. The name Sigma Xi is thus appropriate, coming from the Greek *spoudon xynones* meaning companions in zealous research. Today, there are more than 75,000 members of Sigma Xi, affiliated with more than 500 chapters in the United States and throughout the world. Three of these chapters are at the University of North Carolina at Chapel Hill (founded in 1919),[2] Duke University (founded in 1932), and North Carolina State University (founded in 1944). There is also a chapter in Research Triangle Park (founded in 1991).[3]

The mission of Sigma Xi includes (Sigma Xi 1997) "fostering worldwide interactions of science and technology with society;

encouraging appreciation and support of original work in science and technology; and honoring scientific and engineering accomplishments."

In the fall of 1988, Thomas F. Malone, president of Sigma Xi, initiated discussions to move the national office, with a staff of almost forty, from New Haven, Connecticut.[4] His motivations were practical. New Haven, although the home of Yale University, was not a practical location to convene groups; airport service to the area was unpredictable, and the national office building was old and needed extensive repairs. Malone appointed a headquarters location committee, chaired by Thomas F. McNamara. The committee invited areas with at least one major university to submit proposals for the new national office home.

Approximately 150 proposals were received. Those areas and universities that made the short list were Ann Arbor with the University of Michigan; Atlanta with Emory and Georgia Tech; Dallas with Southern Methodist University, Southwest Medical School, and Texas A&M; Houston with Rice University and the Baylor School of Medicine; New Haven with Yale University; the San Francisco peninsula area with Stanford University and the University of California at Berkeley; Philadelphia with the University of Pennsylvania and Drexel University; and Research Triangle Park.

The Sigma Xi chapters at the three sister universities formed a committee, chaired by Bill Little of the University of North Carolina at Chapel Hill, to represent the Park to the national office.[5] In a letter from the three university chapter presidents of February 15, 1989, McNamara and his committee were invited to visit the Park. The letter stated, "We believe your examination of our area will lead to a recommendation to the Board of Directors to accept our invitation to relocate to America's largest, *most* [emphasis added] successful scientific community." The letter went on to highlight some of the relative advantages of the Park, including quality office space at "prices well below most other metropolitan areas," affordable housing, attractive wage rates for skilled office staff personnel, an educated labor pool, a favorable quality of life and a "sophisticated life style that compares favorably with major metropolitan areas," three major universities, each with a strong chapter, and an active community of industrial scientists.

The committee was so favorably impressed with the Park and the three universities that a site visit was scheduled for April 1, 1989. At this point, the committee had narrowed its search from the 150 or so invitations that Sigma Xi received to six locations, divided into two tiers: Philadelphia, the San Francisco peninsula, and Research Triangle Park in tier 1 and Atlanta, Dallas, and Houston in tier 2 (Malone 1989, Roberson 1989).

Impressed with the Park, and the TUCASI campus in particular, Malone corresponded with Jim Roberson on April 20 to report that the Park was definitely in the top tier group, but additional information was needed from him on several criteria. On May 15, the Sigma Xi chapters at the three sister institutions submitted to Sigma Xi a thirteen-page report that addressed in detail the criteria raised by Malone. Of particular importance to Sigma Xi were the joint activities among the three Triangle universities that the report documented. TUCASI and its residents were, of course, highlighted:

> A distinguishing feature of the Triangle universities is the number of interinstitutional collaborative research activities and facilities in science and engineering, as well as interinstitutional course registration for students. Few, *if any* [emphasis added], other locations in the country can point to such a level of true collaboration. The community spirit in the Triangle is largely responsible for this record. Below are listed some of the major shared activities, most of which are in the Park.
>
> a. The Research Triangle Institute (RTI) was incorporated by the Triangle universities in 1958 as a not-for-profit contract research institute in the Park.
>
> b. The Triangle Universities Nuclear Laboratory (TUNL), located on the Duke University campus, was established in 1965 and is jointly managed and utilized by all three universities. It trains 10% of the nation's nuclear physicists.
>
> c. The Triangle Universities Computation Center (TUCC) in RTP has served all three universities with main-frame computation since 1965. Because of the changes in main-frame computer developments (and affordability) and with the

establishment of the North Carolina Supercomputing Center (see k below), TUCC will be phased out within the next year or so.

d. Triangle Universities Center for Advanced Studies, Inc. (TUCASI) was incorporated in 1975 to foster interinstitutional collaboration and studies among the Triangle universities. It has a campus within the Research Triangle Park and is an excellent vehicle for assembling the talents and resources of all three universities for joint enterprises.

e. The National Humanities Center (NHC), located on the TUCASI campus, was incorporated in 1975 under the aegis of the American Academy of Arts and Sciences to provide for the humanities a center similar to the Center for Behavioral Sciences at Palo Alto and the Institute for Advanced Studies at Princeton. . . . [The NHC] might be drawn upon for some of Sigma Xi's programs for public understanding of science.

f. The Triangle Research Libraries Network (TRLN), with headquarters at Chapel Hill, is a consortium dating back to the late 1970s that has entered the catalogs of all three university libraries into a common database accessible by computer terminal from remote locations (including the Park).

g. The Microelectronics Center of North Carolina (MCNC), located on the TUCASI campus, was incorporated in 1980 and serves five universities in North Carolina, RTI, and a host of industrial associates. It is a state-of-the-art design and fabrication facility that creates interinstitutional and academic-industrial collaboration in the area of microelectronics chips and materials.

h. The MCNC Microwave Network operated by MCNC provides twelve T12 and two 2-way interactive television channels to six locations across the state (including each of the Triangle universities and MCNC) for two-way telecasting of courses, seminars and research conferences.

i. The North Carolina Biotechnology Center (NCBC) was established in 1981 to foster the development of biotechnology in North Carolina. It accomplishes its mission through awarding grants to university programs at public and private universities, assisting start-up companies in biotechnology, catalyzing industrial/academic collaboration in research, and conducting a large educational program directed to the public schools and the general public throughout the state.

j. The Triangle Universities Licensing Consortium (TULCO), organized in 1986 and supported by TUCASI, assists technology transfer from the universities to industry by providing a joint marketing and licensing service for intellectual property development at the Triangle universities. It is located on the RTI campus in the Park.

k. The North Carolina Supercomputing Center (NCSC), under construction on the TUCASI campus, expects completion of its building and delivery of a Cray YMP supercomputer in the fall of 1989.

In addition to emphasizing these joint activities, the report went on to hallmark the state itself:

The State of North Carolina has created an exceptional intellectual climate conducive to scientific research. Although the Research Triangle program was begun totally with private contributions and has been totally privately financed, the state has focused its efforts on the infrastructure of scientific educational activities. In 1963, the North Carolina Board of Science and Technology was established and funded by the General Assembly (and has been funded every year since) as the first state agency in the U.S. to make research grants to public and private universities and colleges to build the scientific base in the state. In 1980, the residential North Carolina School of Science and Mathematics was established as the first in the nation of its kind for talented students throughout the state. In 1982 both the Microelectronics Center of North Carolina and the North Carolina Biotechnology Center were created and have been funded every year since. Approximately $150 million has been funded by the State to support these latter two activities. The most recent step was the appropriation of $18 million in 1986 to establish the North Carolina Super Computing Center. . . . Few, *if any* [emphasis added], states can match this public government emphasis on science and engineering, especially when combined with what has been accomplished at RTP by philanthropy from the private sector.

In June 1989, Sigma Xi announced its plans to move its head-quarters from New Haven to the Research Triangle Park. The Society moved into the Park the following April and is currently in the process of raising funds for its permanent home on the TUCASI campus.

Sigma Xi benefited in several ways by moving to the Park (Ferguson 1998, Keever 1998). The Research Triangle Park Sigma Xi chapter has brought more corporate scientists into the Society, the nearby availability of scientists at both the universities and the Park companies has enriched the Society's resource base for grant reviewers, and the ongoing exchange of ideas between academic and corporate scientists has stimulated Sigma Xi to think in broader terms when organizing its conferences and business/government forums. According to Little (2000a): "TUCASI is an ideal setting for Sigma Xi because the Park represents all of the elements of its membership: academic scientists, industrial scientists, and governmental scientists."

The Park has benefited as well. Sigma Xi's on-campus presence has "provided a vehicle for scientific networking for Park personnel" (Ferguson 1998). In addition, Sigma Xi has donated over the years nearly 14,000 scientific books to the university libraries at the University of North Carolina at Chapel Hill, Duke University, North Carolina State University, and North Carolina Central University. The society's magazine, *American Scientist*, receives more than 1,000 books a year for review consideration. Those not selected for review are so donated. Finally, Sigma Xi, much like the National Humanities Center, is an intangible asset of the Park. It signals to the international scientific community that the universities are stakeholders in the Park as evidenced by their support of Sigma Xi and that they believe the research conducted in the Park is of such a caliber as to merit association with this prestigious organization.

CHAPTER 13

NATIONAL INSTITUTE OF STATISTICAL SCIENCES

> *When you can measure what you are speaking about, and express*
> *it in numbers, you know something about it; but when you cannot*
> *measure it, when you cannot express it in numbers,*
> *your knowledge is of a meager and unsatisfactory kind:*
> *it may be the beginning of knowledge, but you have scarcely,*
> *in your thoughts, advanced to the stage of science.*
>
> —LORD KELVIN

The National Science Foundation (NSF) funded a study in 1988 to examine the current state of statistics, and the NSF–supported panel of the Institute of Mathematical Statistics (IMS) later that same year issued its report *Cross-Disciplinary Research in the Statistical Sciences.*[1] The report recommended that a statistical institute be established "to foster major collaborative efforts between statisticians and other scientists."[2] Toward this end, a joint committee of the American Statistical Association (ASA) and the IMS was constituted to accept proposals from various universities to house a to-be-formed National Institute of Statistical Sciences (NISS).

In March 1990, Jerry D. Campbell, president of TUCASI, submitted a proposal to the ASA/IMS Committee on the Siting of a National Institute of Statistical Sciences, on behalf of the three Triangle universities and the Research Triangle Institute, to establish the National Institute of Statistical Sciences on the TUCASI campus to provide, as stated in the proposal (p. 3) "the requisite structure whereby leading statistical research scholars would be able to work together with other scientists on large-scale cross-disciplinary research projects of national and global importance."

The Triangle universities explicitly supported the proposal by committing three statistics faculty and three graduate students to serve as fellows to the institute at no salary cost during the first five years of its operation. This type of interuniversity cooperation probably would not have occurred had the proposed NISS been on one of the university campuses (Little 2000a).

TUCASI committed approximately ten acres of its 120-acre campus to the institute through a ninety-nine-year lease at the rental price of $1 per year. The Research Triangle Foundation committed $250,000 per year for the first six academic years ($1.5 million in total) in the form of a grant to the proposing consortium. And the state committed up to $2.5 million to cover half the cost of a new 33,000-square-foot building on a matching basis, with the other half to be raised by NISS.

The TUCASI proposal was accepted by the ASA/IMS committee in late 1990, and in 1991 NISS was established as a nonprofit North Carolina corporation. Jerome Sacks, then professor of statistics at the University of Illinois and now professor of Statistics and Decisions Sciences at Duke University, was named director.[3] From its mission statement:[4] "NISS exists to promote, develop and facilitate cross-disciplinary statistical research in problems of national and international importance." Toward this mission, NISS is charged to:

- perform and stimulate cross-disciplinary research involving statistics,
- confront complex, data-driven scientific problems of national importance, and
- provide career development opportunities for statisticians and scientists, especially those in the formative stages of their careers.

NISS, like the other organizations on the TUCASI campus, is both a home for the faculty of the three sister universities and a resource to the companies in the Park. According to Daniel L. Solomon, professor of statistics and dean of the College of Physical and Mathematical Sciences at North Carolina State University (2000): "NISS has created collaborations where scientists from the Park collaborate with students and faculty at the universities . . . and NISS has significantly increased the interaction of faculty in the [three] academic departments. . . . Since NISS there has been more interaction between statistics departments and statisticians in the Park than ever before."

CHAPTER 14

BURROUGHS WELLCOME FUND

*The artist may be well advised to keep his work to himself
till it is completed, because no one can readily help him or
advise him with it . . . but the scientist is wiser not to with-
hold a single finding or a single conjecture from publicity.*

—GOETHE

In 1880, Silas Burroughs and Henry Wellcome formed a partnership known as Burroughs Wellcome and Co.[1] The pharmaceutical
company prospered in the United Kingdom. In 1896, Burroughs
died and Wellcome continued to expand the company. When he
died in 1936, his will called for creating the Wellcome Trust, to be
devoted to research in medicine and allied sciences and to the
maintenance of research libraries and museums.

The Burroughs Wellcome Fund, a U.S. extension of the Wellcome Trust, was created in 1955. The fund was to be supported by
the U.S. Burroughs Wellcome Co. So it was until 1993, when the
fund received a $400 million gift from the Wellcome Trust, thus al-
lowing it to become independent of Burroughs Wellcome Co. The
Burroughs Wellcome Fund remains committed to the belief that
"fostering research by the best and brightest scientists offers the
fullest promise for improving human health today and in the new
millennium."

Among the many projects that the fund has participated in are (Bond 2000):

- partnerships with Sigma Xi to bring together scientists, policy makers, educators, and others to discuss key issues that face biomedical research,
- efforts with the National Institute of Environmental Health Sciences and the North Carolina Department of Health and Human Services to fund studies examining the environmental and biological aftermath of the massive flooding in the eastern part of North Carolina as a result of Hurricane Floyd in 1999,
- the commitment of $3 million of endowment dollars to a venture capital fund started by the North Carolina Biotechnology Center to supply small, promising biotechnology-related companies with an infusion of capital and to attract additional venture capital into North Carolina-based companies, and
- support to academic scientists and programs that provide hands-on science activities to middle and high school students in North Carolina with an investment of nearly $27 million since 1955.

The Burroughs Wellcome Fund deepened its ties to the Park by building a permanent headquarters building on the TUCASI campus; it was dedicated in May 2000. Enriqueta C. Bond (2000), president of the Burroughs Wellcome Fund, said: "As a member of the Research Triangle community, the Burroughs Wellcome Fund is eager to collaborate with our neighbors. Going forward, we hope that our presence [on the TUCASI campus] in Research Triangle Park will have a catalyzing effect to pull together diverse groups of researchers, policy makers, educators, and non-profit organizations to work on projects of mutual interest."

CHAPTER 15

REAPING THE HARVEST

The mind of man is capable of anything—
because everything is in it, all the past as well as all the future.

—JOSEPH CONRAD

REFLECTING ON THE HARVEST

During an interview with *The Leader* in 1969, Governor Luther Hodges offered his opinion about where Research Triangle Park will be by the end of the next decade. Before forecasting, he said (April 16, 1969), "Before I give you [my] predictions . . . I trust that you will not be unkind enough to remind me [of them] in 1979. . . . Almost surely [by the end of the decade] we will not match in any other single year the accomplishments of 1965."

Nineteen hundred and sixty five was the banner year for the Park. As discussed in detail in *A Generosity of Spirit* (1995, pp. 87–93):

The events of 1965 marked the turning point for the Park. . . . Governor Terry Sanford announced on his last day in office, January 6, 1965, that the U.S. Department of Health, Education, and Welfare (HEW) had selected Research Triangle Park for its $70 million Environmental Health Sciences Center. (Today this organization is known as the National Institute of Environmental Health

Sciences.) This announcement marked the end of a three-and-a-half-year effort to obtain that facility. . . . On April 14, 1965, Governor [Dan] Moore joined IBM officials to announce that IBM would locate a 600,000-square-foot research facility on four hundred acres in the Park. IBM had been courted for seven years. "IBM was the turning point," according to Archie Davis (1992). Not only was the Foundation now free of debt, but IBM's presence also validated the mission of the Park. . . . [Also in 1965] Technitrol, Inc., a Philadelphia-based computer electronics research company, committed to move into the Park. And the ground-breaking for the headquarters of the North Carolina State Board of Science and Technology had been scheduled. . . . [And] Beaunit Fibers, a division of Beaunit Corporation, announced in October that it would build a $5 million, 50,000-square-foot research facility on one hundred acres.

By the end of 1965, 1,249 total acres had been sold for development and 1,035 of that acreage had been sold in 1965 alone. Governor Hodges was not being overly bold in his projection that there would not be another development year like 1965.

By the end of 2000, the Research Triangle Foundation had sold for development 4,262 acres of a total of 6,971. Another 275 acres had been donated or sold for infrastructure, and 113 acres had been set aside as a natural area preserve. Therefore, at the end of 2000, nearly 67 percent of the Park's land was obligated.

The companies located in the Park are many of the preeminent public- and private-sector research companies in the world. To name only a few:[1]

- in information technology/telecommunications, Nortel Networks, Cisco Systems, and IBM
- in biotechnology/biopharmaceuticals, Bayer Biological Products, Biogen, and Syngenta (formally Novartis Agribusiness Biotechnology Research)
- in microelectronics, Cronos, Integrated Microsystems (spin-off of MCNC and wholly-owned subsidiary of JDS Uniphase) and Infineon Technologies
- in environmental sciences, the U.S. Environmental Protection Agency and the National Institute of Environmental Health Sciences

- in pharmaceuticals/healthcare, GlaxoSmithKline and BD Technologies

Not only are these research organizations generally prominent financially and by reputation, they are specifically known for the exemplary research of their staff. In 1988, Gertrude B. Elion and George H. Hitchings, both of Burroughs Wellcome, received the Nobel Prize in medicine (Fig. 35); and in 1994, Martin Rodbell, of the National Institute of Environmental Health Sciences, received the Nobel Prize in medicine (Fig. 36). Also noteworthy are the many accomplishments from the Research Triangle Institute. For example, in 2000 Monroe E. Wall and Mansukh C. Wani were awarded the Kettering Prize for their discovery of anti-tumor agents (Fig. 37).

THE BUMPER CROP

Where will the Park be at the end of the next decade? Jim Roberson (2000), president of the Research Triangle Foundation, believes that:

> as Research Triangle Park enters the twentieth-century, it will be as arguably the best known and most successful university-related research park in the United States, and perhaps the world. The Park is at the center of one of the most dynamic economic regions in the country and is, by many accounts, the engine behind the region's exuberant growth, growth which has resulted in straining the infrastructure's ability to provide adequate transportation facilities and public school capacities and [in] increasing the region's cost of living. As the Park moves toward its final build-out, the primary challenge it faces is to be catalytic in finding solutions to the problems an inadequate infrastructure poses. At the same time, it must continue its mission of helping to create quality jobs for North Carolina residents including the graduates of the universities, enhancing the strength and diversity of the region, state, and national economies and ensuring enduring quality of life.

Figure 35. *George H. Hitchings (left) and Gertrude B. Elion, 1988 Nobel laureates.*

Figure 36. *Martin Rodbell, 1994 Nobel laureate.*

Figure 37. *Mansukh Wani* (left) *and Monroe E. Wall, 2000 Kettering Prize recipients.*

APPENDIX A

121

THE MEDICAL COMPLEX

The Research Triangle area is the medical center of the upper South.

The Duke Medical School and Hospital, established in 1930, set highest standards of clinical practice and consultation, training, and investigation.

To this was added, in 1952, the four-year medical school at the University of North Carolina, ten miles away, along with the North Carolina Memorial Hospital, with its attached psychiatric wing and associated Graveley Tuberculosis Sanitorium. Also at Chapel Hill are the distinguished School of Public Health, the new School of Dentistry, and the School of Pharmacy.

HOSPITALS

The two teaching hospitals contain 1,062 beds. The annual outpatient service of these hospitals currently is 162,000.

The Veterans Administration Hospital in Durham, located a few hundred yards from the Duke Hospital, contains 449 beds.

In addition, there are ten other hospitals in Durham and Raleigh, with a total of 3,231 beds.

With this concentration may well be included the four-year Bowman Gray Medical School and teaching hospital at Winston-Salem, 115 miles from the Research Triangle.

At Charlotte, 125 miles away, is another medical center seven hospitals and 1,346 beds. In North Carolina there are 196 hospitals, containing 27,493 beds, the most widespread hospital development in the South.

THE SOUTH AND PHARMACEUTICALS

The economic advance of the South in recent years has opened up a major new market for pharmaceutical products.

Increased per capita income, more widespread education, the breathtaking spread of medical care throughout an urbanizing population—these and other developments have caused a many-fold increase in the consumption of pharmaceuticals.

No major full line pharmaceutical house has acted to take full advantage of this opportunity. The Research Triangle offers a sound basis for major pharmaceutical development.

TRAINING FOR PEOPLE AT WORK

The three institutions have favorable attitudes toward the establishment of programs of work for research scientists who wish to attain either higher proficiency in certain areas, or who wish to attain advanced degrees. Such programs are now in existence.

All programs of this sort are established through normal academic channels, and must meet accepted standards.

ACADEMIC TRAINING

Few areas of the nation can match the Research Triangle in the range and quality of its annual output of young men and women trained in the sciences related to pharmaceutical research.

The School of Pharmacy at the University of North Carolina is the only such school between Maryland and Florida that offers the doctorate in Pharmacy. Current graduate enrollment is 16 with new facilities to increase this number to 30. Annually, about fifty bachelor's degrees in pharmacy are awarded; this number will be doubled beginning in 1963.

The new pharmacy building at the University of North Carolina affords full research facilities, including special laboratories for manufacturing pharmacy, parenteral solutions, and sterile products.

Basic and Allied Sciences in Pharmaceutical Research at Triangle Universities

Anatomy (at 2)	Epidemiology
Animal Pathology	Experimental Medicine
Bacteriology and	Experimental Statistics
Immunology	Genetics
Bacteriology and	Microbiology
Microbiology	Nutrition (at 2)
Biochemistry	Parasitology
Biochemistry and	Pathology (at 2)
Nutrition (at 2)	Pharmacology (at 2)
Biostatistics	Physiology (at 3)
Botany (at 3)	Plant Pathology
Chemistry (at 3)	Preventive Medicine
Crop Management	Psychiatry
and Ecology	Soil Science
Entomology	Zoology

Approximate undergraduate and graduate enrollments in several selected areas, 1959-60, are as follows:

	Undergraduate	Graduate
Pharmacy	370	16
Chemistry	304	107
Zoology	103	59
Botany	228	67
Biochemistry	18	
Biochemistry and Nutrition		26
Nutrition		
Microbiology		10
Plant Pathology		19

RESEARCH

The research facilities and people of the Research Triangle that bear on pharmaceutical research are lodged in the schools and science departments listed above. All have a major teaching function.

It is accurate to say, however, that in general the research emphasis in these schools and departments is equal to the teaching emphasis. They are research oriented.

The range and quantity of current research in these various areas related to pharmaceuticals even that research that has been published or has been supported by grant or contract are too great for listing here.

The following, however, provides a random sample of the sorts and kinds of research on which recent publications have been made, or which are in press.

A study on the prevention of inactivation of quaternery germicides in troches.

New bases of pastilles.

Stabilization of parenteral preparations.

Synthesis of antitussives.

Synthesis of antimetabilites.

Synthesis of antiviral agents.

Improved disintergration of tablets.

Biological testing of antimetobolites.

Synthesis of acetal phosphatides.

Kinetics of proteolytic enzymes.

Kinetics of respiratory enzymes.

Nature of hydrogenases of bacteria.

Metabolic role of phosphoserine.

Nucleotide interconversions (enzymatic).

Sodium and potassium metabolism in muscle.

Mechanism of uremic anemia.

Chemistry of flavin nucleotides.

Metabolic role of glutamine.

Metabolic efforts of dinitrophenols.

Chemistry of connective tissue.

Basis for renal hypertension.

Enzymes of sulfa metabolism.

Enzymatic nucleotide synthesis.

Pathways of nitrogen metabolism.

A study of the factors involved in the observed increase in the incidence of fungus infection following antibiotic therapy.

Investigation of previously unreported toxic metabolites of group A streptococci.

A study of streptococcal hemolysins.

Studies on the nature of the toxic components of psittacosis viruses and their role in the pathogenesis of this disease.

Study of the distribution and mechanism of excretion of phenobarbital.

Study of the metabolic hydroxylation of phenobarbital.

Study of the metabolic hydroxylation of mesantoin, nirvanol, and diphenyl hydantoin.

Development of a method for the assay of small amounts of insulin.

Study of the effects of drugs on intestinal absorption and motility.

Study of the relationship between adrenal cortical function and alcoholic intoxication.

Study of the relationship between the permeation and the metabolism of carbohydrates in different cells.

Study of the metabolism, utilization, and action of methyl ethers of monosaccharides.

Studies of the conditions, dietary and otherwise, which favor the formation of kidney and bladder stones in human subjects.

General investigations of phospholipids from the points of view of both tissue metabolism and synthesis. This investigation has, as one purpose, the understanding of such metabolism under normal conditions and in cardiovascular diseases.

Methods for the fractionation and isolation of proteins and nucleoproteins of the nuclei or normal cells and of cancer cells for the purpose of finding qualitative and quantitative differences. Biosynthesis of nucleoproteins together with a search for inhibitors of such biosynthetic processes in cancer tissue.

Investigations of the metabolism of certain amino acids under normal and abnormal conditions.

Investigation of the role and mode of action of fluorides in prevention of dental caries.

Studies of certain problems of lipid metabolism and of certain phases of the chemistry of the formation of renal calculi.

Relation of nutrition to the growth of children.

Levels of biochemical variables in the blood of groups of people — hemoglobin, alkaline phosphatase, ascorbic acid, Vitamin A.

The Duke University Medical School and Hospital in Durham, N. C.

Medical Hill at the University of North Carolina in Chapel Hill

APPENDIX B

THE RESEARCH TRIANGLE OF NORTH CAROLINA

Duke University
Durham

N. C. State College
Raleigh

The University of North Carolina
Chapel Hill

RESOURCES FOR RESEARCH IN CHEMISTRY

12 mi.

CHEMISTRY BUILDING, DUKE UNIVERSITY

VENABLE HALL, CHEMISTRY BUILDING, UNIVERSITY OF NORTH CAROLINA

24 mi.

30 mi.

*An Extraordinary Concentration
of Research Facilities and Activity
in the Heart of the Upper South*

WITHERS HALL, CHEMISTRY BUILDING, N. C. STATE COLLEGE

*The Institutions Determining the Research Tri-
angle Provide a Stimulating Research Atmosphere
Backed Up by an Extraordinary Combination of
Research Facilities and Professional Training*

The area presents an ideal location for the professional scientist to
live and work . . .

amid congenial surroundings of other scientists in both the
academic and industrial spheres,

with the cultural advantages that play such an important
part in the life of large academic communities,

in the pleasant year-round climate of the Upper South, and

free from the congestion of the larger metropolitan districts.

*The Research Triangle Is Unique in Having in
a Non-Metropolitan Area Three Universities So
Highly Productive in Chemical Training*

Each institution has a chemistry department, fully accredited by the
American Chemical Society, engaged in research programs and chemical
training on both the undergraduate and graduate levels.

DUKE UNIVERSITY and the UNIVERSITY OF
NORTH CAROLINA offer programs leading to the Bache-
lor's, Master's and Doctor's Degrees in Analytical, Inorganic,
Organic, and Physical Chemistry. The Master's and Ph.D.
Degrees in Biochemistry are offered in the Medical Schools.

NORTH CAROLINA STATE COLLEGE offers pro-
grams leading to the Bachelor's and Master's degrees in Agricultural and Biological Chemistry, with Doctorates offered
in the closely related fields of Chemical Engineering, Animal
Nutrition, and Soil Science.

The Chemistry Departments of the three institutions are made up of
approximately 45 regular faculty members directing the instruction and
research programs. Approximately fifteen post doctoral research associates
are maintained on the staffs in the research programs each year.

Currently enrolled in the Chemistry Departments of the
Triangle Institutions are:

250 students working toward the Bachelor's Degree

111 students in graduate study.

Degrees Awarded In Chemistry		
	1953-57	1957
Bachelor's Degrees	280	63
Master's Degrees	71	14
Ph.D. Degrees	85	16

Current enrollments in the allied sciences are:

	Undergraduate	Graduate
Chemical Engineering	153	19
Biochemistry	......	21
Pharmacy and Pharmaceutical Chemistry	245	9
Animal Nutrition	......	5
Soil Chemistry	......	45
Textile Chemistry	40	6

The Research Triangle Is Unparalleled in the South for Its Concentration of Chemical Research

The Chemistry Departments in the Research Triangle recognize a vital connection between high quality instruction and vigorous, productive research. More than 75 publications have come from these laboratories in the past year.

Evidence of the research orientation of the departments is seen in the quality, quantity, and wide range of research in progress. Following is a partial listing of the areas under current investigation:

ANALYTICAL CHEMISTRY

Application of transitory electrode phenomena to analytical chemistry
Complexometric methods of analysis with EDTA and other complexing agents
Polarography of organic substances and metal chelates
Coulometric analysis
Ultraviolet and infrared spectroscopy
Mineral analysis with flame photometry
Spectroscopic analysis for minerals in plant and animal tissues
Gas chromatography

INORGANIC CHEMISTRY

Determination of stability constants of metal chelates and investigation of unusual metal chelates
High temperature chemistry of inorganic salts
Synthesis of high purity inorganic salts
Solution chemistry of inorganic substances, especially hydrolysis and aggregation of cations and anions
Kinetics and mechanisms of inorganic reactions

PHYSICAL CHEMISTRY

Isopiestic and light scattering studies on electrolytic solutions
Determination of magnetic properties of inorganic complex compounds
Theoretical and experimental studies of the thermodynamics of aqueous solutions of electrolytes with added organic compounds
Electrochemical study of battery electrodes with special emphasis on the manganese dioxide electrode
Scattering of high velocity molecular beams
X-ray crystallographic studies
Study of critical phenomena in two component systems
Cryogenics, especially specific heats of solids
Statistical mechanics
Kinetics of photolysis and pyrolysis reactions in the gas phase
Measurement and interpretation of gas solubilities in non-polar solvents
Infrared absorption studies of association in solution
Adsorption of fission products on clay minerals
Physical chemistry and thermodynamics of polymers
Physico-chemical studies of tobacco smoke and investigation of tobacco smoke composition by chromatographic, infrared, ultraviolet, and visible absorption measurements.

ORGANIC CHEMISTRY

The isotope effect of C^{14}
Mechanisms and kinetics of nucleophilic substitutions
Synthesis and mechanisms of rearrangements, condensations, eliminations, etc.
Stereochemistry of catalytic hydrogenation
Studies of direct and indirect fluorination of hydrocarbons, halides, ketones, nitriles, amides amines, and sulfides
Aromatic and heterocyclic fluorine compounds
Synthesis of polycyclic aromatic compounds and other substances with special attention to fungicides and bacteriocides
Organic synthesis including heterocyclic compounds, esp. pyrimidines
Chemistry of "sandwich compounds" like ferrocene
Composition of plant and animal natural products
Residues from spray materials
Carotenoid synthesis in yeast
Plant pigments
Pigments and non-saponifiables in fish oils
Cholesterol metabolism in animals
Fat metabolism
Organic synthesis in general

The Research Triangle Is Endowed with an Unusual Assemblage of Facilities for Chemical Research

LIBRARIES

The combined libraries of the three universities contain over two million volumes, of which more than 31,000 volumes are located in the chemistry departmental libraries. Large additional holdings of chemical journals, monographs, and reference works are found in the libraries of related departments. Just about every chemical journal of interest, including translations of several of the Russian journals, is in at least one of the libraries. Published and kept up to date is a volume listing the complete holdings of all scientific journals in each library, simplifying the locating of any desired journal. Good cooperative service among the three universities allows rapid loan of volumes from one library to another. In addition to the combined resources, the general libraries of the universities participate in interlibrary loan arrangements with the Library of Congress and those at other institutions.

LABORATORIES

The combined physical plants of the three Chemistry Departments occupy more than a quarter of a million square feet of space including:

115 research laboratories ranging in size from one man laboratories to laboratories for small groups

40 instructional laboratories

an ample supply of seminar rooms, classrooms, and large lecture halls.

In addition to usual laboratory facilities, there are several specially constructed or equipped laboratories including:

Three low level radiochemical laboratories
A separately housed radioisotopes laboratory
A stable isotopes laboratory
A dust-free laboratory for light scattering measurements
Spectroscopic laboratories with dark rooms
A high temperature reactions laboratory
Two high pressure hydrogenation laboratories
Instrumental analysis laboratories, some with temperature and humidity control
Complete organic and inorganic microchemical laboratories
Computing laboratory with Remington Rand punched card equipment for punching, sorting, and tabulating
An X-ray crystallographic laboratory

SPECIALIZED EQUIPMENT

Many items of special equipment housed in the chemistry departments, much of which is duplicated at two or more of the institutions, is listed in part below:

Single and double beam recording infrared spectrophotometers
Point and continuous ultraviolet and visible spectrophotometers
Flame photometers
Littrow emission spectrographs
Stigmatic grating emission spectrograph (15000 lines/inch)
Densitometers and comparator microphotometers
Zeiss interferometer for solutions and gases
Light scattering photometer and differential refractometer
Precision polarimeter
Nuclear magnetic resonance equipment
Magnetic susceptability measurement apparatus
Single crystal X-ray diffraction apparatus
High velocity molecular beam apparatus
Dielectric constant measurement apparatus
Recording polarographs
Heat of solution measuring apparatus
Scalers and counters for radioactive systems
Vibrating reed electrometers
Nier 60° mass spectrometer
Precision constant temperature bath for D_2O analysis
Isopiestic measuring apparatus
Osmometers
Chromatographic equipment and fraction collector
Gas chromatography apparatus
Low and high temperature rectification columns
200 tube Craig countercurrent extractor
Elemental fluorine generators
Ketene and ozone generators
Low and high pressure hydrogenation equipment

In other schools and departments of the universities are located several notable facilities:

A 10 kilowatt nuclear reactor	In the School of Engineering at N. C. State College
A 4,000,000 volt Van de Graaf accelerator	In the Department of Physics at Duke University
A Collins liquid helium cryostat	In the Department of Physics at Duke University
An IBM 650 electronic computor	In the Institute of Statistics at N. C. State College
An RCA electron microscope	In the School of Engineering at N. C. State College

SPECIAL SERVICES

In the Department of Chemistry at the University of North Carolina is a completely equipped glass shop with an expert glassblower. Any kind of glass research equipment can be fashioned in this shop.

A full time glassblower is also maintained in the Department of Physics at Duke University.

The chemical laboratories all have either in their plants or within the universities fully equipped machine shops staffed with expert instrument makers and machinists.

A commercial supplier of chemicals and laboratory equipment is located in Durham.

The Research Atmosphere

The community of interest in chemical research extends out from the Chemistry Departments into the many related fields found in the Medical Complex at Chapel Hill including the School of Pharmacy, the Medical School at Duke University, the Departments of Nutrition, Soil Science, and Chemical Engineering, and the School of Textiles at State College. These other schools and departments are actively engaged in chemical research and contribute in large measure to the research personnel in the area.

Researchers of international stature are frequently brought into the area by organizations such as the American Chemical Society, Sigma Xi, various colloquia sponsored by individual departments or jointly among the universities, and other organizations. These meetings are open to the public and are easily accessible from any point in the Research Triangle.

A sampling of some of the speakers in the Triangle Area during the past year includes:

Speaker	From	Topic
T. S. Wheeler	University College, Dublin	Studies in the Chemistry of Flavanoids
Karl H. Hausser	Max Planck Institute	Magnetic and Spectrographic Properties of Radicals of N-Containing Organic Complex Molecules at Low Temperatures
James Franck	University of Chicago	The Role of Chlorophyll in Photosynthesis
C. O'Ceallaigh	Dublin Institute for Advanced Study	K-Meson Studies
H. C. Brown	Purdue University	Chemical Effects of Steric Strain
Raymond S. Boyer	Plastics Division Rohm and Haas	Block and Graft Co-polymers
D. S. Tarbell	Rochester University	Carcinogenic Aromatic Hydrocarbons
Mansel Davies	University of Wales	Aspects of Structure and Interaction of Simple Amides
Harry H. Sisler	University of Florida	Recent Developments in the Chemistry of Hydrazine and Chloramine and Their Derivatives
R. W. Stoughton	Oak Ridge National Laboratories	High Temperature Solution Chemistry
Hermann Flaschka	National Research Center, Cairo, Egypt	The Present Status and Problems of EDTA Titrations
F. O. Rice	Catholic University	Recent Advances in Chemistry—On Jupiter
Lawrence Wilets	Los Alamos National Laboratory	Neutron and Proton Densities and Potentials in Nuclei
Walter Kohn	Carnegie Institute of Technology	Impurity States in Silicon
W. F. Libby	Atomic Energy Commission	Use of Radioisotopes in Teaching
Arnold M. Bass	National Bureau of Standards	Stabilization of Atoms and Radicals at Low Temperatures
I. M. Robinson	E. I. du Pont de Nemours	A New Field of Chemistry: Stereospecific Reactions Using Coordination Catalysts
Roger Williams	Biochemical Institute University of Texas	Chemical Anthropology
F. Hund	University of Frankfort	Elementary Remarks on Field Quantization
Richard T. Arnold	University of Minnesota	Some Reactions of Hydrocarbons Involving Double Bond Shifts
P. S. Skell	Pennsylvania State University	Carbenes—Bivalent Carbon Reaction Intermediates

Contributing to the research activity and atmosphere are several additional research installations including: A tobacco laboratory, a pulp and paper laboratory, and a U. S. Public Health Service Laboratory specializing in the chemistry of organic arsenic and phosphorus compounds and therapeutic agents for treatment of venereal disease.

Partly because of the research activity in the Research Triangle, Union Carbide has located near Raleigh an experimental farm for the testing of agricultural chemicals and pesticides.

Located on the campus of Duke University is the Office of Ordnance Research of the U. S. Army.

The Governor's Research Triangle Committee, Inc.

George L. Simpson, Jr., Director, Box 1488, Raleigh, N. C.

William F. Little, Associate Director for Chemistry
228 Venable Hall, Chapel Hill, N. C.

The Governor's Research Triangle Committee, Incorporated, is a non-stock, non-profit organization whose purpose is to do all that is possible to use and develop the research resources of the Triangle area.

The Committee works solely within the bounds and desires of the three institutions. Its primary purpose is to make industrial and governmental research activities aware of the scientific resources and cultural advantages of the Triangle area.

When asked, the Committee will undertake to arrange a meeting between such industrial and governmental agencies and appropriate people from the three institutions.

The Committee undertakes also to help in carrying forward any projects deemed desirable by one or more of the institutions.

MEMBERS

Robert M. Hanes, President. Honorary Chairman of Board, Wachovia Bank and Trust Company, Winston-Salem, N. C.

A. Hollis Edens, Vice President. President, Duke University, Durham, N. C.

Brandon P. Hodges, Secretary-Treasurer. Counselor, The Champion Paper and Fibre Company, Canton, N. C.

Luther H. Hodges, Governor of North Carolina, Raleigh, N. C.

William C. Friday, President, University of North Carolina, Chapel Hill, N. C.

Robert Armstrong, Vice President, Celanese Corporation of America, Charlotte, N. C.

E. Y. Floyd, Director, N. C. Plant Food Institute, Raleigh, N. C.

Grady Rankin, Attorney, Gastonia, N. C.

C. W. Reynolds, Asst. Works Mgr., Western Electric Company, Winston-Salem, N. C.

William H. Ruffin, President, Erwin Mills, Durham, N. C.

WORKING COMMITTEE

J. Harold Lampe, Dean, School of Engineering, N. C. State College, Chairman.

W. C. Davison, Dean, School of Medicine, Duke University

Marcus E. Hobbs, Dean, Graduate School, Duke University

D. W. Colvard, Dean, School of Agriculture, N. C. State College

Henry T. Clark, Jr., Administrator, Division of Health Affairs, University of N. C.

W. J. Seeley, Dean, College of Engineering, Duke University

Arthur Roe, Director of the Institute of Natural Science, University of N. C.

Malcolm Campbell, Dean, School of Textiles, N. C. State College

Daniel O. Price, Director of The Institute for Research in Social Science, University of N. C.

APPENDIX C

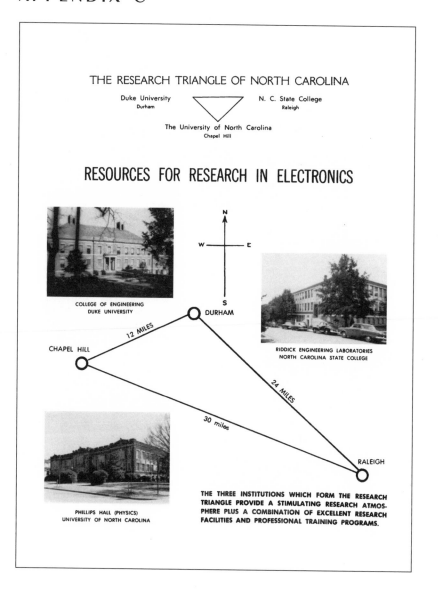

THE RESEARCH TRIANGLE OF NORTH CAROLINA

Duke University
Durham

N. C. State College
Raleigh

The University of North Carolina
Chapel Hill

RESOURCES FOR RESEARCH IN ELECTRONICS

N

W ——— E

S

COLLEGE OF ENGINEERING
DUKE UNIVERSITY

DURHAM

12 MILES

CHAPEL HILL

RIDDICK ENGINEERING LABORATORIES
NORTH CAROLINA STATE COLLEGE

24 MILES

30 miles

RALEIGH

PHILLIPS HALL (PHYSICS)
UNIVERSITY OF NORTH CAROLINA

THE THREE INSTITUTIONS WHICH FORM THE RESEARCH TRIANGLE PROVIDE A STIMULATING RESEARCH ATMOSPHERE PLUS A COMBINATION OF EXCELLENT RESEARCH FACILITIES AND PROFESSIONAL TRAINING PROGRAMS.

THE THREE INSTITUTIONS OF HIGHER LEARNING FORMING THE RESEARCH
TRIANGLE ARE ACTIVE IN RESEARCH IN ELECTRONICS AND IN TRAINING
STUDENTS IN ELECTRICAL ENGINEERING, PHYSICS AND RELATED FIELDS

NORTH CAROLINA STATE COLLEGE

Founded by legislative act in 1887 and opening in 1889, this member of the National Association of Land Grant Colleges and State Universities is composed of

7 schools   48 departments

and offers the master's degree in 35 fields, the doctorate in 18 fields.

Of special interest to the **electronic industry** are the

Electrical Engineering Department granting the B.S., M.S., and Ph.D. degrees.

Physics Department granting the B.S., M.S., and Ph.D. degrees in Nuclear Engineering and Engineering Physics

Also degree programs in Aeronautical, Ceramic, Chemical, Civil, Geological, Mechanical, Metallurgical, and Industrial Engineering, Engineering Mathematics and Experimental Statistics

MEMORIAL TOWER
N. C. STATE COLLEGE

DUKE UNIVERSITY

Founded in 1839 as Union Institute, becoming Trinity College in 1859 and Duke University in 1924, this private institution and member of the Association of American Universities consists of

9 colleges and schools

and offers the master's degree in 24 fields, the doctorate in 19 fields.

Of special interest to the **electronic industry** are the

Electrical Engineering Department granting the B.S. and M.S. degrees

Physics Department granting the A.B., A.M., and Ph.D. degrees

Also degree programs in Civil and Mechanical Engineering, Mathematics, and the School of Medicine

DUKE CHAPEL
DUKE UNIVERSITY

UNIVERSITY OF NORTH CAROLINA

Chartered in 1789 and opened in 1795, the first state university in the United States, this member of the Association of American Universities is composed of

14 colleges and schools

70 departments

and offers the M.S. in 42 fields, the Ph.D. in 27 fields.

Of special interest to the **electronic industry** is the

Physics Department granting the B.S., M.S. and Ph.D. degrees

Also degree programs in Theoretical Statistics, Mathematics, and the School of Medicine

BELL TOWER
UNIVERSITY OF NORTH CAROLINA

RESOURCES OF TRAINED PERSONNEL

The Research Triangle area offers annually a substantial number of young men trained in electronics and related fields both with baccalaureate and with graduate degrees. The enrollment in engineering will increase greatly in the near future. Most of the graduates prefer to live in the area. Enrollment data for the year 1956-57 are as follows:

	Total Enrollment	18,165	
Enrollment in		Undergraduate	Graduate
Schools of Engineering		3,690	127
Electrical Engineering		977	25
Physics		105	69

TRAINING FOR PEOPLE AT WORK

The institutions are conducting special training programs for graduate engineers working in the area. Regular courses are offered in off-campus locations and in the evening by special arrangement when the demand exists. The three institutions are favorable toward the establishment of further programs for research scientists who wish to attain either higher proficiency in certain areas, or who wish to attain advanced degrees.

COMPUTER UNDER DEVELOPMENT AT N. C. STATE COLLEGE

RESEARCH

Although the Electrical Engineering and Physics departments of the Research Triangle have a major teaching function, research in electronics is very active. Research is considered a vital part of the whole program of each department. Research interests and projects are on a high level and cover a wide range.

The following partial list of work currently in progress or recently completed is offered as a sample of the range of activity in electronics in the Research Triangle.

Studies and development of automatic data analyzing
Fundamental analyses of electronic navigating systems (Consolan, L. F. Loran, and Navaglobe)
Superconductivity at millimeter wave frequencies
Millimicrosecond time-difference measurements
A time study of an automatic control system for a nuclear reactor
Instrumentation of a field survey meter for soil moisture determination
Studies of radio transmitting antennas
Investigation of the effect of high temperatures on ferromagnetic materials
Development of testing methods to determine the microwave characteristics of titanates and zirconates
Millimeter and submillimeter wave spectroscopy
A solid scintillation detector for slow neutrons in time of flight spectrometer
Studies of electrical properties of metals at very low temperatures
Mobility of ions in crystals
Development of an analog computer for solution of stochastic problems
A nuclear reactor simulator
A differential pulse amplitude analyzer
Development of electronic means of precision mass measurements by time-of-flight methods
Automatic reactor power level controls
Nuclear resonance experiments on He^3 below 1° Kelvin
Studies of electrical properties of large NaCl crystals
Development of ultrasonic flowmeter to special requirements of measurement of blood flow in medical research
Studies of the properties of longitudinal strain waves in plastic materials
Radiation counting system for recording rapidly varying count rates
Microwave spectroscopy of biological substances
Studies of methods of solution of simultaneous ordinary differential equations with variable coefficients on both analog and digital computers
Direct electron energy losses in thin metallic foils
Instrumentation and calibration of photoelectric nephelometer
X-ray analysis of the homocharge of the electret
Development of regulating system for maintaining temperature of reference saline solution at temperature of subject's body during hypothermia experiments
The fine structure of the microwave absorption of oxygen
A new electronic system for detecting microwave spectra
An instantaneous electronic digital-to-analog converter

CONSULTING

Many faculty members of the three institutions maintain a consulting practice. Members of the engineering and physics faculties have been especially active in this respect. Included in the consulting work in the electronics field have been such subjects as microwave tube design, Doppler radar analysis and design, and guided-missile seeking systems.

MATHEMATICS

The importance of mathematics in modern engineering research is constantly increasing. All three institutions of the Research Triangle have excellent mathematics staffs.

The three institutions complement each other to such a degree that most of the important specialties may be found within the area. Unusual competency is apparent in the fields of applied mathematics, matrix theory, number theory, algebra, topology and analysis.

The development of computers has dramatized the role of mathematics in industrial progress. On the campus of North Carolina State College are located both an IBM 650 digital computer and a GEDA analog computer. Progress is being made in the area to obtain one of the largest computers available.

STATISTICS

The value of statistical methods applied to almost every field of scientific research is unquestioned. The Institute of Statistics operating on the campuses of the University of North Carolina and North Carolina State College is one of the outstanding training and research organizations of the world.

The Raleigh Section of the Institute cooperates with the Department of Experimental Statistics of North Carolina State College. In Chapel Hill, the Institute works with the Department of Statistics of the University of North Carolina, with the Department of Biostatistics in the School of Public Health of the University, with the Psychometric Laboratory, and with the Survey Operations Unit.

The Institute has been successful in encouraging and stimulating research. Recent consulting work includes studying reliability problems of cathode ray tubes and of guidance systems for "Ajax" and "Hercules." The Raleigh Section has conducted short training courses for several years for representatives from industry.

Uniting the strengths of several departments and campuses, the Institute in its membership and staff represents a resource in statistics of great distinction.

THE RESEARCH ATMOSPHERE

LIBRARIES

The combined libraries of the three educational institutions contain over two million volumes. Published and kept up to date is a volume listing the complete holdings of all scientific journals in each library to simplify the locating of any desired journal. Good cooperative service among the three institutions allows rapid loan of volumes from one library to another. In addition to the combined resources, the general libraries of the universities participate in inter-library loan arrangements with the Library of Congress and libraries at other institutions.

LECTURES

Seminars and colloquia are freqeuntly held in the area, open to the public and easily assessible from any point in the Research Triangle. Researchers of international stature are frequently brought into the area by such organizations as the Institute of Radio Engineers, the American Institute of Electrical Engineers, Sigma Xi, various colloquia sponsored by individual departments or jointly among the institutions, and other organizations.

A sampling of some of the technical speakers in the Triangle Area during the past year includes:

Name	From	Topic
Warren Kohn	Carnegie Institute of Technology	Impurity States in Silicon
Nathan M. Newmark	University of Illinois	The Influence of High-speed Digital Computers on Research
Peter Klaudy	University of Graz, Austria	The Behavior of Electrical Contacts
W. Z. Friend	International Nickel Company	Corrosion in Nuclear Materials
George Leddicotte	Oak Ridge National Laboratory	Activation Analysis
Warren Henry	Naval Research Laboratory	Magnetic Interactions in Silicon
Milton C. Edlund	Babcock and Wilcox Co.	Reactor Theory
R. Glover	University of California	Superconductivity in the Millimeter Microwave and Far Infra-Red
Robert J. Walker	Cornell University	Research Problems for Digital Computers
Earle Buckingham	Massachusetts Institute of Technology	Dynamics of Elastic Bodies
Ali Cambel	Northwestern University	Aerothermochemistry of Flame Stabilization
C. R. Russell	General Motors Corp.	Reactor Safety
W. M. Breazeale	Babcock and Wilcox Co.	Research Associated with Reactors
Bern Dibner	Burndy Engineering Co.	The Impact of Science on our Society
J. Wolfowitz	Cornell University	The Minimum Distance Method
William E. Shoupp	Westinghouse Electric Corporation	Developments in Nuclear Power
L. Rosenfeld	University of Manchester	Charge Distribution in Nuclei
Myer Garbor	National Research Council, Ottawa	Magnetic Susceptibilities of Dilute Binary Alloys
Gerald M. Foley	Leeds and Northrup Co.	Control Instruments
A. D. Moore	University of Michigan	Fields from Fluid Mappers

OTHER RESEARCH FACILITIES

Contributing to the research activity and atmosphere are several additional research installations including:

A Tobacco Laboratory   A Pulp and Paper Laboratory

The American Machine and Foundry Company has located a research laboratory in Raleigh.

Located on the campus of Duke University is the Office of Ordnance Research of the U. S. Army.

Also

A 4,000,000-volt Van de Graaf accelerator   In the Department of Physics at Duke University

A 10-Kilowatt Nuclear Reactor   In the School of Engineering at North Carolina State College

An Electron Microscope   In the School of Engineering at North Carolina State College

THE COMMUNITY

THE AREA

The area is an ideal location in which the professional scientist may live and work . . .

amid congenial surroundings of other scientists in both the academic and cultural spheres

with the cultural advantages that play such an important part in the life of large academic communities

in the pleasant year-round climate of the Upper South, and

free from the congestion of the larger metropolitan districts.

ACCESSIBILITY

Two main north-south railroads serve the Triangle, with excellent overnight transportation to Washington and New York. The Raleigh-Durham Airport is almost exactly in the center of the Triangle. Air service is excellent, with several competing airlines. For instance there are 13 daily departures for Washington and 11 for New York.

Washington	67 minutes
New York	2 hours, 15 minutes

CULTURAL ATMOSPHERE

Concerts by national touring artists are frequent; indeed, during the season there is scarcely a week when some excellent program is not available in each of the three communities. Well known attractions appearing within the past year are

Ballet Russe de Monte Carlo	Robert Wagner Chorale
Hungarian String Quartet	Quartetto Italiano
Pittsburgh Symphony Orchestra	Choir Boys of Norway
Jerome Hines	Piatigorsky

and many others

Speakers visit the area under the auspices of many societies, organized lecture series, and endowed lectureships. Some of the outstanding persons speaking here within the past year are

Hon. Harold E. Stassen	Hon. Herbert Morrison
Dr. Ralph Bunche	Justice William O. Douglas
Mrs. Eleanor Roosevelt	Mr. James C. Hagerty
Mr. Robert Frost	Dame Edith Sitwell

and many others

The Duke Players, the Carolina Playmakers, and the Raleigh Little Theatre offer excellent amateur productions throughout the year.

SPECIAL FEATURES

In Raleigh

The **State Art Museum** is considered unique among the museums of the world.

The **Reynolds Coliseum** seating 12,500 persons for sporting events has a skating rink and offers such attractions as ice extravaganzas, professional hockey and tennis, and the circus.

The **State Fair Arena** has received wide publicity as one of the ten outstanding buildings in America today.

In Durham

The **Sarah P. Duke Gardens** are visited annually by thousands for their perennial beauty.

The **Duke Chapel** with its 210-foot tower combines a unique adaptation of English and French Gothic architecture.

The **Duke Medical School and Hospital** comprise an internationally known and respected medical center.

In Chapel Hill

The **Morehead Planetarium** offers daily public demonstrations and lectures, and houses two art galleries, two scientific exhibit rooms and one of only two thirty-five foot orreries of the solar system in the world.

The Governor's Research Triangle Committee, Inc.

George L. Simpson, Jr., Director, Box 1488, Raleigh, N. C.

Wm. D. Stevenson, Jr., Assistant Director for Electronics
327 Daniels Hall, N. C. State College, Raleigh, N. C.

The Governor's Research Triangle Committee, Incorporated, is a non-stock, non-profit organization whose purpose is to do all that is possible to use and develop the research resources of the Triangle area.

The Committee works solely within the bounds and desires of the three institutions. Its primary purpose is to make industrial and governmental research activities aware of the scientific resources and cultural advantages of the Triangle area.

When asked, the Committee will undertake to arrange a meeting between such industrial and governmental agencies and appropriate people from the three institutions.

The Committee undertakes also to help in carrying forward any projects deemed desirable by one or more of the institutions.

MEMBERS

Robert M. Hanes, President. Honorary Chairman of Board, Wachovia Bank and Trust Company, Winston-Salem, N. C.

A. Hollis Edens, Vice President. President, Duke University, Durham, N. C.

Brandon P. Hodges, Secretary-Treasurer. Counselor, The Champion Paper and Fibre Company, Canton, N. C.

Luther H. Hodges, Governor of North Carolina, Raleigh, N. C.

William C. Friday, President, University of North Carolina, Chapel Hill, N. C.

Robert Armstrong, Vice President, Celanese Corporation of America, Charlotte, N. C.

E. Y. Floyd, Director, N. C. Plant Food Institute, Raleigh, N. C.

Grady Rankin, Attorney, Gastonia, N. C.

C. W. Reynolds, Asst. Works Mgr., Western Electric Company, Winston-Salem, N. C.

William H. Ruffin, President, Erwin Mills, Durham, N. C.

WORKING COMMITTEE

J. Harold Lampe, Dean, School of Engineering, N. C. State College, Chairman

W. C. Davison, Dean, School of Medicine, Duke University

Marcus E. Hobbs, Dean, Graduate School, Duke University

D. W. Colvard, Dean, School of Agriculture, N. C. State College

Henry T. Clark, Jr., Administrator, Division of Health Affairs, University of N. C.

W. J. Seeley, Dean, College of Engineering, Duke University

Arthur Roe, Director of the Institute of Natural Science, University of N. C.

Malcolm Campbell, Dean, School of Textiles, N. C. State College

Daniel O. Price, Director of The Institute for Research in Social Science, University of N. C

APPENDIX D

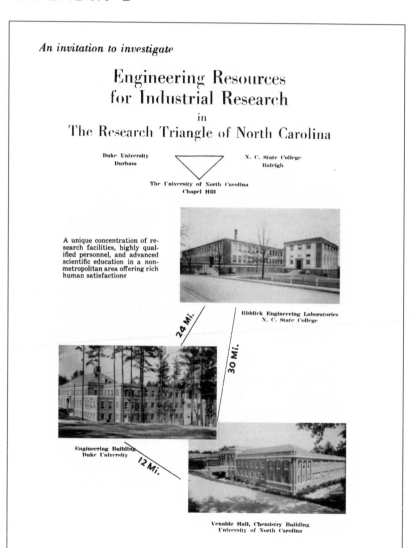

An invitation to investigate

Engineering Resources
for Industrial Research
in
The Research Triangle of North Carolina

Duke University
Durham

N. C. State College
Raleigh

The University of North Carolina
Chapel Hill

A unique concentration of research facilities, highly qualified personnel, and advanced scientific education in a nonmetropolitan area offering rich human satisfactions

Riddick Engineering Laboratories
N. C. State College

24 Mi.

30 Mi.

Engineering Building
Duke University

12 Mi.

Venable Hall, Chemistry Building
University of North Carolina

The Evolution of the Research Triangle

The Research Triangle was not planned. It is a natural consequence of the proximity of three outstanding institutions of higher learning noted for their contributions to basic scientific knowledge. North Carolina State College in Raleigh is a distinguished technological institution whose staff and facilities attract graduate students from all over the nation as well as many foreign lands. Duke University, universally recognized for its sound research programs, is located in Durham, a distance of twenty-four miles from Raleigh. Located in Chapel Hill, a distance of twelve miles from Durham and thirty miles from Raleigh, is the University of North Carolina, the oldest state university. The University of North Carolina, often called the citadel of southern thought, has long been known for its research in both the natural and social sciences. These three institutions determine the Research Triangle, and their combined resources are unique outside of a metropolitan area.

The tradition of research, as well as its practice, is not of recent origin in the three institutions of the Research Triangle. In his inaugural address President Edward Kidder Graham (1914-1918) of the University of North Carolina had this to say about research:

> It is this organic relation to the democratic state that puts the southern state university at the vital center of the state's formative material prosperity. "What are southern universities doing", asks a great industrial leader, "to give economic independence to southern industry." It is a fair challenge, and the state university joyfully acknowledges its obligation fully to meet it. It is a part of the business of laboratories to function in the productive state by solving the problems of embarrassed industry. Science has so faithfully performed this obligation that the main arch of modern industry rests on the laboratory.

How well the challenge stated by President Graham has been met by the three institutions of the Research Triangle is clearly evidenced by the fact that North Carolina, the pioneer state of the South in industrial development, is today the largest industrial state in the region.

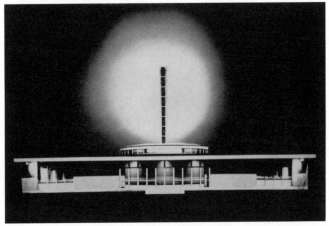

Raleigh Reactor, North Carolina State College

Resources for Research

Personnel

The most important resource for research is obviously personnel of high technical competence. Hence, the most important asset of the Research Triangle is the large pool of highly qualified engineers and scientists on the staffs of the three institutions. Moreover, these staff members are accustomed to mutual consultations and cooperation in the solution of problems that transcend the special interests of an individual investigator. Of particular significance is the fact that a large number of these specialists are called upon to assist many industrial organizations throughout the country in the solution of unusual technical problems. Hence, there is a wide exchange of ideas among the investigators at the three institutions and with industrial investigators.

There are approximately 170 engineers and 182 scientists in the fields of mathematics, physics, chemistry, and statistics possessing unusual competence in specialties which embrace virtually every area of endeavor in engineering and the physical sciences. Some indication of the productivity of these specialists can be gained from the fact that more than 200 publications in engineering, 100 in physics, 75 in chemistry, 60 in mathematics, and 80 in statistics have come from the laboratories of the three institutions during the past year.

Over 400 research investigations in the areas of engineering and the physical sciences are currently in progress at the three institutions. Research at the three institutions extends over a wide range of basic inquiries and is supported by the institutions, foundations, industry, and government by sums of money in excess of $7,000,000. The following sample list of investigations is typical of the nature of research conducted in the Research Triangle.

Aeronautical Engineering

Experimental determination of the circulation strength of wing tip vortices by means of a woolen tuft mounted on the wing tip.

An investigation of a wind-tunnel design suitable for determining possible effects of transient wing deformation on airplane stability.

Experimental procedures for the direct measurement of stress.

An analogy of the special theory of relativity to the study of compressible fluid flow and the prediction of subsonic pressure distribution by the sound-space theory.

Research characteristics of aircraft pressure instruments.

Agricultural Engineering

Mechanization of farming operations, crop processing.

Design and development of a gravity flow unit for metering liquid nitrogen solutions.

Time and effort analysis of seating conditions for tobacco primers.

Chemical Engineering

Investigation of a radioactive tracer technique in a study of wall-adjacent velocities in a flowing fluid.

Method of measuring thermal properties of poor conductors.

Plate efficiency of fractionating columns.

Liquid-liquid extraction.

The application of statistical procedures to a study of the flooding capacity of a pulse column.

Non-newtonian fluids.

Civil Engineering

Flow and fracture of solids.

Plastic design of structural steel.

Design of thin structural shells.

A new method of analysis of statically indeterminate structures.

Mechanism of adsorption by activated sludge.

Study of mechanism of biochemical oxidation of solutions and colloidal suspension of organic matter.

Dissociation of chlorine dioxide in solution.

Improved indicators for contamination of bathing waters.

Mechanism of coagulation in water.

Electrical Engineering

Investigation of the mechanism of dielectric breakdown of plastic insulating materials under high voltage impulses.

Development of method for applying electric radiant heating to industrial processing of textiles.

Evaluation of ferromagnetic materials in terms of the harmonic content of associated magnetic field quantities.

Studies, investigations and applied research concerning rapid analysis of field intensity data.

An instantaneous electronic digital-to-analog converter.

An investigation of the dielectric strength of N-decane.

A mean and variance analog computer.

A microwave frequency standard.

Studies of navaglobe long range electronic navigation system.

Industrial Engineering

Furniture dimension stock from sub-standard logs.

Consistency in speed rating.

Quality control in furniture production.

An investigation of minor method changes in time-study rating.

Cost savings from establishing appropriate dimensional tolerances.

Mechanical Engineering

Determination of the effects of sound waves on the velocity of flame.

An analytical investigation of condensation shock.

Operation of medium-speed diesel engines on heavy fuel.

Determination of diesel engine valve wear and failures.

Thermodynamic and heat transfer properties of liquid metals.

Investigation of secondary fluids for aircraft reactors.

Measurement of the fire resistance of cellular plastic materials.

Total entropy production of chemically irreversible processes.

Cyclic magnetic cooling. Ranque (Hilsch) tubes, and gas liquefaction by means of Ranque tubes.
Phase synchronization of reciprocating internal combustion engines.
Investigation of flame propagation and temperatures in internal combustion engines.
Nonlinear dynamic coupling in a beam vibration.
An analysis of dynamic forces in cam followers.
Investigation of frame and body stresses in buses under road conditions.

Mineral Industries

Use of vibration under low pressure in the forming of oxide and carbide refractory bodies.
Escape of fission products through layers of ceramic materials.
Dielectric properties of ceramic materials.
Investigation of prophyllite refractories.
Slagging of naval boiler refractories.
The effects of hydrostatic pressures on the compaction of shapes which have been previously die formed from non-plastic powders.
An investigation and correlation of the relationship of the linear thermal coefficient of expansion to the brittleness in certain steels.
Vibratory compacting of metal and ceramic powders.
Relation between the elastic moduli of anisotropic crystallites and quasi-isotropic polycrystalline aggregates.
Preliminary investigation of the fission product retention of metal and cermet compacts.

Nuclear Engineering

Research in nuclear reactor instrumentation, calibration, and operation.
Radiation damage in materials.
Neutron activation analysis.
Neutron diffraction studies.
Properties and behavior of positronium.
Accoustical and optical properties of matter.
A portable rate meter and source-counter assembly for measuring soil moisture content by neutron scattering.
Fission-spectrum formula in reactor calculations.
Design analysis for a nuclear power reactor.
The structure of electro deposited nickel.
Observations on the meteorological dispersal of stack gases at the Raleigh Reactor stack.
The fast neutron response of some organic phosphors molded in plastic.
The fast fission factor for hollow natural uranium cylinders.

Physics

Measurement of neutron cross sections including neutron width, charge particle scattering and coulomb excitation, charged particle reactions.
Study of the structure of molecules by microwave spectroscopy and radio frequency techniques.
Solid state studies, particularly as assisted by radiation damage and low temperature.
Study of properties of liquid helium at low temperature.
Studies in high energy physics including new unstable particles—interaction of extremely high energy particles with matter.
Study of superconductivity at high frequencies.
Molecular structure of certain organic molecules.
Study of reactions taking place in flames.
Theoretical studies in nuclear shell structure and beta-rays.
Accoustical and optical properties of matter.
Cosmic rays.
Infrared molecular spectroscopy.
Physics of metals.
Celestial mechanics.
Solid-state physics.

Chemistry

Polarography of organic substances and metal chelates.
Calometric analysis.
Ultraviolet and infrared spectroscopy.
Mineral analysis with flame photometry.
Spectroscopic analysis for minerals in plant and animal tissues.
Gas chromatography.
Determination of stability constants of metal chelates and investigation of unusual metal chelates.
High temperature chemistry of inorganic salts.
Solution chemistry of inorganic substances, especially hydrolysis and aggregation of cations and anions.
Synthesis of high purity inorganic salts.
Kinetics and mechanisms of inorganic reactions.
Isopiestic and light scattering studies on electrolytic solutions.
Determination of magnetic properties of inorganic complex compounds.
Theoretical and experimental studies of the thermodynamics of aqueous solutions of electrolytes with added organic compounds.
Electrochemical study of battery electrodes with special emphasis on the manganese dioxide electrode.
Scattering of high velocity molecular beams.
X-ray crystallographic studies.
Study of critical phenomena in two component systems.
Cryogenics, especially specific heats of solids.
Statistical mechanics.
Kinetics of photolysis and pyrolysis reactions in the gas phase.
Measurement and interpretation of gas solubilities in non-polar solvents.
Infrared absorption studies of association in solution.
Adsorption of fission products on clay minerals.
Physical chemistry and thermodynamics of polymers.
Mechanisms and kinetics of nucleophilic substitutions.
Synthesis and mechanisms of rearrangements, condensations, eliminations, etc.
Stereochemistry of catalytic hydrogenation.
Studies of direct and indirect fluorination of hydrocarbons, halides, ketones, nitriles, amides, amines, and sulfides.
Aromatic and heterocyclic fluorine compounds.
Synthesis of polycyclic aromatic compounds and other substances with special attention to fungicides and bacteriocides.

Statistics

Sample survey theory and methodology.
Design of experiments for industrial research.
Mathematical economics.
Operations research methods.
Design of experiments.
Decision theory.
Stochastic processes.
Multivariate analysis.

Mathematics

Study of spin stabilized rockets during burning.
Matrices with elements in a commutative ring and solution of simultaneous equations.
Stieltzes integrals and Hilbert spaces.
Numerical analysis.
Differential equations, harmonic functions, Fourier series, complex variable.
Function theory.
Theory of numbers.
Theory of entire functions.
Transform theory, probability, statistics.
Functional analysis.
Theory of measure.
Differential geometry, nomography.

Libraries

The combined libraries of the three institutions contain over 2,250,000 volumes and approximately 9,000,000 documents and periodicals. Approximately 140,000 volumes are added annually. Substantially every engineering and scientific journal published anywhere in the world, including translations of several Russian journals, can be found in the combined holdings of the three institutions. Published and kept up to date is a volume listing the complete holdings of all scientific journals in the three libraries, simplifying the locating of any desired journal.

Cooperative service among the three institutions permits rapid loan of volumes from one library to another. In addition to the combined resources, the general libraries of the universities participate in interlibrary loan arrangements with the Library of Congress and those at other institutions. Frequent messenger service, including truck delivery, and a cooperative acquisitions program further cement interlibrary relationships in the region.

Available are batteries of microfilm reading machines microphotographic facilities for reproducing printed and other material. Of special note is the status of the technical holdings at North Carolina State College whose library is a complete depository for all unclassified publications of the Federal Government including all unclassified and declassified publications of the Atomic Energy Commission. This library is also a selective depository for the publications of the Carnegie Institution of Washington and receives exchange publications from many foreign countries in engineering and the physical sciences.

Facilities

The following list of facilities and equipment is intended to merely convey some concept of the scope of the facility resources and is not intended to be an inventory. Only research facilities under the direct jurisdiction of the engineering departments and the departments of mathematics, physics, chemistry and statistics are included. Not included are the extensive research facilities of the School of Textiles, the Wood Technology Laboratories or the Pulp and Paper Technology Laboratories at North Carolina State College. Also omitted are special service facilities used on a school-wide basis such as precision machine shops, photographic laboratories, materials testing laboratories and an experimental foundry at North Carolina State College.

Aeronautical Engineering

Single return closed throat wind tunnel with 46″ x 12″ working section.
Supersonic blow-down tunnel equipped for schlieren and shadowgraph photography.
Aircraft instrument test stand for measuring instrument response and characteristics.

Agricultural Engineering

Individual temperature and humidity controlled rooms.
Research machine shop employing four full-time mechanics.
Time-lapse movie equipment and a high-speed motion picture camera and controls.

Civil Engineering

Beckman Spectrophotometers.
Beckman glass Electrode ph meters.
Thomas copper water baths.
Beggs deformeters.
Photoelasticity apparatus.
Complete equipment for surveying and mapping including optical transit, theodolite, precise level and equipment for standardizing tapes.
SR-4 strain gage equipment.
50,000; 60,000; 150,000; and 300,000-lb capacity testing machines.
50,000-lb Morehouse Proving Ring.
CBR soil testing apparatus.
Triaxial shear apparatus.
Acker soil sampling kit.
Complete sanitary engineering laboratory facilities for the study of waste disposal problems and water treatment.
Charpy-Izod impact testing machines.
Rockwell hardness testing machines.
Krouse fatigue testing machines.
200,000-lb capacity Olsen high-speed tension testing machine.
Complete electronic and mechanical precision measuring instruments.

Chemical Engineering

Fifteen-gallon Blow-Knox pilot plant.
Laboratory equipped with 10 recording potentiometers suitable for making measurements in the range from below 0 to 2500° F. and controlling within this same range.
Pulse column.
Liquid-liquid extraction equipment suitable for studies on efficiency extraction.
202 Tenius Olsen testing machine suitable for compression, tensile and diffraction measurements on plastics, wood, metal, housed in an air-conditioned room.
Small tensile testers.
Precision refractometer for measuring refractive index of liquids to 5 decimal points.
Blackmon ultra-violet spectrometer.
Blackmon Model B Spectrophotometer.
18″ x 3′ stainless steel continuous rotary filter with string discharge.

Electrical Engineering

Two high-voltage laboratories including 500,000-volt, 9,375-watt-second impulse generator; 100,000-volt, 60 cps test equipment; high voltage cathode-ray oscillographs; AC 60-cycle, 150 KV test set; DC 50 KV high voltage sources, transient analyzers, high resistance bridges and 15 KV AC bridge.
Illumination laboratory.
Servomechanisms laboratory.
Electric heating test installation.
Electronics instrumentation.
Photographic dark rooms.
Six-element oscillographs.
High-speed motion picture cameras.
Synchronous sine-wave generators.
Synchronous harmonic generator sets.
Low-frequency servo-mechanism signal generators.
Electric heating test equipment.

Sound recording equipment.
Microwave laboratory equipped for measurements of transmission characteristics in the frequency range 9000 megocycles (3 centimeter wave length) and 3000 megocycles (10 centimeter wave length).
Communications laboratory.
Industrial electronics laboratory.
Electronics Laboratory equipped with vibration and sound intensity measuring equipment in the audio frequency range.
Graphical and Numerical Photoelectronic Analyzer (Granpa).

Industrial Engineering

Complete shock facilities for research on machine work, foundry, and welding.
Time and motion study laboratories.
Wood products laboratory containing general wood shop equipment, a veneer lathe and clipper, glue mixers and spreaders, tape machine and hot presses, testing equipment, preservation tanks, a modern dry kiln, and two portable sawmills.

Mechanical Engineering

Engine test laboratory equipped with water system (fresh and simulated salt water circuits), fuel system with centrifuge and filtering apparatus, and lubricating oil with cleaning system and settling tanks. Fuel storage capacity underground consists of two tanks of 6000 gallons each, above ground, one tank of 3500-gallon capacity. All connected with necessary pumps and piping to provide maximum flexibility. Engines installed:
1 General Motors 16 278-A as a generator set with absorption water rheostat.
1 Fairbanks, Morse 10 cylinder 38D 8½ x 10 fitted to a 2000 HP dynamometer.
1 Cooper Bessemer GSB 10½ x 13½ 900 HP, marine reduction gear attached, no absorption device installed.
2 GM 6-71, Gray conversions, installed and fitted to a water brake of suitable capacity.
1 GM 12 cylinder 567 A, 900 HP, fitted Falk marine gear. No power absorption apparatus fitted.
1 ALCO 12½ x 13 fitted to water brake. 900 HP, 6 cylinder.
3 Lister Blackstone fitted to single cylinder air-compressors and arranged for a speed control study.
2 Superior GDB-8 generator sets 100 KW, and AC and one DC.
2 Cummins 100 KW sets, one AC, and one DC.
2 GM 2-71 arranged as a DC marine propulsion unit with a water brake to absorb the power.
1 International 60 HP fitted to a 150 HP dynamometer.
1 Nordberg model 4 FS-1-AH, single cylinder.
2 Palmer, Model EMD-1, single cylinder.
Dynamometers:
1 Midwest Type 3232, 2000 HP.
1 Midwest Type 758, 50 HP.
1 Sprague, 100 HP.
Other Laboratories and other special equipment:
1 Fuel and lubricating oil test room, capable of carrying out the necessary ASTM tests. Included are bomb calorimeter, electric furnaces, centrifuge, flash point testers, viscosmeters including one of the kinemetic type, distillation apparatus, balances, color determination devices.
1 CFR test engine for Diesel fuels equipped with power absorption dynamometer, smoke meter, exhaust gas analyzer, Cox indicator and Cox recording indicator.
1 Photographic Laboratory with high speed camera, projector, enlarger, developer.
1 Fuel Research Engine for Octane number determination.
Precision devices including 5 Oscilloscopes, strain measuring apparatus, profilometer, gauges, sound level meter and magnaflux bench and demagnetizing attachments.

Special equipment pertaining to diesel engines such as compression pressure gauges, nozzle and injector testers, Bosch fuel pump test equipment, fuel pump calibrator stand.
Strain measuring apparatus consisting of Universal strain amplifiers, oscillographs, recorders, vibrometers, and pickups.
Dynamic and static bearing machines.
Complete bearing and lubrication testing facilities including physical and mechanical properties and bearing friction machine.
Photoelectric equipment.
Air Compressors.
Steam condensing equipment.
Evaporators.
Hydraulic machinery laboratory.
Experimental air ejector with pressure measuring probes.
Low-temperature research laboratory.
Well-instrumented model steam power plant.
Calorimeter rooms for testing heating and refrigerating equipment.
Research grade microscopes.
Photomicrographic equipment.
Polariscopes.
Electromagnets.
Vacuum pumps.
Low-temperature liquid storage vessels.
Heating and air conditioning laboratory including an experimental cold room capable of maintaining temperatures down to —60°F.
Steam turbines.
Gas turbines and propulsion equipment.

Mineral Industries

Microscope and x-ray laboratories including:
RCA Universal electron microscope.
Vacuum evaporation outfit.
Norelco x-ray diffraction-geiger spectrometer outfit.
GE XRD # x-ray diffraction outfits.
240 KVA x-ray radiography unit.
140 KVA x-ray radiography unit.
Pyrochemical laboratories including:
gas and electric furnaces for temperatures up to 400°F.
high temperature load testing equipment.
hydraulic presses up to 50-ton capacity.
extrusion machinery.
dielectric testing equipment.
annealing furnaces.
materials reduction equipment.
automatic temperature controllers and recorders.
Metallurgical laboratories including:
Bausch and Lomb research model metallograph.
Hurlbut counter.
Model L macrograph.
Muffle, tube and hot furnaces for heat testing.
6 KW ajax induction melting furnaces.
Rockwell and Vickers hardness testers.
Gas fired melting furnace.
Size O Whiting cupola.
Large light weight aggregate pilot plant.
Complete facilities for mineral benficiation.

Nuclear Engineering

(See Physics for other facilities)
Burlington Nuclear Laboratory including:
100 kw aqueous homogeneous research reactor.
gamma ray spectrometer.
4 pulse height analyzers.
neutron diffraction spectrometer.
variety of scalers, amplifiers and radiation measuring instruments.
Perkin-Elmer infrared recording spectrograph precision refractometer.
Bellingham and Stanley research polarimeter.
Knorr-Albers microdensitometer.
Bausch and Lomb quartz prism emission spectrograph.
Beckman quartz spectrometer.

Solid fuel reactor (under construction).
Critical assembly (under construction).
Van de Graaf accelerator (under construction).
Radioisotope laboratory.
Geiger counters of many types.

Physics

(See Nuclear Engineering for other facilities)

4,000,000-volt Van de Graaf accelerator.
Collins liquid helium cryostats.
Equipment for the generation, amplification and detection of electromagnetic radiation up to about 300,000 megacycles per second.
Electromagnets of various capacities used in radiofrequency spectroscopy and in low temperature applications.
Oscilloscopes including the writing type.
Recording meters of various kinds.
Geiger counters and crystal counters used in nuclear spectrographs.
Amplifiers, scalers and similar electronic equipment used in nuclear physics studies.
Special electromagnets for study of charged particle nuclear reactions.
Optical spectrographs of various sizes in glass and quartz.
3-meter grating in Eagle mount and a 22-foot Jarrell-Ash spectrograph.
Jarrell-Ash densitometer with recording equipment.
Monochromatic illuminator for both the visible and ultraviolet.
Liquid helium bubble chamber for study of high energy interactions.
Electronic circuits for time-of-flight measurements with resolution of about 8×10^{-10} second.
Perkin-Elmer Model 112 infrared Spectrometers with interchangeable optics of glass, LiF, NcCl and KBr.
Hilger E-1 large quartz spectrometer.
Gaertner L-231 spectrometer.
Proportional counters and ionization chambers.
Enriched BF, neutron counters and photomultiplier detectors including associated electronic equipment.
Cloud chamber ($1' \times 1' \times 2'$).
Research microscopes for nuclear emission studies with automatic scanning devices and plate processing equipment.

Chemistry

In addition to usual laboratory facilities, there are several especially constructed or equipped laboratories including:
Three low level radiochemical laboratories.
A separately housed radioisotopes laboratory.
A stable isotopes laboratory.
A dust-free laboratory for light scattering measurements.
Spectroscopic laboratories with dark rooms.
A high temperature reactions laboratory.

Two high pressure hydrogenation laboratories.
Instrumental analysis laboratories, some with temperature and humidity control.
Complete organic and inorganic microchemical laboratories.
Computing laboratory with Remington Rand punched card equipment for punching, sorting, and tabulating.
An X-ray crystallographic laboratory.
Many items of special equipment housed in the chemistry departments, much of which is duplicated at two or more of the institutions, is listed in part below:
Single and double beam recording infrared spectrophotometers.
Point and continuous ultraviolet and visible spectrophotometers.
Flame photometers.
Littrow emission spectrographs.
Stigmatic grating emission spectrograph (15000 lines/inch).
Densitometers and comparator microphotometers.
Zeiss interferometer for solutions and gases.
Light scattering photometer and differential refractometer.
Precision polarimeter.
Nuclear magnetic resonance equipment.
Magnetic susceptability measurement apparatus.
Single crystal X-ray diffraction apparatus.
High velocity molecular beam apparatus.
Dielectric constant measurement apparatus.
Recording polarographs.
Heat of solution measuring apparatus.
Scalers and counters for radioactive systems.
Vibrating reed electrometers.
Nier 60° mass spectrometer.
Precision constant temperature bath for D_2O analysis.
Osmometers.
Chromatographic equipment and fraction collector.
Gas chromatography apparatus.
Low and high temperature rectification columns.
200 tube Craig countercurrent extractor.
Elemental fluorine generators.
Ketene and ozone generators.
Low and high pressure hydrogenation equipment.

Statistics

IBM 650 electronic digital computer.
Survey operations unit.
Set of International Business Machines for computing.
Complete set of desk calculators.

Mathematics

GEDA Analog Computer.
Complete set of desk calculators of the latest type.
Variplotter.
Donner electronic computers.
IBM 650 electronic computer.

Schematic Map of Research Triangle

Resources for Advanced Training

Educational Facilities

The State of North Carolina supports twelve institutions of higher learning having a combined book value of $182,600,000 and a combined annual operating budget of $46,524,000. Capital improvements authorized for the coming year total slightly less than $22,000,000 exclusive of funding for new dormitories. Over 22,000 students attend these state-supported institutions.

There are twenty-four privately supported senior colleges and universities in North Carolina attended by over 17,000 students. In addition, there are twenty-five privately supported junior colleges and three community colleges which derive part of their support from the state and from the communities in which they are situated. The state also supports three technical institutes which train students for sub-professional work as technical aids, skilled technicians and in the technical trades.

The three institutions forming the Research Triangle have a total enrollment of 18,165 students. Two of these institutions, North Carolina State College and the University of North Carolina are state-supported. Duke University, the third institution, is supported by private endowment.

North Carolina State College

Founded by legislative act in 1887, this member of the National Association of Land Grant Colleges and State Universities is composed of 7 schools and 48 departments. The master's degree is offered in 35 fields and the doctorate in 18 fields. The master's degree and the doctorate are offered in the fields of ceramic, chemical, civil, nuclear and electrical engineering, and in mathematics, physics, chemistry and statistics. The master's degree is offered in the fields of aeronautical, geological, mechanical, metallurgical, and industrial engineering.

Duke University

Founded in 1839 as Union Institute, this private institution and member of the Association of American Universities consists of 9 colleges and schools. The master's degree is offered in 24 fields and the doctorate in 19 fields. The master's degree is offered in the fields of civil, electrical, and mechanical engineering.

The master's degree and the doctorate are offered in mathematics, physics, and chemistry.

University of North Carolina

Chartered in 1789 and opened in 1795, the first state university in the United States, this member of the Association of American Universities is composed of 14 colleges and schools. The master's degree is offered in 42 fields and the doctorate in 27 fields. The master's and doctor's degrees are offered in the related fields of physics, chemistry, mathematics, and statistics.

Resources of Trained Personnel

The Research Triangle trains a substantial number of students in engineering and the allied sciences at both the undergraduate and graduate level. The enrollment in engineering continues to grow rapidly each year and conservative estimates place the engineering enrollment at North Carolina State College alone in the range of 8,500 by the year 1967. Students come from all over the nation and from many foreign lands. Regardless of where they come from originally, most of the graduates prefer to live in the area. The enrollment statistics for the academic year 1956-57 are as follows:

	Undergraduate	Graduate
Aeronautical Engineering	214	—
Agricultural Engineering	91	6
Chemical Engineering	173	20
Civil Engineering	792	17
Electrical Engineering	979	25
Industrial Engineering	282	4
Mechanical Engineering	886	13
Mineral Industries	89	8
Nuclear Engineering	242	40
Totals	**3748**	**133**
Chemistry	250	100
Mathematics	49	36
Physics	90	65
Statistics	2	56
Totals	**391**	**257**

In a typical recent graduating class the following degrees were granted.

	Bachelors	Professional	Masters	Doctors
Engineering	431	9	35	9
Physics	20	—	7	13
Chemistry	63	—	14	16
Mathematics	43	—	13	12
Statistics	—	—	10	43

In addition to the professionally trained personnel is the large number of scientifically trained graduates of the several institutions of higher learning in the State of North Carolina as well as graduates of the technical institutes. The stimulation of working and living within the Research Triangle has consistently drawn a large proportion of these graduates to seek opportunities in the area.

In-Service Training

The institutions of the Research Triangle are conducting special training programs for graduate engineers working in the area. Regular courses are offered in off-campus locations and in the evening by special arrangement when the demand exists. The three institutions are favorably disposed toward the establishment of further programs for research engineers and scientists who wish to attain either higher proficiency in certain areas, or who wish to earn advanced degrees.

Of special note are special short courses offered to meet industrial needs in certain areas of knowledge. The nuclear engineering short course offered annually at North Carolina State College attracts engineers and scientists from all over the nation. Similar short courses are offered in statistics, various areas of engineering and executive training.

An Environment for Research

A Climate for Research

More than any other industrial activity the success of research programs depends upon the intellectual stimulation provided by the environment in which research personnel work. Regardless of the excellence of the physical facilities a climate of thought stimulation and exchange of ideas with other scientists are essential to success in research. The Research Triangle offers an unusually stimulating environment in which the free exchange of ideas among people whose interests cover a wide spectrum of scientific endeavor is traditional.

The not uncommon conflicts between "town" and "gown" are completely absent in the Research Triangle. The communities in the Research Triangle have always maintained a deep pride in the accomplishments of their educational institutions and a sincere interest in the people on the staffs of these institutions. These several factors have made it possible to attract and retain the great faculties of the institutions forming the Research Triangle. Indeed, the three institutions are national and international in the composition of their faculties. Furthermore,

such industrial research installations as those of American Machine and Foundry, Union Carbide, and Liggett and Myers as well as the research organizations of the U. S. Public Health Service and Office of Ordnance Research find the cross-fertilization of ideas present in the Research Triangle highly rewarding.

Relations with the Scientific World

The institutions forming the Research Triangle are noted for the participation of their faculties in the affairs of the national scientific and engineering societies. This participation is one means of bringing into the Research Triangle other points of view while maintaining close contact with the whole world of science. Another means is the invitation of scientists of international stature to participate in the various colloquia sponsored by the universities in the Research Triangle. These colloquia are open to any interested individuals in the area.

A relatively small sample of the scientists and engineers participating in colloquia during the past year include:

Speaker	From	Topic
Warren Kohn	Carnegie Institute of Technology	Impurity States in Silicon
Nathan M. Newmark	University of Illinois	The Influence of High-Speed Digital Computers on Research
Peter Klaudy	University of Graz, Austria	The Behavior of Electrical Contacts
W. Z. Friend	International Nickel Co.	Corrosion in Nuclear Materials
A. D. Moore	University of Michigan	Fields from Fluid Mappers
George Leddicotte	Oak Ridge National Laboratory	Activation Analysis
Warren Henry	Naval Research Laboratory	Magnetic Interactions in Silicon
Milton C. Edlund	Babcock and Wilcox Co.	Reactor Theory
R. Glover	University of California	Superconductivity in the Millimeter Microwave and Far Infra-Red
Robert J. Walker	Cornell University	Research Problems for Digital Computers
Earle Buckingham	Massachusetts Institute of Technology	Dynamics of Elastic Bodies
Ali B. Cambel	Northwestern University	Aerothermochemistry of Flame Stabilization
C. R. Russell	General Motors Corp.	Reactor Safety
W. M. Breazeale	Babcock and Wilcox Co.	Research Associated with Reactors
Bern Dibner	Burndy Engineering Co.	The Impact of Science on our Society
J. Wolfowitz	Cornell University	The Minimum Distance Method
William E. Shoupp	Westinghouse Electric Corporation	Developments in Nuclear Power
Gerald M. Foley	Leeds and Northrup Co.	Control Instruments
L. Rosenfeld	University of Manchester	Charge Distribution in Nuclei
Myer Garbor	National Research Council, Ottawa	Magnetic Susceptibilities of Dilute Binary Alloys
T. S. Wheeler	University College, Dublin	Studies in the Chemistry of Flavanoids
Karl H. Hausser	Max Planck Institute	Magnetic and Spectrographic Properties of Radicals of N-Containing Organic Complex Molecules at Low Temperatures
James Franck	University of Chicago	The Role of Chlorophyll in Photosynthesis
C. O'Ceallaigh	Dublin Institute for Advanced Study	K-Meson Studies
Raymond S. Boyer	Plastics Division Rohm and Haas	Block and Graft Co-polymers
D. S. Tarbell	Rochester University	Carcinogenic Aromatic Hydrocarbons
Mansel Davies	University of Wales	Aspects of Structure and Interaction of Simple Amides
Harry H. Sisler	University of Florida	Recent Developments in the Chemistry of Hydrazine and Chloramine and Their Derivatives
R. W. Stoughton	Oak Ridge National Laboratories	High Temperature Solution Chemistry
Hermann Flaschka	National Research Center, Cairo, Egypt	The Present Status and Problems of EDTA Titrations
F. O. Rice	Catholic University	Recent Advances in Chemisty—On Jupiter
Lawrence Wilets	Los Alamos National Laboratory	Neutron and Proton Densities and Potentials in Nuclei
W. F. Libby	Atomic Energy Commission	Use of Radioisotopes in Teaching
Arnold M. Bass	National Bureau of Standards	Stabilization of Atoms and Radicals at Low Temperatures
I. M. Robinson	E. I. du Pont de Nemours	A New Field of Chemistry: Stereo-specific Reactions Using Coordination Catalysts
F. Hund	University of Frankfort	Elementary Remarks on Field Quantization
Richard T. Arnold	University of Minnesota	Some Reactions of Hydrocarbons Involving Double Bond Shifts

Engineering and Scientific Societies

Because of the heavy concentration of scientific research in the Research Triangle, the area is regularly selected for national and regional society meetings. Of particular note is a recent national meeting of the American Institute of Physics and the International Conference on Gravity. The following societies have one or more sections in the Research Triangle and have regular meetings occuring monthly:

American Society of Mechanical Engineers
American Institute of Electrical Engineers
The Society of the Sigma Xi
American Society of Civil Engineers
American Chemical Society
American Institute of Physics

American Ceramic Society
American Institute of Chemical Engineers
American Institute of Mining and Metallurgical Engineers
Institute of Aeronautical Sciences
Institute of Radio Engineers
American Institute of Industrial Engineers
American Society of Professional Engineers
American Society of Heating and Ventilating Engineers
American Society of Refrigeration Engineers
and many others with chapters associated with the universities.

Local societies include:
Raleigh Engineers Club
Durham Engineers Club
North Carolina Society of Engineers
North Carolina Academy of Science

A Place for Living

Transportation

Two main north-south railroads serve the Research Triangle with excellent overnight transportation to Washington and New York. Located on the main line of these railroads, there are several trains daily. The Raleigh-Durham Airport is almost exactly in the center of the Research Triangle and can be reached from either Raleigh or Durham in less than a half hour. Air service is excellent with several competing airlines. For instance, there are 40 flights leaving daily with 13 daily departures for Washington and 11 for New York. New York is 2 hours and 15 minutes away by air, and Washington is only 67 minutes away by air.

A recent survey rated the North Carolina highway system as second best in the nation. Major north-south highways pass through the Research Triangle. Express highways connect the three cities of the Triangle and an extensive network of paved secondary roads bring even the remotest hamlet within easy access of the major roads.

Cultural Advantages

There are no three cities in the entire State of North Carolina that offer greater cultural advantages than do Raleigh (pop. 80,000), Chapel Hill (pop. 12,000), and Durham (pop. 75,000). In fact, it would be extremely difficult to duplicate the cultural assets of these three cities anywhere outside of a large metropolitan district. Situated in the healthful Piedmont area of the state in relative proximity to each other they provide attractive facilities for residence of professional people.

Churches

In each of the three cities are found congregations of all the principal churches. Religious activities have always been an important part of life in these cities and the surrounding communities. For example, the Institute of Religion, sponsored by the United Church, brings prominent national and international figures to Raleigh each year for a five-week period of lectures and conferences.

Art

Those having an interest in art will find ample expression of such interests in the Research Triangle. The North Carolina Museum of Art, in Raleigh, is unique among art museums in that it receives financial support from the State. The 1947 general assembly appropriated one million dollars for the purchase of paintings, mainly fifteenth to eighteenth century, representing eight major schools of western art and including important works by Peter Paul Rubens, Hans Memling, Van Dyke, Rembrandt, Lochner, Crespi, Belloto, Boucher, Gainsborough, Raeburn, Romney, Gilbert Stuart, Copley, Moran, Ryder, and others. This collection of 200 paintings has been matched by a collection valued at one million dollars, given by the Samuel H. Kress Foundation. The Kress Foundation grant and numerous gifts to the museum provide a broad scope through the impressionists and contemporary works. Many works are exhibited on loan and the exhibits are changed frequently.

In Person Hall at Chapel Hill is an impressive art gallery devoted to modern works which are frequently changed. The Ackland Art Gallery in Chapel Hill houses the famous William Hayes Ackland collection. The rotunda of Morehead Planetarium in Chapel Hill displays an important collection by distinguished artists. The various art collections at Duke University are open to the public.

There is a long tradition of support for art in the Research Triangle as evidenced by a state appropriation in 1831, at a time when the state was poor, to purchase the marble statue by Canova of George Washington. At that time this statue was reputed to be the most expensive work of art in the United States. The tradition of art can still be found in the support given to the art departments of the three universities and flourishing art societies such as the North Carolina Art Society, Durham Art Guild, and the Art Department of the Raleigh Woman's Club which puts on an annual "Sidewalk Art Exhibit". Worthy of note is the four-year art school operated by the Raleigh Art Center.

Theater

Many national companies of New York plays come to the area. Even more stimulating is the great interest in several community theaters which offer excellent productions regularly. Among these community theaters are the Playmakers in their Forest Theater at Chapel Hill, the Durham Theatre Guild in whose productions several former professional actors as well as town and college people participate under the professional direction of Jane Barry Haynes, and the Raleigh Little Theatre which presents

almost continuously productions that are often characterized as the most nearly professional performances by amateurs to be seen anywhere. The Little Theatre seats 800 and has an outdoor arena set in acres of rose gardens. Of special note is the children's Little Theatre soon to be built nearby.

Music

The North Carolina Symphony Orchestra, supported by appropriations from the state treasury, has its home in Chapel Hill. In addition, there are the Chapel Hill Concert Series, the Chapel Hill Choral Club, the Raleigh Civic Music Association, the Raleigh Chamber Music Society, the Durham Civic Choral Society. These organizations offer programs of their own and annually bring outstanding artists to the area. A typical annual offering would include such artists and groups as Heifetz, Curzon, Bachauer, Robert Shaw Chorale, Boston Pops Orchestra, Robert Wagner Chorale, Ballet Russe de Monte Carlo, Hungarian String Quartet, Piatigorsky, Quartetto Italiano, and several others.

In addition to the community music societies, there are excellent university musical groups such as the Graham Memorial Hall Series and the Carolina Folk Festival in Chapel Hill, the Duke Glee Club, the Duke Madrigal Singers, the Duke String Quartet, the Duke Faculty concerts, the Duke Symphony Orchestra, and the North Carolina State College Symphony Orchestra. These university groups, in addition to their own performances, bring outstanding artists to the campus each year. University programs are open to the public at a nominal charge or free. Of particular note is the Grass Roots Opera Company founded in Raleigh by A. J. Fletcher in 1948. This company has grown from a purely local opera production company into a nationally known organization utilizing the talents of the finest young artists in the country.

The three cities have a variety of auditoria suitable for the presentation of any type of musical program.

Literature

For persons with literary tastes the area offers unusual opportunities as evidenced by the fact that a dozen or more active novelists and short story writers have chosen Chapel Hill for their home. Frances Gray Patton, the author of **Good Morning, Miss Dove**, Helen Bevington, William Blackburn, and many other writers make their home in Durham. Similar literary activities are to be found in Raleigh, which boasts of fifty book clubs. There are many writers clubs such as the Scribblers Club, in which professional and amateur writers participate. The State Literary Society in Raleigh awards the Mayflower Cup annually to the North Carolina author of the best literary work of non-fiction and the O'Henry Award to the outstanding author of fiction. The Duke University Press and the University of North Carolina Press are noted for their literary contributions.

Besides the university libraries which are available to the public under some restrictions, there are two public libraries and the state library in Raleigh, and modern public libraries in Durham and Chapel Hill. The area is well served by newspapers and New York City papers, as well as others, are easily obtainable at news stands.

Other Special Features

There are many other items of cultural interest in the Research Triangle. The Sarah P. Duke Gardens in Durham and the Coker Arboretum in Chapel Hill are noted for their perennial beauty and draw thousands annually. The Morehead Planetarium in Chapel Hill offers public demonstrations and lectures daily and contains one of only two thirty-five foot orreries of the solar system in the world.

Those who have architectural interests will be pleased by the many exhibits of the School of Design at North Carolina State College and the many buildings of architectural interest located in the area. One building deserving special note is the State Fair Arena in Raleigh. Of parabolic design, with a roof supported on cables suspended between 90-foot concrete arches and walls entirely of glass, arching against the sky, the building is indeed beautiful beyond description. It received the Gold Medal from the Architectural League of New York in 1952 and the 1953 award of the American Institute of Architects. Rated as one of the ten outstanding buildings in America today, it was designed by the late Matthew Nowicki, a State College professor.

Many speakers visit the area under the auspices of many socities, organized lecture series, and endowed lectureships. Some of the outstanding persons speaking in the area during the past year are: Hon. Harold E. Stassen, Dr. Ralph Bunche, Mrs. Eleanor Roosevelt, Mr. Robert Frost, Hon. Herbert Morrison, Justice William O. Douglas, Mr. James C. Hagerty, Dame Edith Sitwell, and many others.

Many interesting cultural programs, adult education courses and special events are televised on WUNC-TV, a television station operated by the University of North Carolina, State College and the Woman's College.

Carolina Country Club, Raleigh

Schools

Public school facilities in the Research Triangle are excellent. The influence of the three universities and the other colleges (Raleigh alone has six colleges) in the area has had a profound effect on the educational consciousness of the surrounding communities. An unusually high percentage of the high school graduates attend universities; over ninety-percent of the graduates of the central high school in Raleigh are annually admitted to universities all over the country.

Sarah P. Duke Gardens, Durham

In addition to the public schools, there are several parochial and other privately supported schools, which have excellent facilities. Whether private or public, all schools must meet high standards of teaching and physical facilities to satisfy the needs of communities which demand excellence.

Medical Facilities

The Research Triangle with the Duke Medical Center in Durham and the North Carolina Medical Center in Chapel Hill is one of the outstanding medical centers in the nation. North Carolina Memorial Hospital is a 400-bed teaching hospital operated in connection with the University Medical School. Duke Hospital in Durham, also a teaching hospital has 662 beds and draws patients from many states. The Veterans Administration Hospital in Durham, located a few hundred yards from Duke Hospital, contains 449 beds. Virtually any ailment can be diagnosed and treated by nationally recognized specialists connected with these hospitals and their medical schools.

In addition, there are ten other hospitals in Durham and Raleigh with a total of 3,231 beds, including the distinguished Watts Hospital in Durham. To these facilities may be added the Bowman Gray Medical School and teaching hospital at Winston-Salem, 115 miles from the Research Triangle. At Charlotte, 125 miles away, is another medical center—seven hospitals and 1,346 beds.

Recreation

Nearly any type of sport can be enjoyed on a year-round basis in the mild climate of the Research Triangle, ranging from golf, through spectator sports to even indoor ice skating. For example, year-round golf can be enjoyed on any of the fourteen courses located in the three cities. A state park with facilities for camping, boating, swimming, hiking, and picnicking is located between Raleigh and Durham. There are many lakes and rivers in the area to satisfy the angler. The cities in the triangle have extensive systems of public parks equipped with such facilities as swimming pools, picnic areas including barbeque pits, tennis courts, playing fields, ponds, gardens, zoos, and special facilities for the entertainment of children.

Of special interest in the realm of sports are the football and basketball teams of North Carolina State College, Duke University, and the University of North Carolina. The famous William Neal Reynolds Coliseum located on the campus of North Carolina State College is the largest building of its kind in the South. Seating 12,400 spectators, it is the home of the college's basketball games and the annual Dixie Classic. The three universities have exceptional facilities for both indoor and outdoor sports and field teams in all the major sports as well as many of the minor sports.

Those who like mountains will find them only a few hours away from the Research Triangle in Western North Carolina. Camping facilities are maintained by the state near the peak of Mount Mitchell, the highest peak east of the Mississippi. Slightly over an hour away from the Re-

search Triangle is huge Kerr Lake surrounded by pine forests and well equipped for campers, boating, swimming, and fishing. Only a few hours to the east are magnificent strands of beach, deep-sea fishing, and the quaint beauty of Ocracoke, Nags Head and Cape Hatteras.

Among other attractions are a variety of clubs and facilities for the hobby enthusiast. Each of the cities is served by several television and radio stations in addition to the television and radio stations of the university.

Civic Organizations

The cities of the Research Triangle have active groups of various men's civic clubs including Rotary, Kiwanis, Lions, Sertoma, Civitan, Exchange, Toastmasters, American Business, Optimist. For the women there are organizations of Altrusa, Pilot, National Secretaries Association, Women's Clubs, Junior Leagues, Rose Societies, D.A.R., League of Women Voters, and a host of others. Nearly every fraternal order and patriotic organizations have active groups in the area. For example, there are over twenty-five men's clubs in Raleigh and the largest woman's club in the South.

North Carolina Medical Center, University of North Carolina, Chapel Hill

Duke Medical Center, Duke University, Durham

Literature on the Research Triangle:

THE RESEARCH TRIANGLE OF NORTH CAROLINA
RESOURCES FOR RESEARCH IN PHARMACEUTICALS
RESOURCES FOR RESEARCH IN CHEMISTRY
RESOURCES FOR RESEARCH IN ELECTRONICS

Brochures on resources for research in the fields of forest products, textiles, ceramics and cultural opportunities in the Research Triangle are in preparation. Copies of these brochures may be obtained from the Director upon request.

The Governor's Research Triangle Committee, Inc.

George L. Simpson, Jr., Director, Box 1488, Raleigh, N. C.

John F. Lee, Consultant for Engineering
P. O. Box 5356, Raleigh, N. C.

The Governor's Research Triangle Committee, Incorporated, is a non-stock, non-profit organization whose purpose is to do all that is possible to use and develop the research resources of the Triangle area.

The Committee works solely within the bounds and desires of the three institutions. Its primary purpose is to make industrial and governmental research activities aware of the scientific resources and cultural advantages of the Triangle area.

When asked, the Committee will undertake to arrange a meeting between such industrial and governmental agencies and appropriate people from the three institutions.

The Committee undertakes also to help in carrying forward any projects deemed desirable by one or more of the institutions.

MEMBERS

Robert M. Hanes, President. Honorary Chairman of Board, Wachovia Bank and Trust Company, Winston-Salem, N. C.

A. Hollis Edens, Vice President. President, Duke University, Durham, N. C.

Brandon P. Hodges, Secretary-Treasurer. Counselor, The Champion Paper and Fibre Company, Canton, N. C.

Luther H. Hodges, Governor of North Carolina, Raleigh, N. C.

William C. Friday, President, University of North Carolina, Chapel Hill, N. C.

Robert Armstrong, Vice President, Celanese Corporation of America, Charlotte, N. C.

E. Y. Floyd, Director, N. C. Plant Food Institute, Raleigh, N. C.

Grady Rankin, Attorney, Gastonia, N. C.

C. W. Reynolds, Asst. Works Mgr., Western Electric Company, Winston-Salem, N. C.

William H. Ruffin, President, Erwin Mills, Durham, N. C.

WORKING COMMITTEE

J. Harold Lampe, Dean, School of Engineering, N. C. State College, Chairman.

W. C. Davison, Dean, School of Medicine, Duke University

Marcus E. Hobbs, Dean, Graduate School, Duke University

D. W. Colvard, Dean, School of Agriculture, N. C. State College

Henry T. Clark, Jr., Administrator, Division of Health Affairs, University of N. C.

W. J. Seeley, Dean, College of Engineering, Duke University

Arthur Roe, Director of the Institute of Natural Science, University of N. C.

Malcolm Campbell, Dean, School of Textiles, N. C. State College

Daniel O. Price, Director of The Institute for Research in Social Science, University of N. C.

APPENDIX E

An invitation to investigate

Resources for Research In Forestry
and Forest Products
in
The Research Triangle of North Carolina

Duke University
Durham

North Carolina State College
Raleigh

The University of North Carolina
Chapel Hill

12 Mi.

School of Forestry
Duke University

24 Mi.

Venable Hall Chemistry Building
University of North Carolina

30 Mi.

A unique concentration of research facilities, highly qualified personnel, and advanced scientific education in a non-metropolitan area offering rich human satisfactions.

North Carolina State College
School of Forestry

The Research Triangle
and Forestry Research

In the heart of the largest timber-growing region of the United States, the Research Triangle of North Carolina encompasses facilities for forestry research unmatched by any other area in the country . . . centering on:

North Carolina State College

Duke University

The University of North Carolina

. . . For here are two distinguished Schools of Forestry, with a substantial part of their resources devoted to research and the training of research workers.

. . . Here too are located outstanding library facilities, experimental forests, wood products laboratories, and laboratory facilities for research in all phases of forest biology.

. . . And here are found strong supporting programs in chemistry, physics, mathematics, statistics, and economics.

The industrial enterprise or government agency locating its forestry research facilities within the Research Triangle has access to all of these resources. This concentration of research workers and research facilities devoted to expanding the frontiers of knowledge in forestry is unique in the Nation.

Particle Board Tension Test

Vapor Drying Research

Forestry and the South

The role of forests and forest products in the economy of the Nation is far greater than most people realize. Timber-connected activity in 1952 accounted for:

6 per cent of the civilian labor force,

6 per cent of compensation paid to all employees,

5 per cent of our national income.

The South is a major contributor, providing more than half of the Nation's forest products. Lumber, veneer, plywood, furniture, pulp, paper, fiber board, particle board, charcoal and many other commodities are produced in large quantities by southern industries. And this is expected to increase for the twelve southern states contain the largest body of rapidly growing softwoods on the face of the earth.

What forests mean to the regional economy is illustrated by North Carolina's position. With three-fifths of its land forested, the State ranks:

First in the Nation in the manufacture of wooden furniture,

First in the production of hardwood veneer and plywood,

Fifth in the manufacture of lumber.

Growth and Yield Studies

The wood products industries rank second to textiles in the number of employees engaged in manufacture in North Carolina.

Research in Bonded Wood Products

It has been conservatively estimated that the demand for forest products twenty years hence will be about twenty-five per cent greater than at present. Recent and projected expansion of the wood industries, particularly in the South, is an indication that industry shares the confidence of increased future demands.

But to supply this demand, on forest acreage that will probably decrease rather than increase, requires that more trees of higher quality be grown—and more efficient use be made of them.

Statistical Quality Control

Training

Nowhere in the United States is there a concentration of training facilities in all areas of forestry such as exists in the Research Triangle. The forestry schools at North Carolina State College and Duke University are the only institutions in the South offering doctoral programs in forestry. These institutions also offer programs of training leading toward the professional masters degrees and the master of science degree in forestry.

Students entering the forestry graduate programs at North Carolina State College and Duke University come from all sections of the United States and abroad. Many of the finest scholars graduating from the foresty schools of the country are brought to the Research Triangle on graduate scholarships, fellowships and research assistantships to acquire training and proficiency in the methods of forestry research. These trained biologists and technologists are available to the laboratories of the Research Triangle area.

Demand for well-trained research scientists in forestry far exceeds supply. Research laboratories located in the Research Triangle have a unique opportunity to staff their research facilities.

Graduate enrollment and faculty and research workers in forestry and certain allied fields are:

	Graduate Students	Faculty and Research Staff
Forest Soils	5	3
Forest Tree Physiology	10	3
Forest Ecology	3	2
Wood Technology	10	5
Silviculture and Forest Management	20	8
Forest Statistics and Measurements	9	3
Forest Entomology	5	2
Forest Pathology	5	1
Forest Utilization	2	2
Forest Economics	9	2
Industrial Statistics and Operations Research	3	3
Industrial Engineering	2	2
Wood Processing	10	6
Pulp and Paper Technology	2	3
Forest Products Economics	1	2
Forest Tree Improvement	11	2

In addition, there are a large number of staff members and graduate students at the three institutions conducting research in fields closely related to forestry and forest products technology.

High-Frequency Gluing Equipment

Tropical Wood Research

Continuing Education

The Forestry Schools at North Carolina State College and Duke University offer through their graduate programs outstanding opportunities for the staff scientists of forestry research laboratories in the Research Triangle to pursue further graduate education on a part-time basis. Where it is desired arrangements can usually be made to interchange graduate credit between institutions thus offering the full gamut of training opportunities to a single scientist.

Where research workers with advance degrees are scarce the opportunity to up-grade research staff members on the jobs makes it possible to build a strong research organization.

In addition to the formal graduate programs in forestry, the institutions of the Research Triangle offer industrial short courses and conferences designed to acquaint professional forest biologists and forest product technologists with new developments in forestry science. Among the professional conferences held in the Research Triangle during the past few years, the following subjects have been covered:

Forest Management

- Statistical Quality Control
- Industrial Statistics
- Linear Programming
- Forest Tree Improvement
- Veneer Log Grading
- Adhesion and Adhesives
- Wood Drying
- Forest Measurements
- Photogrammetry and Aerial Photo Interpretation
- Industrial Forest Management
- Forest Entomology and Pathology
- Industrial Wastes

Research In Forest Biology

Few places in the country — certainly none in the South — offer facilities for research in forest biology equal to those available within the Triangle. Fully equipped laboratories and greenhouses are specifically designed for research in forest soils, forest tree physiology, forest entomology and pathology, forest genetics, and the gamut of other basic biological sciences.

Within the Triangle there are more than 10,000 acres of forest land owned and managed by these institutions — primarily for experimental and instructional use. Additional forested areas of over 80,000 acres ranging eastward from the Triangle are operated by these institutions and offer a diversity of forest types and conditions representative of a large part of the forest land in the Southeastern United States.

Bark Beetle Studies

Scope of Current Research

The wood-using industry and government agencies, notably the United States Forest Service, the Atomic Energy Commission, the Department of Navy, and the National Science Foundation, have recognized the facilities of the Research Triangle to the extent of contracting for or supporting research projects in forest biology and forest products.

For example:

Twelve major pulp and paper companies in the South are supporting research and teaching in the pulp and paper field.

Thirteen timberland-owning companies are supporting a program of research in forest genetics.

Three major pulp and paper companies are pooling their forest inventory data, thereby permitting more intensive analysis of certain biological relationships.

A partial list of research projects currently in progress that are being actively supported by industrial and governmental agencies includes:

A study of the effects of varying light intensity, soil moisture, and soil fertility on growth of hardwood seedlings.

A study of the absorbing regions of tree roots with respect to water and minerals.

The phytocidal action of 3-amino-1, 2, 4, triazole in the control of honeysuckle.

Rate of photosynthesis of pine seedlings with various temperatures, photoperiods, and light intensities.

Effects of flooding on germination and seedling survival of several species of oaks.

The isolation of growth substances that may regulate the early growth of longleaf pine seedlings.

A study of the effects of day and night temperatures on growth of seedlings of several tree species.

Methods of processing continuous forest inventory data with highspeed computing machines.

Swamp vegetation associations as related to soil and physiographic conditions.

The relation of soil properties and growth of slash pine plantations.

The distribution of certain tree species as related to climatic factors.

An economic classification of planting sites.

The fertilization of loblolly pine plantations.

Regeneration of long leaf pine in the deep sand areas of the Carolinas.

Selection and testing of loblolly, Virginia, and shortleaf pines for desirable qualities.

Microscopic View of Cherry

Study of Wood Properties

Research In Forest Products Technology

The Wood Products Laboratory at North Carolina State College and the Wood Technology Laboratories at Duke University offer research facilities that are unequalled anywhere in the United States.

These institutions have the following laboratory facilities:

Wood Anatomy Laboratory
Wood Chemistry Laboratory
Timber Physics Laboratory
Wood Particle Board Pilot Plant
Veneer Laboratory
Plywood and Laminating Laboratory
Wood Machining Laboratory
Wood Drying Laboratory
Wood Finishing Laboratory
Pulp Laboratory
Paper Testing Laboratory

In addition to these laboratory facilities, the Wood Products Laboratory at North Carolina State College has exercised leadership in the development of methods of statistical quality control, operations analysis, experimental design, and forest products economics. In these areas strong supporting research is provided by the Institute of Statistics, and vigorous departments of economics and mathematics.

Scope of Current Research

Veneering characteristics of selected tropical woods for production of marine-grade plywood.

The physical and mechanical properties of certain Philippine woods.

The treatment of hickory lumber with creosote and pentachlorophenol preservatives.

A study of kiln drying urea-treated green oak lumber.

Volume-weight relationships of loblolly pine pulpwood.

The properties and potential uses of three Costa Rican hardwoods.

Factors causing spring-back in dry formed particle board.

The properties of polyvinyl resin glues.

Development of statistical quality control techniques for plywood manufacture.

Application of linear programming to logging and milling operations.

Factors influencing the quality of urea glue bonds produced using high-frequency gluing.

Development of a test for cold check resistance of furniture finishes.

Tensile Testing Veneer

Development of a substitute for the ten-cycle test for durability of hardwood plywood.

Methods of treating green hardwood veneer to yield protection against destructive organisms.

Development of hardwood veneer log grades.

Development of statistical quality control techniques for the production of dry formed particle board.

The application of linear programming to the scheduling of pulpwood procurement.

Methods of increasing lumber yields in rough mill cut-up operations.

Development of a patched strip core for hardwood plywood.

Factors influencing the rate of drying the hardwood veneers.

Investigating Wood Machinability

The Governor's Research Triangle Committee, Inc.

George L. Simpson, Jr., Director
Pearson H. Stewart, Associate Director
James S. Bethel, Consultant for Forestry
Leon E. Chaiken, Consultant for Forestry
Box 1488, Raleigh, N. C.

The Governor's Research Triangle Committee, Incorporated, is a non-stock, non-profit organization whose purpose is to do all that is possible to use and develop the research resources of the Triangle area.

The Committee works solely within the bounds and desires of the three institutions. Its primary purpose is to make industrial and governmental research activities aware of the scientific resources and cultural advantages of the Triangle area.

When asked, the Committee will undertake to arrange a meeting between such industrial and governmental agencies and appropriate people from the three institutions.

The Committee undertakes also to help in carrying forward any projects deemed desirable by one or more of the institutions.

OFFICERS

Robert M. Hanes, President. Honorary Chairman of Board, Wachovia Bank and Trust Company, Winston-Salem, N. C.

A. Hollis Edens, Vice President. President, Duke University, Durham, N. C.

William C. Friday, Vice President. President Consolidated University of North Carolina, Chapel Hill, N. C.

George Watts Hill, Secretary-Treasurer. Chairman of the Board, Durham Bank and Trust Company, Durham, N. C.

MEMBERS

Luther H. Hodges, Governor of North Carolina, Raleigh, N. C.

Robert T. Armstrong, Vice President and Technical Director, Celanese Corporation of America, New York, N. Y.

E. Y. Floyd, Director, Plant Food Institute of N. C. & Va., Inc., Raleigh, N. C.

R. Grady Rankin, President, Superior Mills, Gastonia, N. C.

C. W. Reynolds, Assistant Works Manager, Western Electric Company, Winston-Salem, N. C.

William H. Ruffin, President, Erwin Mills, Durham, N. C.

G. Akers Moore, Jr., Vice President, Commercial Printing Company, Raleigh, N. C.

Collier Cobb, Jr., Chairman of the Board, Bank of Chapel Hill, Chapel Hill, N. C.

WORKING COMMITTEE

J. Harold Lampe, Dean, School of Engineering, North Carolina State College, Chairman.

W. C. Davison, Dean, School of Medicine, Duke University

Marcus E. Hobbs, Dean Graduate School, Duke University

D. W. Colvard, Dean, School of Agriculture, North Carolina State College

Henry T. Clark, Jr., Administrator, Division of Health Affairs, University of North Carolina

W. J. Seeley, Dean, College of Engineering, Duke University

Arthur Roe, Director of the Institute of Natural Science, University of North Carolina

Malcolm Campbell, Dean, School of Textiles, North Carolina State College

Dan O. Price, Director of the Institute of Research in Social Science, University of North Carolina.

June, 1958

APPENDIX F

DATA RELATED TO THE PARK'S DEVELOPMENT

Data Related to the Park's Development

Year	Acres Acquired	Cumulative Acres Acquired	Acres Sold for Development	Cumulative Acres Sold for Development	Acres Sold or Donated for Infrastructure	Acres Repurchased	Acres for Natural Area Preserves	Developed Square Feet*
1957	1332.60	1332.60	0.00	0.00	0.00	0.00	0.00	0.00
1958	2651.48	3984.08	0.00	0.00	0.00	0.00	0.00	0.00
1959	430.79	4414.87	104.66	104.66	0.00	0.00	0.00	0.00
1960	38.14	4453.01	63.53	168.19	21.96	0.00	0.00	204,000
1961	332.58	4785.59	0.00	168.19	0.00	0.00	0.00	204,000
1962	0.00	4785.59	0.00	168.19	0.00	0.00	0.00	204,000
1963	0.00	4785.59	18.02	186.21	0.00	0.00	0.00	204,000
1964	0.00	4785.59	27.33	213.54	0.00	0.00	0.00	204,000
1965	141.64	4927.23	1035.17	1248.71	6.04	0.00	0.00	384,645
1966	108.29	5035.52	46.00	1294.71	0.00	0.00	0.00	384,645
1967	0.00	5035.52	7.28	1301.99	0.00	0.00	0.00	384,645
1868	0.00	5035.52	106.61	1408.60	0.00	0.00	0.00	384,645
1969	0.00	5035.52	115.17	1523.77	0.00	0.00	0.00	384,645
1970	0.00	5035.52	0.00	1523.77	8.50	0.00	0.00	2,396,512
1971	0.00	5035.52	3.80	1527.57	0.48	0.00	0.00	2,396,512
1972	12.82	5048.34	124.53	1652.10	15.95	0.00	0.00	2,396,512
1973	0.00	5048.34	111.34	1763.44	0.00	0.00	0.00	2,396,512
1974	0.00	5048.34	10.82	1774.26	0.00	0.00	0.00	2,396,512
1975	117.40	5165.74	8.08	1782.34	0.00	0.00	0.00	2,827,412
1976	88.14	5253.88	98.01	1880.35	23.60	19.19	0.00	2,849,412
1977	0.00	5253.88	34.58	1914.93	0.00	40.66	0.00	3,056,412
1978	257.23	5511.11	88.66	2003.59	4.80	0.00	0.00	3,103,812

Year								
1979	0.00	5511.11	215.17	2218.76	0.00	0.00	0.00	3,103,812
1980	32.10	5543.21	159.32	2378.08	0.00	0.00	0.00	6,468,912
1981	0.00	5543.21	25.52	2403.60	0.00	0.00	0.00	6,468,912
1982	194.30	5737.51	22.24	2425.84	9.60	0.00	0.00	7,258,826
1983	388.37	6125.88	272.59	2698.43	8.54	0.00	0.00	8,124,743
1984	109.22	6235.10	188.05	2886.48	9.30	0.00	0.00	9,188,504
1985	406.80	6641.90	239.14	3125.62	0.00	14.05	0.00	10,440,582
1986	31.16	6673.06	101.12	3226.74	0.00	0.00	0.00	10,560,582
1987	0.00	6673.06	10.92	3237.66	0.00	0.00	0.00	11,285,082
1988	0.00	6673.06	118.22	3355.88	72.87	0.00	0.00	11,051,057
1989	4.60	6677.66	0.00	3355.88	0.00	0.00	0.00	11,164,057
1990	113.09	6790.75	216.19	3572.07	20.57	0.00	0.00	11,620,000
1991	1.76	6792.51	44.09	3616.16	3.03	10.92	0.00	13,319,400
1992	0.00	6792.51	21.82	3637.98	0.00	7.97	0.00	13,720,100
1993	0.00	6792.51	0.00	3637.98	0.00	0.00	0.00	13,877,300
1994	0.00	6792.51	117.17	3755.15	0.00	0.00	31.23	13,997,300
1995	1.37	6793.88	25.80	3780.95	0.00	0.00	0.00	14,345,900
1996	29.25	6823.13	52.14	3833.09	11.17	0.00	0.00	15,075,232
1997	0.00	6823.13	127.82	3960.91	3.37	0.00	25.90	15,375,317
1998	63.13	6886.26	53.04	4013.95	33.97	0.00	17.50	15,698,070
1999	0.00	6886.26	145.00	4158.95	0.00	4.54	0.00	16,716,490
2000	85.00	6971.26	102.80	4261.75	21.10	0.00	38.40	17,486,110
Totals	6971.26	6971.26	4261.75	97151.02	274.85	97.33	113.03	

*Notes: No data were available for 1981
Data in italics are estimated
Source: Research Triangle Foundation

APPENDIX G

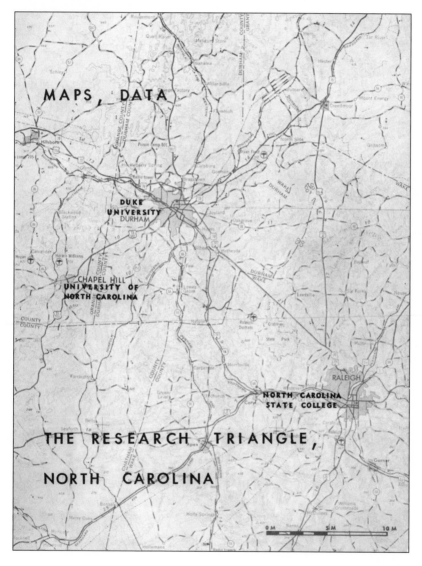

DUKE CHAPEL
DUKE UNIVERSITY

SOUTH BUILDING—ADMINISTRATION
UNIVERSITY OF NORTH CAROLINA

WILLIAM'S HALL—AGRONOMY
GARDNER HALL—BIOLOGY
NORTH CAROLINA STATE COLLEGE

THE RESEARCH TRIANGLE,
NORTH CAROLINA

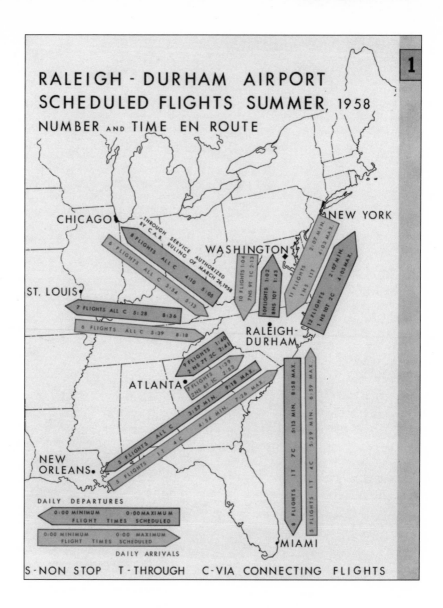

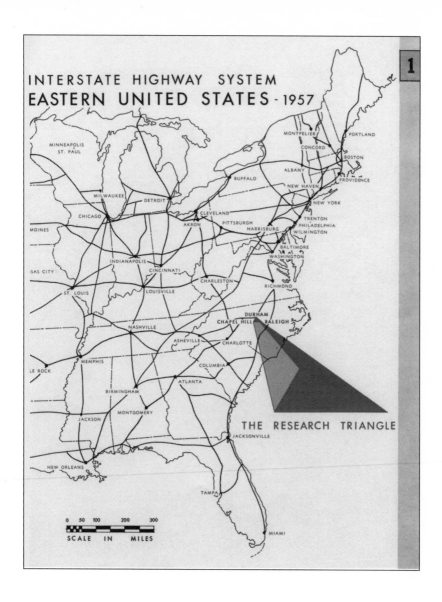

INTERSTATE HIGHWAY SYSTEM
EASTERN UNITED STATES - 1957

THE RESEARCH TRIANGLE

0 50 100   200   300
SCALE IN MILES

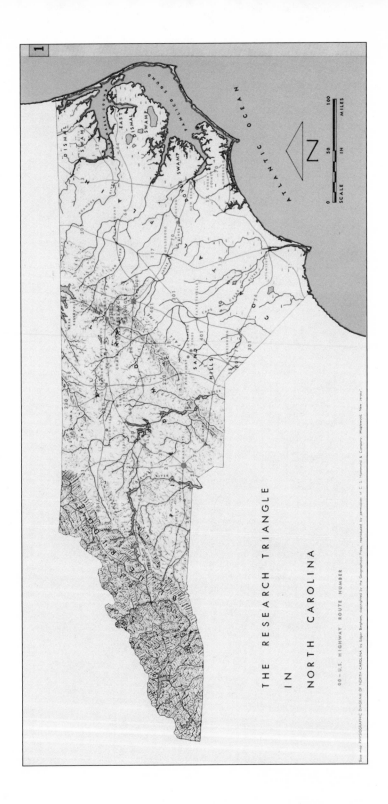

THE RESEARCH TRIANGLE

IN

NORTH CAROLINA

00 - U.S. HIGHWAY ROUTE NUMBER

Base map PHYSIOGRAPHIC DIAGRAM OF NORTH CAROLINA by Edgar Bingham, copyrighted by the Geographical Press, reproduced by permission of C. S. Hammond & Company, Maplewood, New Jersey.

ATLANTIC OCEAN

PAMLICO SOUND

DISMAL SWAMP

SAND HILLS

SCALE IN MILES

0   50   100

176

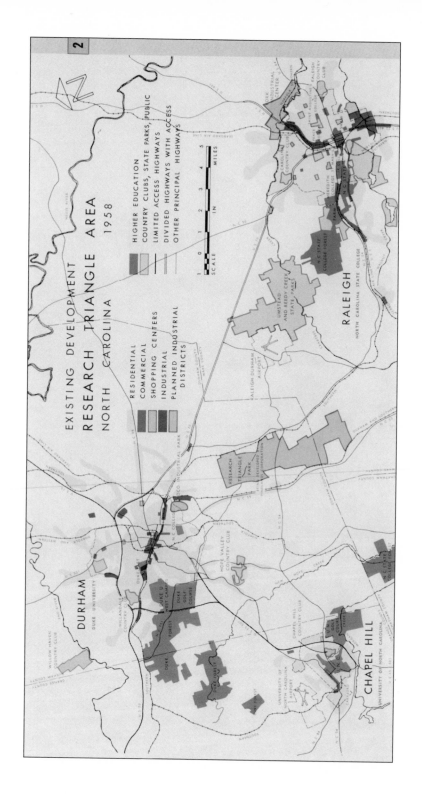

EXISTING DEVELOPMENT
RESEARCH TRIANGLE AREA 1958
NORTH CAROLINA

RESIDENTIAL
COMMERCIAL
SHOPPING CENTERS
INDUSTRIAL
PLANNED INDUSTRIAL
DISTRICTS

HIGHER EDUCATION
COUNTRY CLUBS, STATE PARKS, PUBLIC
LIMITED ACCESS HIGHWAYS
DIVIDED HIGHWAYS WITH ACCESS
OTHER PRINCIPAL HIGHWAYS

SCALE IN MILES
1 0 1 2 3 4 5

DURHAM

CHAPEL HILL

RALEIGH

RESEARCH TRIANGLE PARK

177

DUKE UNIVERSITY

UNIVERSITY OF NORTH CAROLINA

NORTH CAROLINA STATE COLLEGE

A pictorial recognition

UNION BUILDING
AND CHAPEL TOWER

WOMEN'S COLLEGE LIBRARY

MEN'S DORMITORY

UNION BUILDING

WEST CAMPUS

DUKE

DUKE HOSPITAL

WOMEN'S COLLEGE AUDITORIUM

MEDICAL SCHOOL ENTRANCE

MEDICAL SCHOOL

LIBRARY—WEST CAMPUS

UNIVERSITY

KENAN STADIUM,
MOREHEAD-PATTERSON BELL TOWER

GRAHAM MEMORIAL—STUDENT UNION

GRAHAM MEMORIAL IN SPRING

PERSON HALL—ANTHROPOLOGY

FOREST THEATRE

THE UNIVERSITY OF

KESSING POOL

COKER ARBORETUM

PLAYMAKERS' THEATRE

MOREHEAD PLANETARIUM

OLD EAST DORMITORY, PLAYMAKERS
THE OLD WELL, SOUTH BUILDING

NORTH CAROLINA

COLLEGE UNION

CLASSROOM BUILDING
UNDER CONSTRUCTION 1958-59

WATAUGA HALL—BOOKSTORE

WITHERS HALL—CHEMISTRY

D. H. HILL LIBRARY

NORTH CAROLINA

RICKS HALL
AGRICULTURAL EXTENSION

THE MALL

BROOKS HALL—SCHOOL OF DESIGN

MEMORIAL TOWER

PULLEN HALL—AUDITORIUM
PRIMROSE HALL—UTILITY

STATE COLLEGE

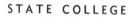

3

RESEARCH TRIANGLE INDUSTRIAL CONSTRUCTION COSTS

September, 1958

INDUSTRIAL CONSTRUCTION COSTS IN THE RESEARCH TRIANGLE—CHAPEL HILL, DURHAM, AND RALEIGH— ARE ABOUT 64% OF THOSE IN NEW YORK CITY.

Based on Dow Service Real Estate Valuation Calculator, F. W. Dodge Corporation, which reports that industrial construction costs in Raleigh are 64 per cent of those in New York. The Dow Service biannual survey of construction costs includes representative cities throughout the country. Chapel Hill and Durham, being very close to Raleigh, are not included in the published survey.

Courtesy: Durham's Committee of 100
Raleigh Chamber of Commerce

RESEARCH TRIANGLE RESIDENTIAL CONSTRUCTION COSTS

1958

Custom-built houses are erected in the Triangle area for from $10.00 to $12.00 per square foot.

Speculative houses meeting FHA requirements as a minimum are built in the Triangle area for from $8.00 to $10.00 per square foot.

Lots in Triangle area residential developments served by all utilities—including water, sewer, electricity, and paved street—range in price from $40.00 to $65.00 per front foot.

Lots served with electricity and graded streets only range in price from $10.00 to $25.00 per front foot.

RENTAL

RENTAL

RECENTLY BUILT HOMES

IN THE TRIANGLE AREA

RESEARCH TRIANGLE POPULATION

	CITY 1950	CITY 1958[1]	URBANIZED AREA 1950	URBANIZED AREA 1958	COUNTY 1950	COUNTY 1958
Chapel Hill	9,177	15,800	15,000(a)	28,600	. . .	. . .
Orange County	. . .	. . .	. . .	. . .	34,435	43,800
Durham	71,311	88,500	73,368	112,900	. . .	. . .
Durham County	. . .	. . .	. . .	. . .	101,639	119,300
Raleigh	65,679	86,000	68,743	112,400	. . .	. . .
Wake County	. . .	. . .	. . .	. . .	136,450	158,600
Total	146,167	190,300	157,111	253,900	272,524	321,700

[1]Including additions to corporate areas.

Sources: 1950 (except a)—U. S. Census
1950 (a)—Estimate by Chapel Hill Planning Board.
1958—Urban estimates by appropriate planning departments.
1958—County estimates by Public Health Statistics Section, North Carolina
Board of Health.

7

RESEARCH TRIANGLE LABOR FORCE

	DURHAM COUNTY		ORANGE COUNTY		WAKE COUNTY	
	May 1950	January 1959	May 1950	January 1959	May 1950	January 1959
Total Labor Force	43,800	47,525	12,500	11,975	52,600	67,000
Employed	40,900	44,025	12,125	11,275	51,600	62,400
Nonagricultural	38,900	42,300	9,850	9,275	42,700	55,100
Manufacturing	13,400	12,825	2,650	1,540	4,750	6,920
Service	7,300	7,460	800	450	7,600	5,545
Trade	6,800	6,795	1,450	1,300	9,400	11,335
Government	1,200	3,630	2,800	3,500	5,800	13,300
Construction	3,300	2,715	800	500	2,400	3,930
Transportation-Communication-Public Utility	1,300	1,950	375	120	4,000	3,600
Finance-Insurance-Real Estate	1,500	1,555	300	365	1,850	3,100
Misc.—Others[1]	4,100	5,370	675	1,500	6,900	7,370
Agricultural	2,000	1,725	2,275	2,000	8,900	7,300
Unemployed	2,900	3,500	375	700	1,000	4,600

[1] Includes self-employed domestics, unpaid family workers, not reported, etc.

Source: Employment Security Commission of North Carolina

RESEARCH TRIANGLE LABOR SUPPLY

Available Labor Supply[1] Within 20 Miles of the Center of the Triangle
February, 1959

	Total		White		Other	
	Male	Female	Male	Female	Male	Female
Skilled	225	70	190	65	35	5
Semi-Skilled	855	1,325	555	785	300	540
Trainable[2]	2,125	3,880	1,405	2,555	720	1,325

[1]Those persons who are referable to and suitable for a production type job in a new or expanding industry which affords wages and working conditions equal to or slightly better than the industrial pattern of the area. Recruitment would be from such groups as: (1) the unemployed and underemployed; (2) housewives available, if suitable job opportunities existed; (3) workers now commuting to employment at a distant point who prefer local employment; (4) youths expected to join the labor force; and (5) other lesser segments of the labor force.

[2]Includes otherwise unabsorbed portions of high school graduates.

Source: Employment Security Commission of North Carolina

7

RESEARCH TRIANGLE PUBLIC UTILITIES—A SUMMARY

1958

	Water		Sewer Treatment Capacity	Electricity	Telephone[1]
Chapel Hill	499 3 2.5	MG* MGD** MGD***	2.25 MGD	University Service Plant	Chapel Hill Telephone Co. Durham—35[2]
Durham	4600 15.6 9	MG* MGD** MGD***	27 MGD	Duke Power Co.	General Telephone Company[3] Atlanta—9 Charlotte—23 New York—11 Washington—11
Raleigh	3840 13 8.87	MG* MGD** MGD***	12 MGD	Carolina Power and Light Co.	Southern Bell Telephone & Telegraph Co. Atlanta—18 Charlotte—42 New York—21 Washington—15

DIDCO Industrial Park is in the Durham service area.

Research Triangle Park	5	MGD available from Durham in 18" line		Duke Power Co. and Carolina Power and Light Co.

York Industrial Center is in the Raleigh service area.

---

* Impounding reservoir capacity.
** Filtration consumption.
*** Average consumption.

[1]Number of direct toll circuits to indicated cities.
[2]All long distance calls routed through Durham.
[3]Long distance system in Durham owned and operated by Southern Bell.

Natural Gas—Public Service Company of North Carolina, serving the area with a 10" high pressure line, purchases from the Transcontinental Gas Pipe Line Company, which buys from fields in Louisiana and Texas.

All rates and other details available on request.

8

RESEARCH TRIANGLE GOVERNMENT OR CONTROL

1959

	Type of Government or Control
Chapel Hill	Council-City Manager
Durham	Council-City Manager
Raleigh	Council-City Manager
Orange County	County Commission
Durham County	County Commission-County Manager
Wake County	County Commission
DIDCO Industrial Park	Non-Profit Corporation in Durham City
Research Triangle Park	Private Corporation in Durham and Wake Counties
York Industrial Center	Prviate Corporation in Wake County

9

RESEARCH TRIANGLE CLIMATOLOGY SUMMARY

	Durham	Raleigh (airport)	Miami	New York[1]
Mean daily maximum temperature—January	53°F	51	74	40
Mean daily minimum temperature—January	31	32	63	26
Mean daily maximum temperature—July	89	89	87	82
Mean daily minimum temperature—July	67	68	76	67
Difference—indicating relative night time cooling	22	21	11	15
Mean annual precipitation	40 in.	45	47	42
Mean annual number of days with minimum temperature of 32° or below	78	51	0	92
Mean annual amount of snowfall	6 in.	7	0	30
Mean total number of heating degree days, base—65°	3333	3369	173	5050

[1]Based on temperatures atop a skyscraper near the waterfront; not entirely comparable with other data.

Details available on request.

Source: Raleigh-Durham Airport Station Weather Bureau

Design outside temperature for air-conditioning	95	95	91	95
Design outside temperature for heating	10	10	35	0

Source: ASHVE Guide

10

RESEARCH TRIANGLE PUBLIC SCHOOLS

PUPIL-TEACHER RATIOS, 1957-1958

Pupils per Teacher	Elementary[1]	Junior High School[2]	Senior High School[2]
Chapel Hill	33.4	(JHS begins 58-59)	24.8
Durham	30.3	26.9	22.7
Raleigh	31.3	27.6	24.0

[1]Only full-time teachers counted; special teachers, art, music, library, etc., excluded. Pupil load from average daily membership.

[2]Only teachers of 3 or more periods a day counted. Pupil load from total enrollment.

Source: North Carolina Department of Public Instruction

PERCENT OF HIGH SCHOOL GRADUATES ENROLLED IN COLLEGE

	CHAPEL HILL		DURHAM		RALEIGH	
	Chapel Hill	Lincoln	Durham	Hillside	Needham-Broughton	J.W.Ligon
1955	59		55		80	36
1956	62		54	36*	90	44
1957	69	44*	54	46	73	35
1958	60	36	55	44	78	60

Data as of September first after June graduation

All schools are accredited by the Southern Association of Secondary Schools and Colleges.

*First year of record keeping.

Source: North Carolina Department of Public Instruction

QUALIFICATION OF TEACHERS, 1957-1958

	CHAPEL HILL		DURHAM			RALEIGH		
	Elem.	SHS	Elem.	JHS	SHS	Elem.	JHS	SHS
Total number of teachers	58	35	236	124	84	284	133	97
Percent of Teachers								
With master's degree	31	30	36	28	35	21	30	44
With bachelor's degree	66	66	66	71	64	79	70	56
Other	3	0	0	0	1	0	0	0

Source: North Carolina Department of Public Instruction

11

RESEARCH TRIANGLE PRIVATE SCHOOLS

Number of Grades in Private Schools, 1957-1958

	Chapel Hill	Durham	Raleigh
Catholic Elementary		1 - 9	1 - 8
Catholic Secondary			9 - 12
Calvert Method		1 - 7	
Junior Colleges			11 - 14
Other		1 - 8	1 - 6

(Private kindergartens are in each city)

Source: North Carolina Department of Public Instruction

11

THE RESEARCH TRIANGLE RETAIL PRICES

		U. S. City Average[1] December, 1958	Triangle Area[2] December, 1958
		Cents	Cents
FOOD			
Fruits and vegetables:			
Frozen:			
Strawberries	10 oz.	26.6	22.5
Orange juice concentrate	6 oz.	28.9	24.75
Peas, green	10 oz.	20.0	19.5
Beans, green	9 oz.	23.0	19.5
Fresh:			
Apples	1 lb.	12.4	14.5
Bananas	1 lb.	17.8	14.5
Oranges, size 200	doz.	69.9	37.0
Lemons	1 lb.	18.8	37.0
Grapefruit*	each	12.6	12.5
Peaches*	1 lb.		
Strawberries*	1 pt.		
Grapes, seedless*	1 lb.		25
Watermelons*	1 lb.		
Potatoes	10 lb.	51.6	39
Sweet potatoes	1 lb.	13.4	14.5
Onions	1 lb.	9.4	8.33
Carrots	1 lb.	14.0	12.5
Lettuce	head	18.1	19
Celery	1 lb.	15.1	7.5
Cabbage	1 lb.	7.7	8.33
Tomatoes	1 lb.	30.6	33
Beans, green	1 lb.	22.4	22.5

*priced only in season.

Canned:			
Orange juice	46-oz. can	46.2	39
Peaches	#2½ can	35.1	35
Pineapple	#2 can	35.5	35
Fruit cocktail	#303 can	27.4	27
Corn, cream style	#303 can	18.4	19.5
Peas, green	#303 can	21.0	19.5
Tomatoes	#303 can	16.1	12.5
Baby foods	4½ to 5 oz.	10.1	9.33
Dried:			
Prunes	1 lb.	38.2	39
Beans	1 lb.	17.5	17
Cereals and bakery products:			
Flour, wheat	5 lb.	54.9	59
Biscuit mix	20 oz.	26.8	27
Corn meal	1 lb.	12.9	17
Rice	1 lb.	18.6	17
Rolled oats	18 oz.	20.4	21
Corn flakes	12 oz.	25.7	25
Bread, white	1 lb.	19.6	15.5
Soda crackers	1 lb.	29.3	29
Vanilla cookies	7 oz.	24.4	23

[1] Table 7: Average retail prices of selected foods, Consumer Price Index, Bureau of Labor Statistics, December, 1958.
[2] Chain store actual prices.

12

THE RESEARCH TRIANGLE RETAIL PRICES

FOOD		U. S. City Average[1] December, 1958 Cents	Triangle Area[2] December, 1958 Cents
Meats, poultry and fish:			
Round steak	1 lb.	104.9	99
Chuck roast	1 lb.	63.4	57
Rib roast	1 lb.	81.2	83
Hamburger	1 lb.	54.7	59
Veal cutlets	1 lb.	135.9	139
Pork chops, center cut	1 lb.	89.1	89
Bacon	1 lb.	72.8	69
Ham, whole	1 lb.	67.7	63
Lamb, leg	1 lb.	77.3	75
Frankfurters	1 lb.	66.1	65
Luncheon meat, canned	12 oz.	53.3	49
Frying chickens, ready-to-cook	1 lb.	42.0	35
Ocean perch, fillet, frozen	1 lb.	46.6	43
Haddock, fillet, frozen	1 lb.	58.4	53
Salmon, pink, canned	16 oz.	61.6	53
Tuna fish, canned	6-6½ oz.	33.8	35
Dairy products:			
Milk, fresh, (grocery)	1 qt.	24.2	27
Milk, fresh, (delivered)	1 qt.	25.4	27
Ice cream	1 pt.	29.6	27
Butter	1 lb.	74.4	79
Cheese, American process	1 lb.	57.9	59
Milk, evaporated	14½ oz. can	15.1	15
Other foods at home:			
Tomato soup	10½ to 11-oz. can	12.4	11.66
Beans with pork	16-oz. can	15.1	15
Pickles, sweet	7½ oz.	27.0	19
Catsup, tomato	14 oz.	22.5	21
Coffee	1 lb. can	85.3	85
Coffee	1 lb. bag	66.3	81
Tea bags	pkg. of 16	24.1	25
Cola drinks, carton	36 oz.	28.3	27
Shortening, hydrogenated	3 lb.	93.0	93
Margarine, colored	1 lb.	29.1	28
Lard	1 lb.	22.6	21
Salad dressing	1 pt.	37.9	37
Peanut butter	1 lb.	56.6	53
Sugar	5 lb.	56.9	43
Corn syrup	24 oz.	26.3	27
Grape jelly	12 oz.	27.9	24.5
Chocolate bar	1 oz.	5.2	4.17
Eggs, Grade A, large	doz.	58.8	55
Gelatin, flavored	3 to 4 oz.	9.1	8.75

[1]Table 7: Average retail prices of selected foods,
Consumer Price Index, Bureau of Labor Statistics,
December, 1958.
[2]Chain store actual prices.

FUEL	All Cities[3] Combined	Triangle[4] Area
100 gallons of Fuel Oil #2	$15.42	$15.20
Gasoline (per gallon)		
regular	.295	.309
premium	.335	.339

[3]Table 2: Average retail prices for coal, fuel oil, and gasoline,
Retail Prices and Indexes of Fuels and Electricity, Bureau of Labor Statistics,
December, 1958
[4]Actual prices.

RESEARCH TRIANGLE COST OF AN EVENING
FOR TWO AT THE THEATRE

	Triangle	New York City
	$13.05	$24.30
Two tickets, top price	$ 8.00 (@ $4.00, actual price "No Time for Sergeants" January, 1958)	$16.10 (@ $8.05)
Travel	$ 3.30 (residence location assumed at center of Triangle — 15 miles from each campus; 30 mi. round trip @ 11c)	2.70 (1 round trip Darien, Conn.— Grand Central, New York. Other fare accounted for as regular commutation cost.)
Parking	0	0
Taxi	0	1.75
Baby Sitter	$ 1.75 (3½ hours @ 50c)	3.75 (5 hours @ 75c)
Total	$13.05	$24.30

12

THE RESEARCH TRIANGLE OF NORTH CAROLINA

CALENDAR OF CULTURAL EVENTS

ACADEMIC YEARS 1956-1957 AND 1957-1958

Duke—Duke University
UNC—University of North Carolina
NCS—North Carolina State College

PROFESSIONAL ENTERTAINMENT

A. Artists Series of Music and Dance

Guimar Novaes, pianist . October 9, 1956—Raleigh
Eileen Farrell, soprano . . October 10, 1956—UNC
Boris Christoff, basso . . November 8, 1956—Raleigh
Ballet Russe de Monte
   Carlo . . . . November 13, 1956—Duke
Gregor Piatigorsky, cellist
   . . . . December 12, 1956—Raleigh
An Evening with Johann
   Strauss . . . . . . January 14, 1957—Duke
Claramae Turner, contralto
   . . . . January 14, 1957—Raleigh
Chicago Opera Ballet . . January 22, 1957—UNC
Pittsburgh Symphony Orchestra
   . . . . February 8, 1957—Duke
Pittsburgh Symphony Orchestra
   . . . . February 11, 1957—Raleigh
Okernkirchen Children's Choir
   . . . . February 21, 1957—UNC
Roger Wagner Chorale February 22, 1957—Raleigh
Singing Boys of Norway . . March 8, 1957—Raleigh
Gina Bachauer, pianist . . March 15, 1957—Duke
Ballet Russe de Monte
   Carlo . . . . March 19, 1957—Raleigh
Witold Malcuzynski, pianist March 28, 1957—UNC
Jean Madeira, contralto . . April 15, 1957—Duke
Gregor Piatigorsky, cellist April 23, 1957—Raleigh
Victoria de los Angeles, soprano
   . . . . October 10, 1957—UNC
Zinka Milanov, dramatic soprano
   . . . . October 15, 1957—Raleigh
NBC Opera . . . . . . November 19, 1957—Duke
Cavalcade of Song . . November 21, 1957—Raleigh
Fred Waring and his Pennsylvanians
   . . . . December 9, 1957—Raleigh
Berl Senofsky, violinist . December 10, 1957—Duke
Ballet by Kovach and Rabovsky
   . . . . December 12, 1957—UNC
Bach Aria Group . . . . January 13, 1958—Duke
Jan Peerce, tenor . . . . February 6, 1958—UNC
National Ballet of Canada
   . . . . February 19, 1958—Raleigh
Virtuosi di Roma Orchestra
   . . . . February 27, 1958—UNC
Gina Bachauer, pianist . February 27, 1958—Raleigh
Leon Fleisher, pianist . . February 27, 1958—Duke
Westminster Choir . . . . March 3, 1958—Raleigh
Pittsburgh Symphony Orchestra
   . . . . March 11, 1958—UNC
Chicago Opera Ballet . . . March 17, 1958—Duke
List and Glenn, pianist and violinist
   . . . . March 28, 1958—Raleigh

B. North Carolina Symphony Orchestra

Little Symphony . . . . February 26, 1957—Raleigh
Little Symphony . . . . . March 25, 1957—Raleigh
Children's Concert . . . May 6, 1957—Chapel Hill
Full Symphony . . . . . May 9, 1957—Raleigh
Children's Concert . . . . May 9, 1957—Raleigh
Children's Concert . . . May 10, 1957—Durham
Full Symphony . . . . . May 13, 1957—Durham
Full Symphony . . . May 19, 1957—Chapel Hill
Full Symphony . . . . April 23, 1958—Durham
Children's Concert . . . April 30, 1958—Chapel Hill
Full Symphony . . . April 30, 1958—Chapel Hill
Children's Concert . . . . May 2, 1958—Durham

Full Symphony . . . . . . May 2, 1958—Durham
Children's Concert . . . . May 7, 1958—Raleigh
Full Symphony . . . . . . May 7, 1958—Raleigh

C. Chamber Music Series—Duke

Robert Masters Piano Quartet . October 20, 1956
Hungarian String Quartet . . November 17, 1956
Budapest Quartet . . . . . January 18, 1957
Quartetto Italiano . . . . . January 19, 1957
Smetana Quartet (Prague) . . March 9, 1957
Rococo Ensemble . . . . April 13, 1957
Alfred Deller Trio (England) . . October 26, 1957
Hungarian String Quartet . . . November 2, 1957
Barylli String Quartet (Vienna) . December 7, 1957
Amadeus String Quartet (London) February 1, 1958
Koeckert String Quartet (Munich) . March 1, 1958

D. Chamber Music Guild—Raleigh

Quintetto Boccherini . . . . . November 2, 1956
Quartetto Italiano . . . . . . January 18, 1957
University Quartet . . . . . . February 1, 1957
Rococo Ensemble . . . . April 12, 1957
Hungarian String Quartet . . . November 1, 1957
Barylli String Quartet (Vienna) . December 6, 1957
Amadeus String Quartet (London) January 31, 1958
Koeckert String Quartet (Munich) . March 7, 1958

E. Drama

"Peer Gynt" . . . . November 15, 1956—Duke
   Canadian Players
"The Best of Steinbeck" November 30, 1956—Duke
   Constance Bennett, Tod Andrews
   Frank McHugh, Robert Strauss
"Charley's Aunt" . . . . . March 1, 1957—NCS
   Players, Incorporated
"Henry IV", Part One . . . March 2, 1957—NCS
   Players, Incorporated
Nine by Six . . . . October 11, 1957—NCS
   Barter Theatre of Virginia
"The Rivalry" . . . . . December 6, 1957—UNC
   Agnes Moorhead, Raymond Massey
"No Time for Sergeants" . January 10, 1958—UNC
"Othello" . . . . January 31, 1958—Duke
"Shadow and Substance" . February 21, 1958—NCS
   Dublin Players
"Juno and the Paycock" . February 22, 1958—NCS
   Dublin Players
"Back to Methuselah" . . . March 1, 1958—UNC
   Tyrone Power, Faye Emerson
   Arthur Treacher

Summer Stock—Durham

"The Happiest Millionaire" . . June 23-28, 1958
   Jeffrey Lynn
"Janus" . . . . June 30-July 5, 1958
   Lillian Roth
"Angel Street" . . . . July 7-12, 1958
   Shepperd Strudwick
"Monique" . . . . July 14-19, 1958
   Lisa Ferraday
"Middle of the Night" . . . July 21-26, 1958
   Joanne Dru
"Picnic" . . . . July 28-Aug. 2, 1958
   Scott Brady
"The White Sheep of the Family" . .
   . . . . August 4-9, 1958
   Edward Everett Horton
"Inherit the Wind" . . . . August 11-16, 1958
   Walter Abel

F. Arts Council—Duke

Edgar and Dorothy Alden, violinists
   . . . . September 28, 1956
Elizabethan Evening . . . . December 11, 1956
John Langstaff, baritone . . . January 8, 1957
Beveridge Webster, pianist . . . May 7, 1957
Wilton Mason, pianist . . . September 27, 1957
An Evening of Contemporary Art . January 10, 1958
Cora Kelson, pianist . . . . . . March 9, 1958

G. Miscellaneous

Ice Capades of 1956
   . . . . September 24-29, 1956—Raleigh
Exploring Secrets of Underwater
   World, color film,
   Dimitri Ribicoff, Submarine Research
   Institute, Cannes, France October 2, 1956—NCS
Katherine Anne Porter, readings
   . . . . October 19, 1956—NCS
Mantovani and his Orchestra
   . . . . December 6, 1956—UNC
Anshel Brusilov, violinist . January 11, 1957—Duke
Dr. Eta Harich-Schneider, harpsichordist
   . . . . February 4, 1957—Duke
Jose Greco and his Company of
   Spanish Dancers . . . February 9, 1957—Duke
Don Cossack Choir . . . . February 9, 1957—UNC
Frankel-Ryder Dance Drama
   Company . . . . . February 15, 1957—Duke
Challenge of Everest, color film,
   Norman G. Dyhrenfurth . March 12, 1957—NCS
An Evening with Mark Twain March 26, 1957—UNC
   Henry Hull
Jose Limon and Dance Company
   . . . . April 11, 1957—UNC
Jose Limon and Dance Company
   . . . . April 12, 1957—UNC
Four Freshmen . . . . . . October 11, 1957—Duke
Fun with the Mind . . . . October 22, 1957—NCS
   Dr. Franz Polgar
Page Full of Stars . . . . October 25, 1957—Duke
   Don Shirley Trio, etc.
Ice Capades of 1957—October 25-30, 1957—Raleigh
New York Pro Musica Antiqua
   . . . . November 26, 1957—Duke
Iva Kitchell, dance satirist December 3, 1957—UNC
John Jacob Niles, balladeer
   . . . . December 17, 1957—Duke
Lotte Goslar, pantomimist . January 17, 1958—NCS
Lotte Goslar, pantomimist . January 30, 1958—UNC
Louis Armstrong, trumpeter February 11, 1958—Duke
Alex Templeton, pianist . . . April 17, 1958—UNC
Victor Borge, pianist . . . April 24, 1958—Raleigh
Rey de la Torre, classic guitarist
   . . . . April 29, 1958—Duke
Israeli Troupe . . . . May 7, 1958—UNC
   Israel song and dance
A Night of Mark Twain . . . May 8, 1958—Duke
   Hal Holbrook

II. LECTURES

Dr. Will Durant . . . . . . October 9, 1956—Duke
   Philosopher, Historian
Dr. Melvin Rader . . . . October 23, 1956—Duke
   Philosopher, Author
Arthur C. Clarke . . . . November 13, 1956—NCS
   Space Travel Scientist
Archibald Henderson . . November 15, 1956—UNC
   President, G. B. Shaw Society
Eleanor Roosevelt . . . November 26, 1956—Duke
   Journalist
Caroline London . . . . November 28, 1956—Duke
   Novelist
Dr. Alphonso Elder . . . December 4, 1956—Duke
   Lawyer, Artist
Sara Mashkawitz-Varkonyi December 5, 1956—Duke
   Artist
V. K. Krishna Menon . . December 10, 1956—Duke
   Indian Representative to United Nations
Herbert Morrison, M. P. . December 13, 1956—Duke
   British Labor Party Leader
Dr. Alexander C. Soper . . February 1, 1957—Duke
   Far Eastern Art Lecturer
Bruce Catton . . . . . . February 7, 1957—Duke
   Historian
Dr. Karl Gruber . . . . February 21, 1957—UNC
   Austrian Ambassador to United States
Henry Steele Commager . . March 12, 1957—UNC
   Historian

Harold Stassen .... March 12, 1957—Duke
   Special Assistant to President
Robert Frost .... March 18, 1957—UNC
   Poet
Dame Edith Sitwell .... March 21, 1957—UNC
   Poet
Patrick Murphy Malin.... March 27, 1957—UNC
   American Civil Liberties Union
James C. Hagerty .... April 4, 1957—Duke
   White House Press Secretary
Dr. George Catlin .... April 4, 5, 6, 1957—UNC
   Political Scientist
William O. Douglas ...... April 16, 1957—Duke
   Justice of the United States Supreme Court
Walter Cronkite .... April 23, 1957—Duke
   News Commentator
Dr. Ralph Bunche .... May 14, 1957—UNC
   Under Secretary of the United Nations
Adlai Stevenson .... September 28, 1957—UNC
   Lawyer
Edward P. Morgan .... October 21, 22, 1957—UNC
   ABC Commentator
Reginald Sorenson, M.P. ...October 24, 1957—Duke
   Author
Norman Thomas .... October 28, 1957—UNC
   Socialist
Robert F. Kennedy .... November 12, 1957—UNC
   Counsel for Special Senate Committee
Dr. Gerald Clemence .... November 12, 1957—Duke
   Principal Astronomer, U. S. Naval Observatory
James T. Farrell .... December 17, 1957—Duke
   Author
Abba Eban .... January 8, 1958—UNC
                January 9, 1958—Duke
   Israeli Ambassador to United States
Eleanor Roosevelt .... January 12, 1958—UNC
   Journalist   January 13, 1958—NCS
Hubert Humphrey .... February 12, 1958—UNC
   United States Senator
Dr. Fayez Sayegh .... February 20, 1958—Duke
   Spokesman for Arab States
   Delegation Office
Ogden Nash .... March 4, 1958—NCS
   Poet
Walt Kelly .... March 11, 1958—Duke
   Creator of "Pogo"
Robert Frost .... March 14, 1958—UNC
   Poet
Luther H. Hodges .... March 16, 1958—UNC
   Governor of North Carolina
Dr. Charles L. Dunham ...March 16, 1958—UNC
   Director, Division of Biology
   and Medicine, A.E.C.
Henry Jackson .... March 16, 1958—UNC
   United States Senator
John Sparkman .... March 17, 1958—UNC
   United States Senator
Malcolm Cowley .... March 17, 1958—UNC
   Writer
Dr. Katharine McBride ...March 17, 1958—UNC
   President, Bryn Mawr College
Sergei Striganov .... March 18, 1958—UNC
   Charge d' Affairs, USSR Embassy
Victor Reuther .... March 18, 1958—UNC
   United Auto Workers
Jonathan Daniels .... March 18, 1958—UNC
   Editor
J. Spencer Love .... March 18, 1958—UNC
   Burlington Industries
Dr. Benjamin Fine .... March 21, 1958—UNC
   Dean, Yeshiva University Graduate School
Harry Ashmore .... March 21, 1958—UNC
   Editor
Irving Koslowe .... March 25, 1958—NCS
   Rabbi at Sing-Sing
Sir Leslie Munroe .... April 17, 1958—Duke
   President General of the United Nations
   General Assembly

e. e. cummings .... May 1, 1958—Duke
   poet
Victor Andrade .... May 6, 1958—Duke
   Bolivian Ambassador to United States
Walt Kelly .... May 8, 1958—UNC
   Creator of "Pogo"
Arnold J. Toynbee .... May 12, 1958—Duke
   Historian

III. INSTITUTION MUSIC SERIES

A. Duke Symphony Orchestra Concerts—Duke

Soloist, Anshel Brusilov, violinist ...January 10, 1957
Soloist, Lorne Munro, violoncellist ...April 18, 1957
Soloist, Loren Withers, pianist ...November 22, 1957
Piano Concerto Concert .... March 13, 1958
Spring Concert .... April 18, 1958

B. Duke Concert Band—Duke

Winter Concert .... December 6, 1956
Spring Concert, David Bar-Illan,
   pianist .... April 5, 1957
Lawn Concert .... May 12, 1957
Winter Concert .... December 5, 1957
Spring Concert, Percy Grainger, pianist April 8, 1958

C. Durham Civic Choral Society—Durham

Winter Concert .... December 4, 1956
Spring Concert .... May 3, 1957
Winter Concert .... December 3, 1957
Spring Concert .... April 14, 1958

D. Duke Glee Clubs—Duke

Men's Glee Club Concert .... May 10, 1957
Joint Concert of Men's and
   Women's Glee Clubs .... October 18, 1957
Men's Glee Club Concert .... February 25, 1958
Women's Glee Club Concert ...... April 19, 1958

E. Duke Madrigal Singers—Duke

Spring Concert .... April 22, 1957
Milton and Music .... May 8, 1957

F. Duke Miscellaneous—Duke

Little Symphony Orchestra Concert
                      November 29, 1956
Faculty Chamber Music Concert ...December 14, 1956
Chamber Music Concert .... January 4, 1957
Nereidian Water Show .... Dec. 5 and 7, 1957
Faculty Chamber Music Concert ...February 21, 1958

G. University of North Carolina
Les Petites Musicales—UNC

Willis Palmer, pianist .... November 11, 1956
Jan Saxon, soprano .... November 18, 1956
The Magic Flute, edited version,
   Norman Cordon .... December 2, 1956
Duke Madrigal Singers .... December 16, 1956
Martha Fouse, soprano .... January 13, 1957
Students of Walter Golde, pianists March 24, 1957
Herb Shellans, balladeer .... October 13, 1957
Francis Hopper, harpsichordist .... October 27, 1957
Emily Kellam and Suzann Davids, duo harpists
                      February 9, 1958
Paul Doktor, violist, and Raphael Puyana,
   harpsichordist .... March 5, 1958
Martha Fouse, soprano .... March 20, 1958
Lily Keleti, pianist .... March 23, 1958
Ethel Casey, soprano .... March 30, 1958
William Leland, pianist .... April 13, 1958
Gene Strassler, tenor .... April 20, 1958
Francis Hopper, organist .... May 4, 1958

H. University of North Carolina
Tuesday Evening Series—UNC

Lilian Pibernik, pianist .... November 13, 1956
Wilton Mason, pianist .... January 15, 1957
Lillian Freundlich, pianist .... February 19, 1957
Die Fledermaus, Grass Roots
   Opera Company .... October 22, 1957
Die Fledermaus, Grass Roots
   Opera Company .... October 25, 1957—NCS

13

William S. Newman, pianist . . . . November 5, 1957
Chamber Music Concert . . . . November 19, 1957
"King David", University Chorus January 14, 1958
Robert MacDonald, pianist
January 16, 1958 (Thursday)
Robert Baker, organist . . . . February 4, 1958
Percy Grainger, pianist with University
Symphonic Wind Ensemble and UNC Chorus
February 11, 1958
Sonata recital, Edgar Alden, violinist,
William Newman, pianist . . February 18, 1958
Alice Riley, soprano . . . . March 18, 1958
"The Mikado", concert
production . . . . April 25, 1958 (Friday)
Hollins College and UNC Choral Groups

I. University of North Carolina

Music Groups Concerts—UNC

University Symphony Orchestra . . November 27, 1956
University Chorus Christmas
Concert . . . . December 18, 1956
University String Quartet . . . . March 2, 1957
University Concert Band . . . . March 19, 1957
"Dido and Aeneas", Concert by Men's Glee
Club and Women's College Chorus April 9, 1957
Band Lawn Concert . . . . April 28, 1957
University Symphony Orchestra . . . . April 30, 1957
Concerts of American Music, Phi Mu
Alpha Sinfonia Fraternity . . . . May 2, 1957
Band Lawn Concert . . . . May 5, 1957
University Chorus . . . . May 14, 1957
University Chorus Christmas
Concert . . . . December 17, 1957
University Glee Club . . . . March 4, 1958
University Concert Band . . . . April 1, 1958
University Chorus . . . . April 15, 1958
University Symphony Orchestra . . . . April 22, 1958
University String Quartet . . . . May 6, 1958
Band Lawn Concert . . . . May 18, 1958

J. North Carolina Museum of Art

Chamber Music Concerts—Raleigh

Emily Kellam, Suzann Davids, duo harpists
Ethel Casey, soprano . . . . January 26, 1958
Walter Golde, pianist
Ethel Casey, soprano . . . . February 16, 1958
May Mukle, cellist . . . . March 16, 1958
University String Quartet . . . . April 13, 1958
Emily Kellam,
Suzann Davids, duo harpists . . . . . May 25, 1958

K. North Carolina State College Miscellaneous—NCS

State College Glee Club . . . . November 4, 1956
Raleigh Symphony Orchestra . . November 11, 1956
Christmas Concert . . . . December 2, 1956
State College Symphonic Band January 12-13, 1957
State College Glee Club . . . . March 17, 1957
Raleigh Symphony Orchestra . . . . . . April 7, 1957
State College Symphonic Band . . . . . . May 5, 1957
State College Glee Club . . . . November 3, 1957
Raleigh Symphony Orchestra . . November 24, 1957
State College Symphonic Band . . December 6, 1957
Christmas Concert . . . . December 8, 1957
State College Glee Club . . . . January 10, 1958
State College Symphonic Band . . February 21, 1958
Raleigh Symphony Orchestra . . . . . . March 2, 1958
State College Glee Club . . . . March 2, 1958
State College Chamber Music Concert March 4, 1958
State College Symphonic Band . . . . March 14, 1958
Air Force Symphony Orchestra . . . . March 22, 1958
State College Glee Club . . . . April 11, 1958
Raleigh Symphony Orchestra . . . . . . May 4, 1958
State College Symphonic Band . . May 6 and 8, 1958
State College Symphonic Band May 13 and 15, 1958

IV. STUDENT AND LITTLE THEATRE DRAMA

A. Carolina Playmakers (professional training)—UNC

"Androcles and the Lion" . . . . November 14-18, 1956
"Desire Under the Elms" . . . December 14-18, 1956
"Brigadoon" . . . . March 1-3, 1957
"Stranger in the Land" . . . . March 27-30, 1957
"Peer Gynt" . . . . May 10-12, 1957
"The Lark" . . . . October 16-20, 1957
"Teahouse of the August
Moon" . . . . November 15-17, 1957
"What Every Woman Knows" . December 11-15, 1957
"View from the Bridge" . . . . . . March 12-16, 1958
"Comedy of Errors" . . . . May 9-11, 1958
"Sabrina Fair" . . . . June 27-28, 1958

B. Miscellaneous—UNC

"Esther Wake" . . . . December 5, 1956
A melodrama of colonial North Carolina,
commissioned by North Carolina Society
for Preservation of Antiquities
"A Christmas Carol" . . . . December 9, 1956
Annual reading
"Henry IV" . . . . March 11, 1957
Graham Memorial Players
"Thieves Holiday" . . . . March 30, 31, 1957
All student musical
Carolina Dramatic Arts Festival . . April 11-13, 1957
One-act plays
"A Christmas Carol" . . . . December 15, 1957
Annual reading
Out of the South . . . . March 28-29, 1958
Eight Paul Green one-act plays
Carolina Dramatic Arts Festival . . April 24-26, 1958
One-act plays
"No Squares Allowed" . . . . May 2-3, 1958
All student musical

C. Duke Players—Duke

"The Reclining Figure" . . . . November 1, 1956
"The Father" . . . . December 5, 1956
"The Infernal Machine" . . . . February 22-23, 1957
"Misalliance" . . . . March 7-8, 1957
"The Private Life of the
Master Race" . . . . April 5-6, 1957
"Teahouse of the August Moon"
October 31, November 1, 1957
"Uncle Vanya" . . . . December 11, 1957
"Volpone" . . . . March 7, 1958
"The Lark" . . . . May 1-2, 1958

D. Miscellaneous—Duke

"I'm Emir Here" . . . . April 25-26, 1957
"Magnolias and Madness" . . . . April 24-25, 1958

E. Miscellaneous—Allied Arts, Durham

Allied Arts Follies . . . . March 15-16, 1957
Allied Arts Follies . . . . March 13-14, 1958

F. Raleigh Little Theatre—Raleigh

"Anniversary Waltz" . . . . October 12-18, 1956
"Street Car Named Desire"
November 30-December 6, 1956
"Desperate Hours" . . . . January 25-31, 1957
"The Play's The Thing" . . . . . . March 15-20, 1957
"Teahouse of the August Moon" . . . May 3-9, 1957
"Ah, Wilderness", amphitheatre July 22-28, 1957
"Reclining Figure", amphitheatre . October 15-20, 1957
"Pajama Game" . . . . December 3-8, 1957
"Witness for the Prosecution" . . January 28-February 2, 1958
"Solid Gold Cadillac" . . . . March 18-23, 1958
"Matchmaker" . . . . May 6-11, 1958
"The Tender Trap", amphitheatre June 23-29, 1958
"In The Summer House", amphitheatre
July 21-27, 1958

G. Miscellaneous—NCS

"Time Out for Ginger" . . . . November 2, 1956
(Goldsboro Goldmasquers)
East Carolina Playhouse . . . . . November 16, 1956
College One-Act Play Night . . . . December 7, 1956
State College Drama Club . . . . May 3, 1957

College One-Act Play Night . . . . November 15, 1957
One-Act Play Festival . . . . February 28, 1958
State College Drama Club . . . . May 9-10, 1958

V. ARTS EXHIBITS

A. North Carolina Museum of Art—Raleigh

French Painting of the Nineteenth
Century . . . . June, July 1956
(31 works from 10 U. S. galleries)
Southern Highlands Handicraft
Guild . . . . August 1957
Fourth Miami National Ceramic
Exhibition . . . . September, October 1956
Rembrandt and his Pupils . . November, December 1956
(30 paintings and 127 other works by Rembrandt
and 80 paintings by his pupils)
Nineteenth Annual North Carolina
Artists' Competition . . . . December 1956
North Carolina Artists'
Competition Finalists . . . . January 1957
Recent Acquisitions . . . . February, March 1957
Panel's Choice (contemporary American Art
chosen by a New York panel) . . . . April 1957
Ceramic Artist, Hajime Katn . . . . . . April 1957
Hammer Brothers Collection . . . . May 1957
(50 16th and 17th century paintings by
Dutch, Flemish and Italian masters)
Art Rental Gallery . . . . June 1957
(Subsequent rental galleries held every three months)
Contemporary British Paintings
and Sculptures . . . . July, August 1957
Paintings by Enrique Montenegro . . . August 1957
contemporary
Rowlandson Drawings . . . . . September, October 1957
Little International . . . . November 1957
(26 smaller canvases of contemporary
artists throughout world)
Recent Acquisitions . . . . November 1957
Bradley Walker Tomlin . . . . December 1957
contemporary American painter
Twentieth Annual North Carolina
Artists' Competition . . . . December 1957
Mother and Child Theme in Art . . . December 1957
E. L. Kirchner, German Expressionist . January 1958
African Sculpture . . . . February 1958
Family of Man . . . . March, April 1958
(Edward Steichen Museum of Modern
Art Photographic Exhibition)
Chiaroscuro Woodcuts . . . . May 1958
(16th-18th centuries woodcuts)
Midwest Designer-Craftsmen . . . . June 1958

B. Duke—Duke

Toulouse-Lautrec . . . . November 1956
Japanese prints from Ukeyo-e School . February 1957
Prints of contemporary Japanese . . . February 1957
Contemporary American Glass . . . . . . March 1957

C. Person Art Gallery—UNC

Reproductions of Old Masters . . . . . September 1956
(for rent)
Chagall prints . . . . October, November 1956
Prints from UNC's Jacocks and
Burton Emmett Collections . . . . . January 1957
Annual exhibit of North Carolina Chapter of
American Institute of Architects . . February 1957
Indian Art from Museum of
New Mexico . . . . March 1957
Prints by Old and Modern Masters . . . April 1957
20th Annual North Carolina
School Art Exhibit . . . . May 1957
Reproductions of old masters . . . . . September 1957
(for rent)
Cape Cod Artists . . . . October 1957
Contemporary Sculptures . . . . November 1957
Fifty Pieces of African Art . . . . January 1958
Original Graphics by Modern Masters . February 1958
Contemporary French Artists, prints . . March 1958
Angelo Testa Fabrics and Designs . . April, May 1958

D. Morehead Art Gallery—UNC

Works of English Artist
Geoffrey Jenkinson............December 1956
Mobiles and Stabiles by
G. W. Owen of Mexico....January, February 1957
Works of Robert L. Blake
of Durham...............January, February 1957
North Carolina in pictures ....March 1957
Adult Beginners in Art ....March 1957
Water Colors of the United States .....April 1957
Paintings by Robert Dance
of Kinston..................September 1957
Paintings by Geoffrey
Jenkinson ....September-November 1957
A History of Pharmacy
in Oil Painting ....December 1957
North Carolina Photographers
Annual Exhibit ....January 1958
Paintings by Rachael Wells
of Miami ....February, March 1958
Works by Sylvia Carewe..............April 1958
Paul Flora Drawings ....May 1958
North Carolina Press Photographers .....May 1958

E. Allied Arts Center—Durham

Annual Show, Durham County
Artists.......................November 1956
North Carolina Chapter American
Institute of Architects ....November 1956
Camera Intra-Club.................January 1957
Art Guild Students................January 1957
Annual Juried Show ....February 1957
Schools Art.......................March 1957
Creative Art......................April 1957
Paintings by Murray Jones.............May 1957
Camera Club......................May 1957
Camera Intra-Club ....October 1957
Street Show.....................November 1957
Schools Art.................March, April 1958
Juried Show of Paintings ....April 1958
Art Students......................May 1958
Juried Show of Photographs ....May 1958

F. Sidewalk Art Exhibit

by Chapel Hill Painters...May 1958—Chapel Hill

G. College Union—NCS

38 Latin American Prints
(IBM exhibit).......September-October 1956
California Painting................November 1956
Christmas Sale ....December 1956
22 Paintings of the Western
Hemisphere ....January 1957
25 Years of A. H. Maurer..........February 1957
Good Design Show ....March 1957
Works by Rudy Pozzatti...............April 1957
Fact and Fantasy '56................May 1957
5th Year Design Show ....May 1957
French Art Exhibition Posters ......September 1957
25 Years of A. H. Maurer..........October 1957
Polish Cutouts....................October 1957
Sarasota Art ....November-December 1957
History of Photography ....November 1957
Polish Photography ....January 1958
Works by Leslie Laskey...........February 1958
Good Design Show ....March 1958
The Edwardians ....April 1958
Young Italian Artists................May 1958
Margaret Bourke-White...............May 1958

VI. MOTION PICTURES

A. Art Film Festival ....May 9, 1957—Duke
B. Quadrangle Pictures show motion picture   Duke
films on Wednesday and Saturday nights.
These are generally in foreign and art
film classifications.
C. Graham Memorial Activities Board shows   UNC
foreign, historical or experimental films
on Thursday evenings.

D. Graham Memorial Activities Board 'shows   UNC
motion picture films of recent outstanding
quality on Friday and Saturday evenings.
E. The College Union shows motion picture   NCS
films of recent outstanding quality on
Saturday and Sunday evenings.
F. The Design Film Committee shows motion   NCS
picture films in art and design classifications on Tuesday evenings.

VII. MOREHEAD PLANETARIUM PRODUCTIONS—UNC

"Our Sun".........September 25-October 22, 1956
"Mister Moon".....October 23-November 19, 1956
"Star of Bethlehem"
November 20-December 31, 1956
"1957 Celestial Preview"
January 1-January 28, 1957
"Satellites".....January 29-February 25, 1957
"Weather Whys".....February 26-March 27, 1957
"Easter, the Awakening".....March 28-April 29, 1957
"Signals from the Stars".....April 30-May 27, 1957
"Science Fiction".........May 28-July 1, 1957
"A Trip to Venus".....July 2-September 23, 1957
"Children of the Sun"
September 24-October 21, 1957
"Harvest of the Skies"
October 22-November 25, 1957
"Star of Bethlehem"
November 26-January 6, 1957-1958
"Star Scouting".....January 7-February 3, 1958
"Devils, Demons and Stars"
February 4-March 10, 1958
"Easter, the Awakening".....March 11-April 14, 1958
"Things that Fall from the Sky"
April 15-May 12, 1958
"End of the World".....May 13-June 30, 1958
"Land, Sea and Sky"...July, August, September 1958

VIII. UNIVERSITY CHAPEL PROGRAMS—Duke

A. Guest Preachers

Dr. Douglas V. Steere............September 23, 1956
The Reverend Maldwyn Edwards....October 21, 1956
Dr. Harold Bosley..............December 2, 1956
Dr. John Baillie...................January 6, 1957
Dr. H. R. Niebuhr................February 3, 1957
Dr. B. D. Napier.................February 17, 1957
Dean Jerold C. Brauer............March 17, 1957
Dr. E. C. Blake....................April 7, 1957
Dr. George P. Hedley..............May 5, 1957
Bishop G. Bromley Oxnam.........October 13, 1957
Dr. Paul J. Tillich............November 17, 1957
Dr. Hugh Anderson.............December 15, 1957
Dr. James A. Jones.............January 26, 1958
Dr. Clavis G. Chappell.........February 9, 1958
Dr. William G. Pollard............March 2, 1958
Bishop Rajah B. Manikam.........March 16, 1958
Bishop Nolan B. Harmon...........April 27, 1958
Dean Liston Pope.................May 11, 1958
Dr. Harold Bosley.................June 1, 1958

B. Guest Organists

E. Power Biggs..............November 4, 1956
Robert Elmore ....February 3, 1957
Carl Weinrich.................November 3, 1957
Eugene Mauney................February 2, 1958
University Organist in recital 1st Sunday in each
month. Carillon recitals daily.

C. Special Choir Events

"The Messiah".........December 2 and 9, 1956
"Elijah".....................May 5, 1957
"The Messiah"...............December 8, 1957
"Requiem".....................May 4, 1958

Note: Events at Duke University, Durham, University of
North Carolina, North Carolina State College, and
Raleigh are included in this calendar. Events of both
national and local origin are scheduled also at other
institutions in the Triangle area: Meredith College, North
Carolina College, Peace College, Shaw University, St.
Augustine's College, St. Mary's College.

RESEARCH TRIANGLE FOUNDATION OF NORTH CAROLINA
BOX 1488, RALEIGH, NORTH CAROLINA

The Research Triangle Foundation of North Carolina is a nonprofit organization whose purpose is to encourage the development and use of the research resources of the Research Triangle area of North Carolina. The Foundation works within the bounds and desires of the three institutions, Duke University, the University of North Carolina, and North Carolina State College.

The Foundation has assisted in the establishment of the Research Triangle Institute, a corporation organized for the purpose of establishing and operating facilities for research in the physical, biological, medical, mathematical, agricultural, economic, and engineering sciences, and the contracting for the conduct of investigation and research in such sciences.

Research Triangle Institute — George R. Herbert, President
Box 490, Durham, North Carolina

The Foundation has as a wholly owned subsidiary the Research Triangle Park, a 4,300-acre campus in the center of the Triangle area for the location of industrial and governmental research facilities.

Research Triangle Park — James B. Shea, Jr., Executive Vice President
Pearson H. Stewart, Vice President—Planning
Box 1488, Raleigh, North Carolina

RESEARCH TRIANGLE FOUNDATION OF NORTH CAROLINA

Maps and Data published spring, 1959, jointly by the Research Triangle Foundation of North Carolina and the North Carolina Department of Conservation and Development

Rev. 2/60

THE RESEARCH TRIANGLE
REGIONAL PLANNING COMMISSION

James Ray, Chairman	Raleigh
E. K. Powe, First Vice-Chairman	Durham County
Orville Campbell, Second Vice-Chairman	Chapel Hill
Mrs. Adelaide Walters, Secretary	Alderman, Chapel Hill
Arthur Clark, Treasurer	Durham
James E. Briggs	Raleigh
Edwin B. Clements	Durham County
William Enloe	Mayor, Raleigh
E. J. Evans	Mayor, Durham
Ben W. Haigh	County Board Chairman, Wake County
Dr. R. J. M. Hobbs	County Board Chairman, Orange County
Frank Kenan	County Board Member, Durham County
Don Matheson	Orange County
Hubert C. Sears	Wake County
Dr. George L. Simpson, Jr.	Orange County

Pearson H. Stewart .... Executive Director
Research Triangle Regional Planning Commission
P. O. Box 1488 .... Raleigh, N. C.

THE COMMISSION GRATEFULLY
ACKNOWLEDGES THE COOPERATION
AND ASSISTANCE OF THE FOLLOWING:

The City of Durham	and	Durham County
The City of Raleigh	and	Wake County
The Town of Chapel Hill	and	Orange County

The North Carolina State Board of Health
The North Carolina State Department of Water Resources
The North Carolina State Highway Commission

The United States Geological Survey
The United States Soil Conservation Service

The School of Forestry .... Duke University
The Institute of Government ...... University of North Carolina
The School of Public Health ...... University of North Carolina

BELL TOWER
N. C. STATE COLLEGE

DUKE CHAPEL
DUKE UNIVERSITY

GUIDES for the RESEARCH TRIANGLE

Prepared with the assistance of the Department of City and Regional Planning, University of North Carolina Chapel Hill, North Carolina

THE OLD WELL
UNIVERSITY OF NORTH CAROLINA

CONTENTS

THE RESEARCH TRIANGLE REGIONAL PLANNING COMMISSION
September 1960

The Research Triangle

As shown on the map on the opposite page, Raleigh, Durham, and Chapel Hill form the vertices of a triangular area at the northeast extremity of the sixteen county region known as the Piedmont Industrial Crescent.

A major college or university is located in each of these communities: North Carolina State College in Raleigh, Duke University in Durham, and the University of North Carolina at Chapel Hill. The more than eight hundred research personnel in these institutions create a concentration of research competence in the Research Triangle, as the area has come to be called, that is unique in the South.

On the conviction that academic research bears a close relationship to industrial and governmental research, a 4,600 acre tract of land near the center of the Triangle has been purchased for a park to be devoted entirely to research. Development of the park is under the control of a private corporation, the Research Triangle Park, a wholly-owned subsidiary of the non-profit Research Triangle Foundation.

At present, construction of the administration building and statistics laboratory for the Research Triangle Institute, a separate non-profit organization, and of a laboratory for the Chemstrand Research Center is underway. The Chemstrand research facility is the first industrial research laboratory to be located in the park.

It is expected that the Research Triangle Park will serve not only as a source of employment within the immediate Triangle

CHEMSTRAND RESEARCH CENTER, INCORPORATED

RESEARCH TRIANGLE INSTITUTE ADMINISTRATION BUILDING

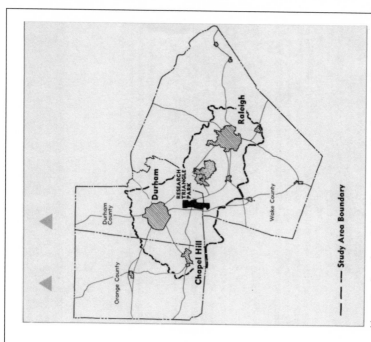

Map showing the relationship between the Research Triangle Study Area and the three-county Research Triangle Region.

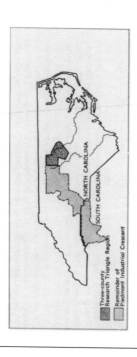

Three-county
Research Triangle Region

Remainder of
Piedmont Industrial Crescent

Area, but also as a magnet for the development of new industry in the region and the state.

This report presents a general view of the requirements that will be generated by future urban development of the Research Triangle Area, and explores ways of meeting these requirements. A Study Area has been delineated around Raleigh, Durham, and Chapel Hill, including land where most new development will occur. As used here, the terms "Triangle" or "Triangle Area" refer specifically to this Study Area. The term "Research Triangle Region" designates the larger area of Wake, Durham, and Orange counties.

The way in which land is used now, whether for houses, stores, factories, farms or other purposes, has an important bearing on its most desirable use in the future.

The map on the opposite page indicates the existing uses of land in the Research Triangle Study Area. These uses are broken down into four broad categories: residential, public and semi-public, wholesale and industrial, and commercial. As can be seen from the yellow areas on the map, residential uses, which account for approximately 35 percent of all the developed land, are concentrated around the communities of Raleigh, Durham, and Chapel Hill. There is, however, a significant amount of development scattered in random fashion along the major roads.

As shown by the green areas on the map, a large proportion of the developed land in the Triangle Area (approximately 31 percent) is devoted to public and semi-public uses. The largest of these areas represent Duke University, the University of North Carolina, North Carolina State College, Umstead State Park, and the Raleigh-Durham Airport. Such relatively open land can sometimes serve not only to provide amenity to surrounding areas but also to guide development into suitable areas or to provide a buffer between incompatible uses. The location of Umstead Park, for example, prevents construction of homes along one aircraft approach lane, thus avoiding the undesirable effects of aircraft noise on residential areas.

The Research Park dominates the central section of the Triangle Area and represents by far the largest area devoted to the industrial category of land use (research being classified as an industrial use for the purposes of this study). Other industrial areas are primarily concentrated in Raleigh and in Durham. Urban renewal may make available a few new industrial tracts inside these cities. But since the largest percentage of land in possible urban renewal areas is in small scattered holdings, too small for modern industrial needs, it is almost inevitable that most new industry will be located on the periphery of existing communities. The development of the York Industrial Center in the northeast part of Raleigh illustrates this trend.

The majority of commercial development is located in the main downtown areas or in centers (such as Raleigh's Cameron Village) near the downtown areas. As in other parts of the country, however, there is a trend toward the location of new large retail areas outside the central sections of towns and cities. In the Triangle Area this is evident in the construction of Northgate shopping center north of Durham, and in the Eastgate shopping center just east of Chapel Hill. Such outlying centers could grow at the expense of the central business areas unless a conscious effort is made, perhaps through urban redevelopment, to make the centers of towns attractive for new commercial development.

Approximately three-quarters of all the land in the Study Area is still undeveloped for urban purposes. Subtracting "marginal" land which, because of its steep slope, frequent flooding, or other reasons, is suitable for use only as natural open space, there is still a large amount of land (approximately 65 percent) which could be used for future development. Lack of space won't be a problem in the Triangle for a long time.

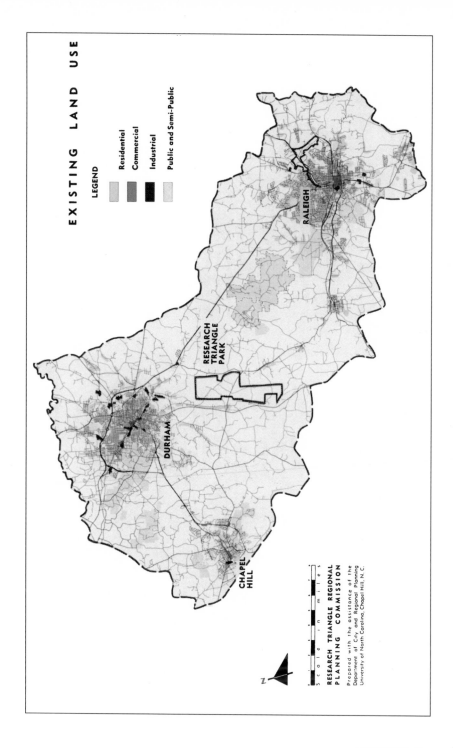

EXISTING LAND USE

LEGEND

Residential
Commercial
Industrial
Public and Semi-Public

RALEIGH

RESEARCH
TRIANGLE
PARK

DURHAM

CHAPEL
HILL

N

Scale in miles

RESEARCH TRIANGLE REGIONAL
PLANNING COMMISSION

Prepared with the assistance of the
Department of City and Regional Planning
University of North Carolina, Chapel Hill, N. C.

economy

One of the ways of measuring the economic health of a region is to compare its economy with that of a larger region within which it is contained. The graph on this page shows the relationship between the three-county Research Triangle Region and the Piedmont Industrial Crescent (see location map on page 3 for the outline of this region). Three economic indices, value added by manufacture, retail sales, and wholesale sales have been used for comparative purposes. As can be seen, the relationship of economic activity in the Triangle to that in the Piedmont Crescent differs somewhat for each index. All three indices show a decline in the region's position in relation to the Crescent from 1929 until 1947. The Triangle Region's relative position began to improve with respect to value added by manufacture in 1947, and with respect to wholesale sales in 1954. The Triangle Region's share of Crescent retail sales continued to decline slightly throughout the period.

The trends shown by the graph are not to be construed to mean that the Triangle Region has suffered a decline in absolute terms. They do indicate, however, that at least until recently the region's economy has been growing less rapidly than that of the Piedmont Crescent as a whole.

Based on past trends, then, there is some indication that the Triangle Region may be entering a period of more rapid economic growth. Since the trends shown on the graph do not reflect the potential impact of employment in the Research Triangle Park, successful development of the Park will provide further assurance of an accelerated rate of growth.

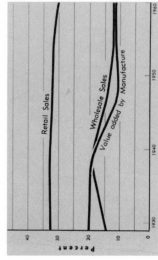

RESEARCH TRIANGLE COUNTIES AS A PERCENT OF THE PIEDMONT INDUSTRIAL CRESCENT

Viewing the economy in another way, employment in the Research Triangle Region increased approximately 33 percent from 1940 to 1950 and approximately 25 percent in the last decade. Based on these trends and assuming successful development of the Park, it is estimated that present employment (approximately 125,000) will be doubled by 1980 in the three county region.

population

As shown on the accompanying graph, current estimates, based on preliminary 1960 Census figures for the three Triangle counties, indicate that the Triangle Study Area now contains approximately a quarter of a million people. Discounting for the moment the potential effect of the Research Park, projections of recent trends indicate that by 1980 the Study Area might contain from 360,000 to 410,000 people. Considering additional employment to be provided by the Research Triangle Park, these projections need adjustment upward.

Although estimates contain a large element of uncertainty, it is considered reasonable to expect that by 1980 the Research Park might employ some 30,000 people. If it were assumed that each employee represented one family, this would mean that the Research Park would account for an additional 110,000 people (using a family size of 3.6 which is the national average). Based on experience in other parts of the country, however, it is possible that the park would create an even larger increase in population since the influx of new people into the area would create new employment opportunities in business, service, and retail activities, which, in turn, would attract more people into the area. In short, a population increase created by new employees in the park might bring about a further population increase. The amount of this "multiplier effect" is extremely difficult to determine and since the basic estimates of park employment are round numbers in the first place, it is reasonable and perhaps safer to ignore this effect.

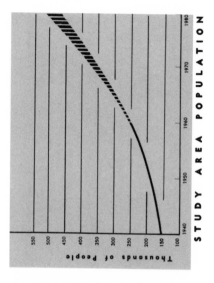

STUDY AREA POPULATION

Returning to the figures used previously, if the increment for the Research Park is added to the original population projection, an overall estimate is derived. Conservatively, then, it is estimated that the total population of the Study Area in 1980 might range from 470,000 to 520,000.

limits to growth?

The Research Triangle faces a serious limitation in its capacity for growth unless solutions can be found for its water supply and sewage disposal problems.

The map of the Triangle Area on the facing page illustrates, in exaggerated form, the drainage divide which separates the watersheds of the Neuse and Cape Fear Rivers. Also shown are two lakes which have been proposed for the area by the Army Corps of Engineers. As currently proposed, the lake on the Neuse River to the north of the Triangle would be a major water supply source and a means of providing flood control. The lake to be formed by damming the Haw River below the Triangle would be primarily for flood control and navigation. The major portion of this lake would actually be created on New Hope Creek.

Water Supply

The principal communities of the Triangle are now well supplied with water. Water resources will not be adequate in the near future, however, if population continues to grow and if the rate of water consumption, both for individual and industrial needs, continues to increase.

The region has demonstrated forethought in developing plans for new sources of water, the most important being the proposed reservoir on the Neuse River. The principal need now,

therefore, is the translation of those plans into reality and consideration of the mechanics of distributing water from the Neuse River to the various parts of the region. It should be remembered, however, that such a reservoir can only even out the irregularities of water flow in the river during the year. The capacity of this source of water is still limited by the average yearly flow of the river. If an adequate flow is to be maintained in the river for users further downstream, it is obvious that far less than the average yearly flow is available for use in the Triangle Region. For this reason it is not too early to begin to examine possible needs for an additional water supply, and to evaluate such a potential source as Kerr Lake which extends across the border between Virginia and North Carolina.

Sewage Disposal

An even more serious problem than obtaining new sources of water is finding ways to properly dispose of greatly increased volumes of sewage effluent. Essentially this problem is caused by the limitations in sewage treatment processes. Even a well designed and well operated sewage treatment plant providing secondary treatment can only remove up to ninety or ninety-five

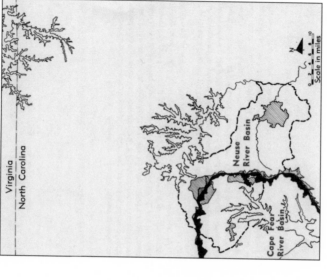

Drainage Basins in the Research Triangle Area

Virginia
North Carolina

Neuse
River Basin

Cape Fear
River Basin

N

Scale in miles

percent of the waste material. Thus, a city of 100,000 people, for example, having excellent treatment facilities, can be discharging to receiving streams effluent containing the equivalent of the untreated wastes from a city of 10,000 people.

Within the Triangle Area this limitation on the effectiveness of treatment is particularly critical because the streams are either too small (in the Cape Fear watershed) or too valuable as water supply sources (as in the Neuse watershed) to receive much additional sewage effluent. The following is a summary of the situation.

Raleigh and Durham currently depend on the Neuse River basin as a source of water and on the Neuse and streams in the Cape Fear basin as means of carrying off treated sewage effluent. The Neuse has recently been given an "A-2" classification (suitable for use as a source of drinking water) by the North Carolina State Stream Sanitation Committee. This means that the water in the river must meet high quality requirements. Although natural forces acting in the river can perform the necessary purification to make the river a suitable source of drinking water, this ability is limited, and the Neuse is rapidly approaching this limit in the Triangle Region.

Even with the highest degree of treatment available, the Neuse River will not be able to receive a great volume of additional sewage from the Raleigh and Durham areas and still meet the assigned quality standards. If the Neuse is to be maintained as a source of drinking water for cities further down the river, sewage created by a large increase in population in Raleigh and in the part of Durham lying in the Neuse basin must be finally disposed of without impairing the quality of water in the river.

In addition to its use of the Neuse River to carry off some of its sewage effluent, Durham discharges treated effluent into two streams, New Hope Creek and Third Fork Creek, which ultimately drain into the Cape Fear River. These creeks have nearly reached the limits of their capacity to receive this sewage and still meet the standards of the "D" classification (suitable for agriculture and industrial cooling and process water) assigned to them by the State Stream Sanitation Committee.

Chapel Hill draws its water from Morgan Creek (University Lake) and disposes of part of its effluent downstream in the same creek and part in Bolin Creek. These creeks, lying within

the Cape Fear basin, have also been given a "D" classification at the point where sewage effluent is discharged. If the assigned quality standards are to be met, increased growth around Chapel Hill will require another way of disposing of the increased volume of sewage.

As a final factor in the problem of sewage disposal, septic tanks, although currently used to a limited extent in the area, operate very unsatisfactorily due to the impervious clay subsoil which underlies much of the Triangle Region. Even if use of septic tanks is continued, a substantial increase in population could not be serviced by this means without violating public health standards.

Possible Solutions

Since the Haw River, as presently classified, still has the capacity to receive additional sewage, effluent from the Neuse side of the drainage divide could be collected, treated and pumped to the Cape Fear watershed. This effluent, together with sewage from areas already in the Cape Fear watershed, could then be carried by an outfall sewer as far down the Haw River as necessary to reach a stream flow with the requisite assimilating capacity.

With this solution, however, two serious difficulties immediately arise. First, pumping of effluent from the Neuse basin over the drainage divide to the Cape Fear basin would require installations which are very costly to build and maintain. Second, removal of water from one watershed for disposal in another is a violation of riparian rights. Without state legislation authorizing such a transfer, cities further down the Neuse would have a legal right to enjoin the removal of water naturally flowing in the river.

It is possible that numerous small dams located on various tributary streams, upstream from sewage discharge points, could serve to increase minimum flow levels, thereby increasing the capacity of the streams to accept sewage, and avoiding the necessity of a long outfall sewer. Construction of these dams would, of course, be extremely expensive, and it might still be necessary to pump some sewage from the Neuse to the Cape Fear basin, involving the problem of riparian rights mentioned previously.

Following a different approach, the volume of sewage effluent to be discharged into streams could be drastically reduced through the use of individual dwelling sewage disposal systems that recirculate treated water for toilet use. Systems of this kind have been developed. If they were required in new homes con-

structed in the area, the volume of sewage discharged might be sufficiently reduced so that streams in the area could handle the effluent load. Individual recirculation systems are unfamiliar to the average citizen and there might, understandably, be resistance to their use. With public understanding, however, such a solution might be feasible.

Finally, consideration might well be given to encouraging new development in other portions of the Triangle Region outside the immediate Study Area so that the dilution capacity of additional streams might be utilized. The Hillsboro area, for example, is on a portion of the Eno River which has a significant amount of dilution capacity, and will soon be linked to the Research Triangle Park by new highway facilities.

Previously, it has been indicated that the population of the Triangle Study Area may reach a half million people by 1980. If the area is to accommodate this population safely and without abdicating its responsibility to other parts of the state, it is obvious that the problem of disposing of sewage effluent must be solved. This report suggests possible approaches to the solution, but undoubtedly there are others. A detailed study by competent experts will be needed to determine which solution or which combination of solutions will be most effective and most economical.

guided growth

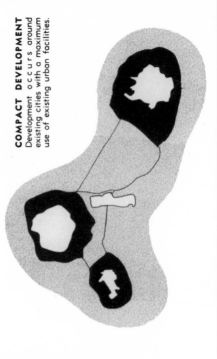

COMPACT DEVELOPMENT
Development occurs around existing cities with a maximum use of existing urban facilities.

If haphazard growth is to be avoided, there must be some concept of what is wanted in its place. Although the interrelationships of the various elements of a region are extremely complex, there are certain basic principles governing the desirable location of the uses of land. Development, for example, should be located so that a plentiful supply of water is available and so that maximum use can be made of natural drainage areas to carry off sewage. Residential areas should be separated from industrial or other uses which adversely affect residential property values and the desirability of these areas as a place to live. The most efficient and direct means of transportation should be provided among homes, stores, and industries where the largest volume of travel exists.

It is never possible, of course, for every element to be perfectly located. Location of drainage courses, for example, may indicate the desirability of residential development in one area, while proximity to existing areas of employment may indicate the desirability of development in another area. Since any pattern or guide for development is a way of representing schematically a desirable physical organization of land uses, it must inevitably contain some compromises.

The following pages discuss three alternative patterns for guided growth in the Triangle Area as identified in land development research at the Urban Studies Center, University of North Carolina. These are not the only possible patterns, nor should it be inferred that a single pattern must be followed rigidly throughout the Research Triangle. They represent alternatives, however, which take into consideration existing conditions in the Triangle. There has been no attempt to forecast a date at which the extent of development depicted in the three proposed schemes might occur. The schemes should be thought of as conceptions of what the Triangle Area might look like when an optimum level of development is reached. The population associated with these patterns varies from three to four times the present population of the Study Area.

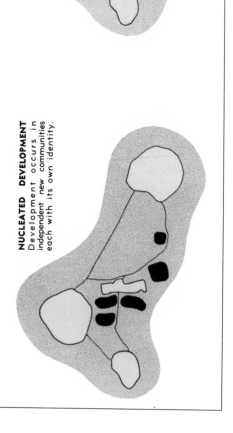

NUCLEATED DEVELOPMENT
Development occurs in independent new communities each with its own identity.

CORRIDOR DEVELOPMENT
Development occurs along utility corridors constructed parallel to natural drainage courses.

The first alternative for guided growth to be examined is the expansion of the existing cities of Raleigh, Durham, and Chapel Hill in a compact scheme of development. In this alternative, urban growth would be accommodated by extension of existing urban areas and by increased density of development. A mixture of various types of apartment buildings and single family residences could provide this increase in density without sacrificing a desirable amount of open space for amenity and recreation.

Commercial development in the compact scheme would call for the revitalization and strengthening of existing central business areas. Additional outlying regional shopping centers would be discouraged in order to reinforce compact residential growth. Industrial parks would be located on the periphery of the major urban concentrations permitting use of the relatively large sites suited to modern industrial requirements.

Two forms of transportation would be used. Travel to and from the central business, governmental, or cultural areas would be provided by an efficient form of bus or rail transit, while travel to the outlying industrial areas would be principally by private automobile. The use of mass transit would require a minimum amount of expansion of the present highway facilities.

One major advantage of the compact pattern is that maximum use could be made of existing facilities. As growth required extension of these facilities, costs of construction and administration would be less than if entirely new facilities were provided outside the urban areas. A second advantage is that a maximum amount of land would be preserved for agricultural, forestry, and recreational uses, creating a clear distinction between town and country.

Two main types of governmental action would be needed to bring about the compact pattern of development. First, careful control would be exercised over the extension of water and sewer lines and such community services as fire and police protection. By insuring maximum development of land within areas already receiving these services and by extending services selectively to new areas, growth would occur in concentric rings around Raleigh, Durham, and Chapel Hill, and scattered haphazard growth would be kept to a minimum. Second, region-wide policies on zoning and subdivision regulations would need to be adopted to preserve agricultural and other open areas and encourage development around the urban centers.

scheme "A" -- compact

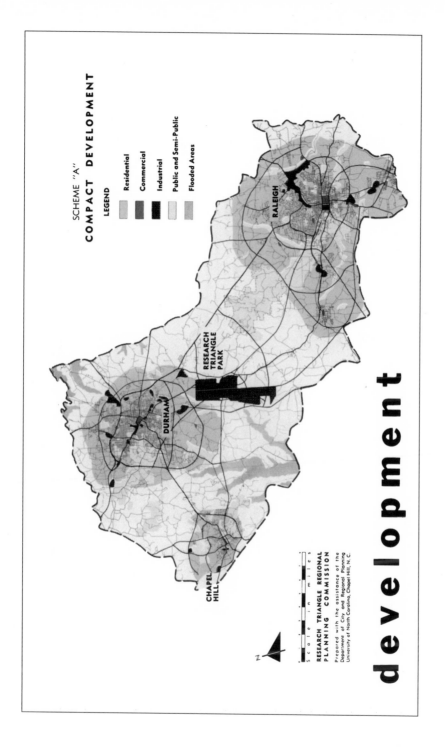

SCHEME "A"
COMPACT DEVELOPMENT

LEGEND

Residential
Commercial
Industrial
Public and Semi-Public
Flooded Areas

RALEIGH

RESEARCH
TRIANGLE
PARK

DURHAM

CHAPEL
HILL

N

Scale in miles

RESEARCH TRIANGLE REGIONAL
PLANNING COMMISSION

Prepared with the assistance of the
Department of City and Regional Planning
University of North Carolina, Chapel Hill, N. C.

development

Another possible pattern of orderly growth is the formation of new towns in the Triangle Area. These towns would be comparable in size to the existing town of Chapel Hill and would each contain from 15 to 25 thousand people. The residential areas would be similar to the better suburban developments today. They would consist mostly of single family homes at a density of two to three homes per acre. Each town would contain a number of "neighborhoods" of from one to two thousand homes centered around an elementary school and local shopping facilities serving the neighborhood.

A town center containing stores, business and governmental offices, and educational and medical facilities serving the whole town would form the nucleus of each community. Although these towns would be relatively self-contained and would each possess an individual identity, they would still depend on the centers in Raleigh and Durham for regional shopping facilities, including, for example, major department stores and various kinds of specialty shops.

With this scheme, industrial development might be handled in several different ways. New industries might be located on the periphery of the three existing communities. Industrial groupings might be located on sites completely separated from any community and so placed to permit easy access by automobile from any part of the Triangle Area. Finally, industry might be made an integral part of the new towns, making each town a relatively independent economic, as well as social unit.

Industry so organized would be located to insure that industrial and residential areas would not adversely affect each other.

Automobiles would serve as the primary means of transportation. A net of limited access highways would tie together the various communities and industrial sites, with particular emphasis being placed on highways permitting rapid, "congestion free" driving to and from work.

The building of an efficient utility system for the new towns and the area as a whole would be one of the key problems to be faced. It would be most desirable to locate the new towns within the natural watersheds of the area, assuring optimum operation of gravity sewers. This would probably mean several small sewer systems for each of the towns, all of which might be tied into a larger system designed to handle the sewage of the whole area. At least initially, water and sewer lines would probably have to be extended from the existing cities, with access to utility lines restricted to the new communities and industrial areas to insure that string development does not occur among the new towns.

As in the compact scheme, region-wide zoning and subdivision regulations would be needed. However, these regulations would differ from those required for compact development in that they would encourage growth in the existing cities only to the point of filling in undeveloped areas within their present corporate limits. Growth over and above this amount would be guided to the new nucleated communities.

scheme "B" -- nucleated

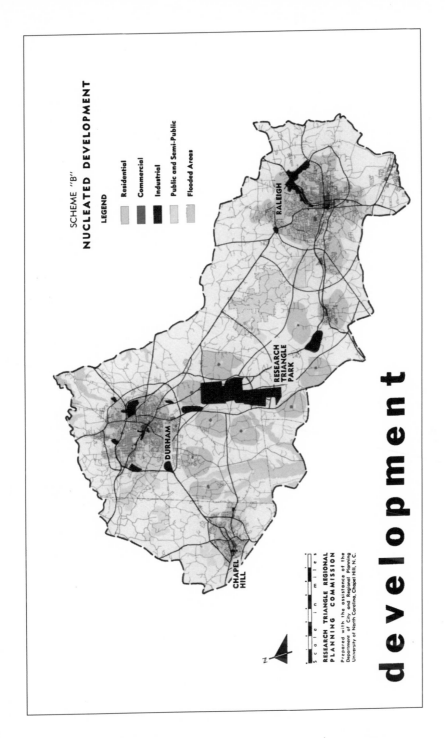

SCHEME "B"
NUCLEATED DEVELOPMENT

LEGEND

Residential
Commercial
Industrial
Public and Semi-Public
Flooded Areas

RALEIGH

RESEARCH
TRIANGLE
PARK

DURHAM

CHAPEL
HILL

N

Scale in miles

RESEARCH TRIANGLE REGIONAL
PLANNING COMMISSION

Prepared with the assistance of the
Department of City and Regional Planning
University of North Carolina, Chapel Hill, N. C.

development

With a corridor pattern, development would be encouraged along natural drainage courses, permitting disposal of sewage into trunk sewers which could take advantage of gravity flow to deliver sewage for treatment in a central plant at the juncture of a number of drainage courses. Sewer lines, water mains, and other utility lines, together with collector highways and transit routes would form what is called a utility corridor. These corridors are conceived also as parkways which weave permanent open spaces in the pattern of land development.

The individual residential developments serviced by a utility corridor might be visualized as vertebrae attached to a central spinal cord, each one of which would be comparable in size to a large modern subdivision, and would contain from three to four thousand people. Each of these developments would contain churches, an elementary school, facilities for local convenience shopping, and a system of neighborhood parks and playgrounds. More extensive community facilities such as junior and senior high schools, civic auditoriums, and government office buildings would be located in an expanded section of the corridor right-of-way, forming an "alcove" adjacent to the corridor. Such groupings of public buildings would be spaced along the corridor at intervals appropriate to the numbers of people being served and the travel time required to reach them.

Regional shopping facilities and offices for various business purposes would be located where the corridor intersects with main intercity arteries serving the Triangle Region. Industry is visualized as occurring in park-like development separated from the residential areas but within easy access of corridor highways and utilities.

The particular advantage offered by the corridor form of development is that it facilitates provision of high quality urban services while maintaining a relatively low residential density, similar in nature to our best suburban areas today. It is designed to permit maximum use of the automobile and yet avoid the congestion such use implies in densely concentrated areas.

In order to establish this pattern of development, public rights-of-way would be purchased along drainage courses, and highways, water, sewer and other utility lines installed. Access to all of these utilities would be controlled just as is now done for highways. Coupled with appropriate zoning of the three counties in the study area, such a course of action would assure that development would occur where it could be most efficiently serviced.

scheme "C" -- corridor

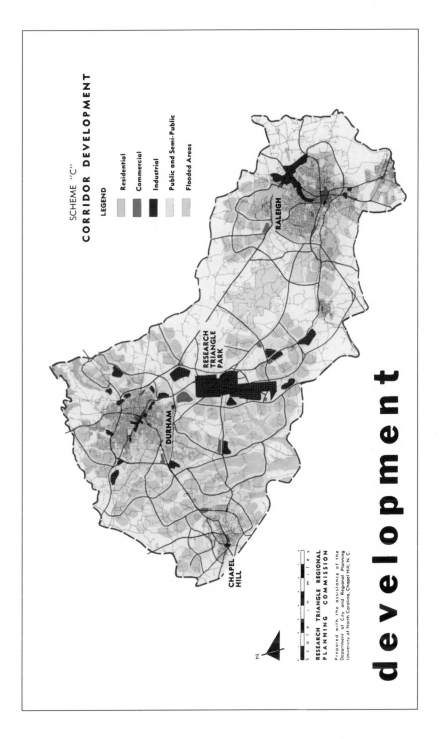

SCHEME "C"

CORRIDOR DEVELOPMENT

LEGEND

Residential
Commercial
Industrial
Public and Semi-Public
Flooded Areas

RALEIGH

RESEARCH
TRIANGLE
PARK

DURHAM

CHAPEL
HILL

N

Scale in miles

RESEARCH TRIANGLE REGIONAL
PLANNING COMMISSION

Prepared with the assistance of the
Department of City and Regional Planning
University of North Carolina, Chapel Hill, N.C.

development

a comparative

New development anywhere in the Triangle Area will affect the whole region. For this reason it appears desirable that at least two important governmental functions be carried out on a region-wide basis, regardless of the scheme or combination of schemes of development which is followed.

(1) Because of the financial and jurisdictional problems involved in distributing water to and disposing of wastes from the various city and county areas in the Triangle Region, all three development schemes are predicated on the existence of some form of inter-city, inter-county organization to develop and administer utility services for the region as a whole.

(2) Since the most desirable form of development for the Triangle Region may bear no relation to existing city limits or county lines, it is essential that criteria for zoning districts, subdivision regulations, and other controls over land use be determined by regional considerations rather than by the boundaries of local governmental units.

DEVELOPMENT POLICIES

COMPACT DEVELOPMENT

Fill up existing incorporated areas.

Annex new areas after existing areas are fully developed.

Provide for higher density residential areas.

NUCLEATED DEVELOPMENT

Fill up existing incorporated areas.

Channel new development into separate incorporated towns.

CORRIDOR DEVELOPMENT

Fill up existing incorporated areas.

Establish and construct utility corridors to encourage development along drainage courses.

summary

UTILITIES	INDUSTRIAL AREAS	COMMERCIAL AREAS	TRANSPORTATION
Use existing facilities to fullest extent. Extend facilities only after existing service areas fill up. Enlarge existing treatment facilities or build new ones to serve only compact areas.	Provide for industrial parks on periphery of city.	Provide neighborhood shops in residential areas. Concentrate region-serving facilities in existing downtown areas. Revitalize and strengthen downtown areas.	Increase capacity of mass transit facilities to and from downtown areas. Develop inter-city limited access highways.
Provide limited access lines to new centers. Provide unified system for sewage disposal for new centers.	Reserve carefully selected locations in new towns separated from residential areas, in industrial parks, on periphery of city, or in isolated areas.	Provide neighborhood shops in residential areas. Provide local shopping in new town centers. Retain region-serving facilities in existing downtown areas.	Develop limited access highways linking towns with each other and with industrial parks. Facilitate automobile access to all points. Provide for a rapid transit system between centers.
Develop corridor systems of utility lines. Provide for unified system of sewage disposal.	Provide for industrial parks separated from other development.	Provide neighborhood shops in residential areas. Develop local highway shopping centers and new regional shopping centers in strategic locations.	Develop an inter-city system of limited access highways and connector parkways along corridors.

tools for guiding growth

Zoning and Subdivision Regulation

There are a number of ways in which development may be guided to form a desirable pattern. To the average citizen in the Triangle Region, the most familiar of these methods is probably zoning. Too frequently throughout the United States zoning has been used to fix a pattern of growth once it has occurred. For zoning to be most effective, it should be used to guide the way land is to be used before development occurs. In this way the "rules of the game" are clearly set forth and many of the inequities and hardships created by attempting to force existing development into a "strait jacket" are avoided. In order to zone ahead in a rational manner, it is important that a plan be adopted and that there be a high degree of co-operation among the counties and municipalities in the Research Triangle Region.

A second device which is used for guiding growth is the control of land subdivision. Besides controlling the way land may be cut up into lots and tracts, these regulations may prescribe the conditions under which a municipality or county may agree to provide services to new subdivisions. These conditions are concerned with such matters as the width of streets and the manner in which utilities are installed. Municipalities in the Triangle Region have the authority to prescribe these conditions for areas which come within a certain distance of the city limits. Beyond this distance, responsibility lies with the counties. Here again it is important that cities and counties agree on the standards which are to be met.

Utility Policies

In conjunction with zoning and subdivision regulations, municipal policies governing extension and financing of new utility lines have an important effect in determining where new devel-

opment will occur. Within the Triangle, Durham, for example, currently follows a policy of extending water and sewer lines to areas outside the city limits on condition that such areas be annexed to the city. Raleigh, while it does not make annexation a condition of utility extension, requires that developers of new areas finance the entire capital costs of utility extensions. Where a developer extends utility lines to an area some distance beyond existing development, the costs of construction not directly related to his own acreage are returned to him by the city from "acreage fees" received from developers of the intervening areas along the utility lines.

Both of these policies tend to encourage development around existing areas. The emphasis in Durham is placed on insuring that the city does not service areas from which it does not receive taxes, while with the type of policy followed by Raleigh, emphasis is placed on insuring the financial responsibility of developers and encouraging them to look to the future effects of their developments on surrounding areas.

These, of course, are not the only policy choices available, and it should be pointed out that the effectiveness of such policies will depend on the degree to which new development is dependent on municipal services. If septic tanks, for example, are freely allowed, even though their operation is unsatisfactory and they must ultimately be replaced by public sewers, non-extension of public sewers will only serve to encourage the use of septic tanks outside the cities' area of jurisdiction rather than to encourage development within areas already served by public sewers.

Other Devices

Outright purchase of land by municipalities, counties or the state can be used to provide parks or open areas. Land acquisition is sometimes used in particular situations to prevent development where it is dangerous, unsanitary or otherwise undesirable or to provide buffer areas between incompatible land uses.

An old, but little tried device, is the purchase of development rights through an easement. Acquisition of easements for utility lines, for approaches to airport runways, for roadways, floodways, and drainage structures are well known examples of the use of this device to permit use of land for specified purposes. Examples of the use of this device as a means of controlling land development are less common. However, the right to subdivide one's land is a property right which can be purchased, given necessary state enabling acts, without purchase of the actual land itself.

If a government, for example, were to purchase development rights from the owner of a two-hundred acre farm, the farm owner would continue to own and farm his land as before. The only thing he would give up would be his right to subdivide his property. The advantage of this use of the easement to the community is that the benefits of open space can be assured without payment of the full cost of the land. This may be particularly appropriate when the land has not yet been subject to the impact of added speculative value. The advantage to the individual is that he can then only be taxed on the value of his property as farm land. He cannot be placed in the position of having to subdivide unwillingly because his property taxes have been forced sky high by nearby development. By judicious use of easement purchases to prevent urban development in various parts of the region, a skeletal framework for desirable devel-

opment could be assured at reasonable cost to the region and with complete fairness to all landowners.

These methods, while certainly not the only ones, are the most important that governments can use to guide future development. It is clear that the methods can not be used reasonably and fairly without a regional plan of development, and that such a plan can not be brought into being without a very high degree of co-operation among all the governmental units in the Research Triangle Region.

To secure a sufficiently high degree of co-operation, some formal organization may be necessary. In some parts of the country new governmental units have been formed to attain the degree of co-ordination necessary for efficient administration of services on a region-wide basis. The formation of sanitary districts, as in Chicago, or of water districts, as in Southern California, are examples of this. The Metropolitan Transit Authority of Boston is another example of a new governmental unit created to administer a certain type of service for a whole region. In the Triangle Region where water supply and sewage disposal needs present a problem requiring a regional solution, formulation of a regional district or authority might be an effective way of meeting these needs.

There are, of course, a great many factors which must be studied before it can be determined what new forms of government, if any, will be desirable in the future. This discussion is intended only to point out that forms of government should be appropriate to the needs they serve, and that changing needs may require new governmental forms.

the next steps

In the preceding sections some of the alternative patterns of guided growth have been presented together with a brief summary of how the region might achieve these various patterns. It is clear that growth in the Research Triangle Region will create regional problems which can ultimately be solved only by regional planning. The immediate question is where to begin.

On the basis of this preliminary appraisal, it seems apparent that development of an adequate water supply and determinations as to satisfactory methods for sewage disposal are the most critical problems facing the Triangle Region. As suggested in the section entitled "Limits to Growth", solutions intimately affect not only the Triangle Area, but other areas of the state as well. The conclusion seems inescapable that an exhaustive study of the Neuse and Cape Fear river basins will be required before rational decisions can be made concerning the use of water, and thus, concerning the Triangle Region's capacity for development. This is a necessary first step since final decisions as to the most desirable pattern or patterns of growth cannot be made until questions about water supply and sewage disposal are answered.

A second step, essential for the development of a sound regional plan, is a detailed examination of the costs of various land development schemes and of the form of government which could most efficiently provide public services in each scheme.

In the meantime, it is important that citizens throughout the Triangle Region be made aware of the decisions that will have to be made to formulate a regional plan of growth, and the bases on which these decisions should be made. At present, people in the Region are well aware of the opportunities for growth. Most people, however, are not aware of the problems which must be solved.

In conclusion, it should be said that the decisions which must be made will not be easy ones. Suppose, for example, that careful analysis indicated the desirability of policies severely limiting growth in portions of the area. Governmental decisions to establish such policies would require great courage, and could only be made with full public understanding of the regional considerations on which they were based.

THIS REPORT WAS PREPARED WITH THE ASSISTANCE OF THE FOLLOWING GRADUATE STUDENTS OF THE DEPARTMENT OF CITY AND REGIONAL PLANNING, UNIVERSITY OF NORTH CAROLINA, CHAPEL HILL

Arthur J. Bolek
Ronald G. Bracegirdle
Roy J. Butner
George P. Cardis
Theo H. Carraway
Jayanta Chatterjee

Lawrence B. Christmas
A. Kent Clement
John A. Crislip
Edward L. Falk
Raymond J. Green
John R. Hitchcock

C. Eugene Hix
Gerald A. Holtenhoff
Jonathan B. Howes
Jeanette Lamoureux
Ray R. Lester
Ralph W. Miner

John T. Morse
David C. Neville
William G. Roberts
Jerry B. Schneider
Phillip L. Tallon

Robert M. Hanes Memorial Building

RESEARCH TRIANGLE PARK

December 16, 1960

———

Presiding --- Honorable Luther H. Hodges
Governor of North Carolina

Invocation --- Dr. Mark Depp
Pastor Centenary Methodist Church
Winston-Salem, N. C.

Robert March Hanes of North Carolina
1890 - 1959

"A certain nobleman took his journey into a far country to receive a kingdom."

Guiding spirit of the Research Triangle effort as Chairman of the Research Triangle Committee, Incorporated

And in addition and at various times, among other positions and honors:

An officer	— United States Army — Second Lieutenant to Major
A member	— House of Representatives, North Carolina General Assembly
A member	— Senate, North Carolina General Assembly
President	— Wachovia Bank and Trust Company
Honorary Chairman of the Board	— Wachovia Bank and Trust Company
President	— North Carolina Bankers Association
President	— American Bankers Association
President	— Association of Reserve City Bankers
Director	— Economic Affairs for Germany, Economic Cooperation Administration
Chairman	— Commerce and Industry Division, North Carolina Department of Conservation and Development
Director	— North Carolina State College Textile Foundation
Director	— North Carolina State College Engineering Foundation
President	— North Carolina Business Foundation
Trustee	— Consolidated University of North Carolina
Trustee	— Morehead Foundation
Trustee	— Salem College
Trustee	— Winston-Salem Teachers College
Chairman	— Fifth Federal Reserve District of the Committee for Economic Development
Member	— Business Advisory Council, United States Department of Commerce
Educated	— Woodberry Forest School The University of North Carolina The Graduate School of Business Administration, Harvard University

Honorary LL.D., University of North Carolina

"And a man shall be as a hiding place from the wind, and a covert from the tempest; as rivers of water in a dry place, as the shadow of a great rock in a weary land."

Robert March Hanes, citizen of North Carolina.

A man of good humor and of sternness, of ability and of humility, of frankness and with reserve — such a man was Robert Hanes.

A man of leadership and a man ready to work — such a man was Robert Hanes.

A man willing to state and support his position with forthrightness and pride and a man willing to listen and learn — such a man was Robert Hanes.

In the main stream of the development of North Carolina, Robert Hanes was ambitious for his state and active in promoting the public good and the general welfare. He was active in developing North Carolina's resources — human, natural, commercial, industrial.

A tireless servant of his country, Robert Hanes accepted the responsibilities of leadership and service that his profession, his government, his civic associations demanded and was more than diligent — and cheerful — in executing these responsibilities.

Robert Hanes, the entire State of North Carolina says of you, "You have served your State well."

Luther H. Hodges

Governor

RESOLUTION

WHEREAS, Robert M. Hanes, as a climax to a lifelong interest in supporting sound programs for the development and progress of the State of North Carolina, led the Research Triangle idea to the threshold of success on which it stands today; and

WHEREAS, he, with a few others, had the foresight nearly five years ago to recognize the unique potential of the Research Triangle idea; the courage to begin development with then meager resources; the strength and character necessary for such a venture during difficult times; and the supreme human qualities of humility, pride and humor with which to endow the idea in his last official public act;

THEREFORE, BE IT RESOLVED, That those now charged with the responsibility of carrying forward the Research Triangle program are deeply in his debt.

RESOLVED FURTHER, That those so charged pledge themselves to the successful completion of the task he so nobly helped to begin.

UNANIMOUSLY APPROVED BY THE BOARD OF DIRECTORS OF THE RESEARCH TRIANGLE FOUNDATION OF NORTH CAROLINA THE RESEARCH TRIANGLE PARK AND THE RESEARCH TRIANGLE INSTITUTE.

RESEARCH TRIANGLE FOUNDATION OF N. C.
Archie K. Davis, President

RESEARCH TRIANGLE PARK
G. Akers Moore, Jr., President

RESEARCH TRIANGLE INSTITUTE
George Watts Hill, Chairman

April, 1959

APPENDIX J

ALL ORGANIZATIONS LISTED ON THE WALL OF PARK PLAZA,
THE COMMEMORATIVE PARK LOCATED ON THE CORNER OF
HIGHWAY 54 AND DAVIS DRIVE

1959
Research Triangle Foundation
Research Triangle Institute
Research Triangle Regional
  Planning Commission (now
  Triangle J Council of
  Governments)

1960s
American Association of Textile
  Chemists & Colorists
Beaunit Corporation
Burroughs Wellcome (now
  GlaxoSmithKline)
Chemstrand Research Center
First Citizens Bank
GTE (now Verizon)
Hercules Inc.
International Business Machines
  (IBM)

The Leader
National Center for Health
  Statistics
National Laboratory for Higher
  Education/Regional Education
North Carolina National Bank
  (now Bank of America)
NC Board of Science & Technology
National Institute of Environ-
  mental Health Sciences
NC Science & Technology
  Research Center
Technitrol, Inc.
Teer Associates
Triangle Service Center
Triangle Universities Computation
  Center
USDA Forest Service
Wachovia Bank of North Carolina,
  Inc.

1970s

Airco Special Gases (now BOC Gases)
Andrews, Congressman Ike
Appraisal Associates
Aquatics Control
Becton Dickinson Research Center (now BD Technologies
Burroughs Wellcome Fund
Carolina Copy Center and Office Supply, Inc.
Carolina Traffic Consultants
Chemical Industry Institute of Toxicology (now CIIT Centers for Health Research)
Circle Tours, Inc.
Comprehensive Accounting Services
Computer Sciences Corporation
Cooper USA, Inc.
CRS Sirrine, Inc./J.E. Sirrine
Data General Corporation (now EMC^2)
Data Processing Associates
Diener and Associates
Eastern Airlines
ERA Realty One
Federal Express Airlines
First Citizens Bank
First Federal Savings & Loan
Foundation for Educational Development, Inc.
Gay & Taylor
Governor's Inn (now Radisson Governor's Inn)
Greensboro Printing Service
International Fertility Research Program (now Family Health International)
International Trade Center

JAYCOR
Leadership Communications, Inc.
Microelectronics Center of North Carolina (now MCNC)
Meridian Travel Service, Inc.
Monsanto, Inc.
National Driving Center, Inc.
National Humanities Center
National Institute of Statistical Sciences
National Toxicology Program
Newcomb Co., Inc.
North Carolina Alternative Energy Corporation
North Carolina State Education Assistance Authority
Northern Telecom (now Nortel Networks)
Northrup Services Inc. (now ManTech Environmental Technology, Inc.)
Olsten Staffing Services
Pease, J.N. & Associates
Research Engineers, Inc.
Reynolds & Reynolds Company
SDC Integrated Services
Security Alarms of North Carolina
Southern Growth Policies Board
Southern Testing & Research Laboratories, Inc.
Sperry Univac Technical Services Division
Systems Research & Development Corporation
Treasure Cove
Triangle Fire & Rescue Equipment Company
Triangle Universities Center for Advanced Studies Inc.

Troxler Electronic Laboratories, Inc.
US Army Research Office
US Environmental Protection Agency
US Postal Service
University of North Carolina Institute for Transportation Research & Education
Wright, J. Meade, CPA

1980s

American Health & Life
American Travel
Analytical Sciences
Andrews, A.B. & Company, Inc.
ANF Enterprises, Inc.
BASF Corporation, Agricultural Products
Battelle Scientific Services Program
Bell Northern Research (now Nortel Networks)
Better Business Bureau of Eastern NC
Bio-Medcom International, Inc.
Boeing Computer Services
Break Time Snack Bar/Legend's Café
Burke-Taylor Associates/Burke-Wall Associates
Business Telecom
C. Edison, Inc.
Carolina Group Insurance Services, Inc.
Carolina Livery Service MHG, Inc.
Cedalion Systems, Inc.
Center for New Business Executives, Inc.
Ciba-Geigy (later Novartis Agribusiness, now Syngenta)

Comp-Aid Inc.
Compuchem Environmental Corporation
Compuchem Laboratories
Computer Circuitry Group
Computer Data Systems, Inc.
CRC Systems
Daniel's & Daniel's
Datatronics Inc.
Discount WATS Lines, Inc.
Diversified Control Systems, Inc.
DuPont Company
Dynamit Nobel Gracie Silicon
DynCorp/Program Resources, Inc.
Eastman Kodak
Ericsson GE Mobile Communications (now Ericsson Inc.)
Ferbee, Walters & Associates
Flynt, Paul, Associates, Inc.
Fraser Morrow Daniels & Company
Friendship Force
FWA Group
GE Microelectronics Center/GE Semiconductor
General Dynamics – Communications Systems
Glaxo, Inc. (now GlaxoSmithKline)
Glaxo Wellcome Foundation
GoGo Tours
GTE Government Systems
Hansel, John R. D.M.D.
Heins Systems, Inc.
H-Three Systems Corporation
Human Resource Consultants
Instrument Society of America (now ISA)
Intel Corporation
International Genetic Sciences

International Visitors Council
ITEL/MRI Systems, Inc.
Jaakko Poyry, Inc./Poyry-Bek Inc.
Johnson Travel Corporation
JWG Associates
Keller Consulting Group
Kobe Steel USA Inc.
Latimer, John D. & Associates
Learning Unlimited Corp.
Leland Computer Service, Inc.
LITESPEC Optical Fibre LLC
Management Applications
Manpower Temporary Services
Manhattan Associates
McBee Loose Leaf Binders
McMahon Research Laboratories, Inc./McMahon Biotechnology & McMahon Electro-Optics Inc. (now Gretag McBeth)
Mobius Group (now CheckFree Investment Services)
Myrick Relocation Center
NC Beacon
NC Educational Information Centers
New Britain Tool
North Carolina Biotechnology Center
Occucare Inc.
Park Dematology
Park Medical Center
Park Opthalmology
Performance Analysis Corporation
Personnel Pool of Raleigh/Durham
Pinkerton's Inc.
Plasma Energy Corporation
Practical Management, Inc.
Quadtek, Inc.
Radian Corporation

Reichhold Chemicals (now Reichhold Inc.)
RS&H Architects-Engineers-Planners
Rudd Group/Clyde Rudd & Associates
SCI Systems, Inc.
Semiconductor Research Corporation
Siecor Corporation
Southeastern Educational Improvement
Southern Emergency Medical Associates
State Farm Insurance
Sumitomo Electric Lightwave Corporation
Symbolics, Inc.
Synertech Group
TAB Products Co.
Tracor Jitco, Inc.
Travelhost Magazine
Triangle Inspection Services, Inc.
Triangle Research Collaborative, Inc.
Triangle Transit Authority
Triangle Universities Licensing Consortium (TULCO)
TRW, inc./TRW Environmental Engineering
UAI Technology, Inc.
Underwriters Laboratories Inc.
Union Carbide Agricultural Products (subsequently Rhone Poulenc, and then Advantis CropScience)
Unisys
University of NC Center for Public Television
Vaughn Associates, Inc.

Voice-Tel of Central North Carolina
Wesson, Taylor, Wells &
    Associates, Inc.
Winston Printing Company
Xonics, Inc.

1990s
1-800-9-Analysis, Inc.
Able Waterproofing of NC, Inc.
Adsystech Inc.
Alternate Realities Corporation
American Data Technology
Applied Communications Concepts
Arty P's
Audio Services
Aurora Funds, Inc.
Bayer Biological Products
Bekaert Advanced
    Materiels/Flexible Circuits
    Ventures
Bekaert Fibre Technologies
Biogen, Inc.
BioStratum Inc.
BioTraces, Inc.
Centura Bank
ChiraChem International Chemical
    Company (now Asymchem
    International Inc.)
Cisco Systems
CitySearch, The Triangle (now
    trianglecitysearch.com)
Columbia Staffing Services Group
Comtrex Corporation
Corning BioPro (subsequently,
    Covance Biotechnology Services,
    Inc., now Azko Nobel, Diosynth)
Columbia Staffing Services
Council for Entrepreneurial
    Development
CPKD Solutions, LLC

Cronos Integrated Microsystems
    (now JDS Uniphase)
Cynex Software, Inc.
Datawatch Corporation, Triangle
    Software Division
Delta Pharmaceuticals
Delta Products Corporation
Diamond Books/Info Café
Disability Advocates
Duke Mass Spectrometry
DynTel
Eisai, Inc.
Eli Lilly, Sphinx Pharmaceuticals
    Division
Endocrinology
The Enrichment Center at RTP
Enterprise Research, Inc.
Entrepreneurial Assistance, Inc.
Environmental Health Research &
    Testing, Inc.
Epiteleo (now Mi-Co)
F-1 Consulting
The Fast Italian
First Flight Venture Center
First Union National Bank
FTL Systems, Inc.
Ganymede Software, Inc.
GEL Environmental Consulting,
    Inc.
Gene Quest
Gene Tec Corporation
Glaxo Wellcome Inc. (now
    GlaxoSmithKline)
Governor's Institute on Alcohol &
    Substance Abuse
Harris Communications Company
Harris Semiconductor
    (subsequently Harris
    Corporation/Harris
    Microelectronics Center)

Howard Associates LLC
Hultquist, Steven J.
ICES of North Carolina Ltd.
IFC Kaiser Consulting/K.S. Crump
  Group
Impact
Improvement Systems, Inc.
Industrial Microwave Systems Inc.
Innovative Sputtering Technology
  (now Innovative Specialty Films)
Insight Industries
Intek Labs
InterBank Leasing and
  Investments, Inc.
International Union of Pure and
  Applied Chemistry (IUPAC)
INET Technology, Inc.
Intercardia (now Incara
  Pharmaceuticals)
Ivex Corporation
JMC (USA), Inc.
Journal of Vacuum Science &
  Technology
Kirkman, Steven T., CPA
Kohl Research, Inc.
Kultech, Inc.
Leadership Triangle
Learning Machines, Inc.
Lineberry Research Associates
Link Technology, Inc.
Listing Services Solutions Inc.
  (now Lssi Corporation)
Magnequench Technology Center
Mallet Technology, Inc.
Managed Care Resources, Inc.
Martin Marietta Corporation (now
  Lockheed Martin)
Medco Research Inc.
Mechini & Associates

Motor & Equipment
  Manufacturers Association
Motorola MOS 15
National Council of the Paper
  Industry for Air and Stream
  Improvement
Nanoprobes, Inc.
Natural Pharmacia International,
  Inc.
NeoButler, inc.
NetEdge Systems, Inc. (later
  Larscom, Inc.)
Network Development Group
Newbass Technical Services
NJC Enterprises
North Carolina Healthcare
  Information and
  Communications Alliance, Inc.
North Carolina Technological
  Development Authority, Inc.
Novel Pharmaceutical, Inc.
Panasonic Technologies/Kyushu
  Matsushita
Paradigm Genetics, Inc.
Penny's Too
Pharmakopius International
  Group
Praegizer Industries, Inc.
Quick Color Solutions
Red Hat Software
RESOURCE/SOLUTIONS, Inc.
Robb, Joseph A. & Associates
Saffron Technology
SageWorks, Inc.
SARCO, Inc.
Scholastic Inc.
Scurria, Mark S., D.D.S.
SDI
Sigma Xi

SilentPower Technologies
Corporation
Smart Communications
Software Development, Europe,
Inc.
Sports Media Technology
Corporation
SRC Education
Alliance/Competitiveness
Foundation
Technical Systems Integrators, Inc.
Triangle Community Foundation
Triangle MLS, Inc.
Trinity Consultants
United Therapeutics Corporation
Var.Code
VenSouth Capital Group
Whitcom International
Corporation
Worldwide Clinical Trials
Xanthon
ZenBio

2000s
Advanced Engineering & Research
Associates

AlphaVax
AXA Advisors
Caspian Networks
ClearReason, Inc.
Db Tag
FullSeven Technologies
Infineon Technologies
IT Parade.com
Kev Ventures, Inc.
Market Driven Corporation
Merix Biosciences
Millennium Designs, Inc.
Norak Biosciences
NTRnet Systems Inc.
NUMED International
Transportation
OSV/Cognosci, Inc.
Overture Networks, Inc.
Quantum Logic Devices
Schwartz Biosciences
Synergy Vaccines
SyneCor
Transportation Partners.com
Webwide Information Systems,
Inc.

NOTES

CHAPTER 1 *Planting the Seeds*

1. North Carolina State College of Agriculture and Engineering became North Carolina State University at Raleigh in 1965.

2. Author's emphasis.

3. See Internet site http://www.rtp.org.

4. Companies and individuals from across the entire state pledged for this effort, with the largest amount coming from the Winston-Salem area (Foundation archives). This important point is emphasized again in Chapter 4.

5. On December 28, 1958, the Research Triangle Committee's charter was amended, its name changed to the Research Triangle Foundation of North Carolina. Also on the morning of the January 9, 1959, luncheon, Robert M. Hanes was elected chairman and Archie Davis was elected president.

6. The Research Triangle Institute was incorporated as a nonprofit organization on December 29, 1958. The morning of the January 9, 1959, luncheon, George Watts Hill of Durham Bank and Trust Company was elected chairman, and George R. Herbert, previously of the Stanford Research Institute, was elected president.

7. It was fortuitous that the very first contact made by Bill Little on behalf of the Research Triangle was with Bruce Ballentine of Chemstrand on February 7, 1957, while Ballentine was in Chapel Hill recruiting doctoral chemists for his company (Little 1957). This was also the first contact between Chemstrand and the Research Triangle organization. Following up a

year later, Little had technical brochures on chemistry, engineering, and pharmacy to present to Ballentine, and from there the Chemstrand story is recorded in *A Generosity of Spirit*. The news of Chemstrand locating in the Park received praise from around the state. In prepared press releases, U. S. Senator Sam Ervin, Jr., said, "This . . . will mean a great deal to the promotion of this important research center in our State and will afford the Chemstrand Corporation real opportunity for the future development of its far-reaching textile operations." U. S. Senator B. Everett Jordan said, "This new project will bring many scientists and specialists to live in our State and will add greatly to the wave of industrial expansion that is now coming our way in North Carolina."

8. Today, this organization is known as the National Institute of Environmental Health Sciences.

CHAPTER 2 *Planning for Growth*

1. The primary data are in Appendix F.
2. See in Appendix F.
3. See Appendix F.
4. See 1959 N.C. Session Laws, Chapter 642.
5. This Act was ground breaking in the sense that it created the first multicounty planning commission in the state, and it was a precursor to the concept that led to the Councils of Government. There are currently eighteen Councils.
6. This was increased to 15 percent in August 1963.
7. These data come from Appendix F.
8. Senator Kenneth Royall of Durham worked closely with Davis on how to handle Durham's attempt in early June 1985 to annex the Park's land.
9. See 1985 North Carolina Session Laws, Chapter 435.

CHAPTER 3 *Measuring the Park's Growth*

1. These data come from Appendix F.
2. Interestingly, and contrary to popular conception, Research Triangle Park is not simply a park of large tenants. According to Little (2000a), working from the Park's 2000–2001 *Owners & Tenants Directory*, the median size organization in the Park in 2000 has twenty or fewer employees.
3. This percentage does not take into account acreage that has been optioned.
4. Interestingly, Stewart projected in 1961 that there would be room in the Park for a maximum of 79,780 employees. Stewart's estimate was based on 10 percent developed floor space rather than the current 15 percent. See Chapter 2.

1. This event was sponsored by the Research Triangle Foundation, whose leaders dated the birth of the Park on January 9, 1959, for purposes of celebrating its fortieth anniversary.

2. Hobbs also chaired in 1955 the Inventory Preparation Subcommittee within the Working Committee. In January 1956, the committee reported that it had identified, on the staffs of the three Triangle universities, approximately nine hundred individuals in fields that could eventually be related to the broadly defined mission of the Research Triangle.

3. According to Roberson (2000), the Foundation conducted a survey in 1986 of Park companies. Among other things, the survey findings showed that Park companies purchased goods and services in nearly all one hundred counties in the state.

4. This is the most complete time series of data available on per capita state income. See Internet site http://www.ospl.state.nc.us.

5. In all likelihood this reflects technology-based industrial growth based on the technology culture created by the Park.

CHAPTER 5 *Why Has the Park Been a Success? A First Look*

1. As discussed in *A Generosity of Spirit*, Pineland's Corporation was liquidated to the Research Triangle Foundation on August 31, 1965.

2. The Triangle Service Center, Inc., was authorized to borrow up to $1.3 million at the Foundation's board meeting on January 25, 1966. The Foundation ended up borrowing only $1.2 million from sixteen banks and insurance companies.

3. The 1965 North Carolina legislature made a grant of $750,000 to the Foundation on behalf of the National Environmental Health Science Center in consideration of the Foundation's gift of land for the Center.

4. Nello L. Teer Company signed a franchise agreement in 1969 with Triangle Service Center, Inc., the for-profit arm of the Research Triangle Foundation. According to Teer (2000), this agreement was for twenty years and contained a list of services the Park desired, and time frames for the construction of the Governors Inn Hotel, several banks, and the service center. The first improvements were completed in the fall of 1972. At about this time, Nello L. Teer put his real estate development assets into a company known as Teer Enterprises, Ltd. Between 1969 and 1979, the hotel, five banks, a U.S. post office, a travel agency, an office products store, and a delicatessen were completed in addition to buildings at 50 Park Offices and at 100 Park Offices. In 1979, construction of 200 Park Offices began (tenants were Nortel, Olsten, and Battelle), followed by 300 Park Offices (tenants were RTI, Nortel, GE Microelectronics, and a dental practice). In 1980, 400 Park Offices housed GTE Government Systems,

and IBM was housed in other offices. In 1980, the Nello L. Teer Company was sold to the Koppers Company. In 1985, the lease to the service center complex was sold to a partnership set up by Integrated Resources of New York. The partnership was named Research Triangle Associates Limited Partnership. Afterward, the management of the service center was transferred to Teer Associates, a company started by Robert D. Teer, Jr., in 1986. In 1997, the partnership was sold to Starwood Real Estate Investment Trust of Connecticut.

5. The three Triangle universities are listed here and throughout the book in alphabetical order.

CHAPTER 6 *Why Has the Park Been a Success? A Second Look*

1. Developed square footage is a more meaningful metric than buildings, but the AURRP no longer publishes comparable statistics on that measure. The last time such data were reported was in 1991. In that year, Research Triangle Park ranked first followed by Stanford Research Park.

2. This emphasis on TUCASI as the unique differentiating aspect should not be interpreted to mean that the fact that there are *three* major research universities within a 20-mile radius of the Park has gone unnoticed. It has not; however, it would be somewhat ambitious to posit that two research universities are twice (or even n-times) as important as one, and three are three times as important as one. While Duke University, North Carolina State University, and the University of North Carolina are preeminent institutions, so are Stanford University, Princeton University, and others. But on the other hand, the three universities do provide an extensive networked library that Park tenants can access (Little 2000a).

CHAPTER 7 *TUCASI: A "Park" within a Park*

1. Author's emphasis.

2. John Caldwell in a 1982 report on the development of TUCASI quoted these remarks by Davis; however, the date of the Davis quotation is not known. Minutes of the Foundation's board of directors from November 6, 1974, suggest that this idea had been discussed earlier among the Foundation's leadership.

3. In an internal memorandum dated October 9, 1974, from R. E. Fadum, Dean of Engineering at North Carolina State University to Earl G. Droessler, Dean of Research Administration, Fadum wrote: "In response to Chancellor Caldwell's request that members of the Administrative Council solicit suggestions as to an appropriate and meaningful use for a 100-acre site in the Research Triangle Park . . . [t]hree ideas emerge:

(1) The establishment of an institute for technology assessment.
(2) The establishment of an institute for advanced studies.

(3) It would be most appropriate to name the facility after [Governor] Luther Hodges, not only because of his involvement in the establishment of the Research Triangle Foundation but also because of his interest in the kinds of activities that would be encompassed in the above two areas."

4. William Bevan, Juanita Kreps, and George Pearsall represented Duke University; Earl G. Droessler, Vivian T. Stannett, and Jackson A. Rigney represented North Carolina State University; and Hugh Holman, William F. Little, and Lyle V. Jones represented the University of North Carolina. William M. Lehmkuhl, S. M. Cozart, and Alex Galloway, Sr., represented the Foundation.

5. Six exhibits were attached to the 1975 proposal submitted to the Foundation by the Committee of 13. The proposed centers are described here in the order that they were appended to the committee's proposal. One idea suggested by Fadum that was not included in the proposal was for an institute for technology assessment modeled after the Office of Technology Assessment recently established by the U. S. Congress.

6. As illustrated in Chapter 2, based on data in Appendix F, 5,166 acres had been acquired by the Foundation by the end of 1975 compared to 6,971 within the Park by the end of 2000. In 1975, 1,782 acres, or 34.5 percent, had been sold for development. By the end of 2000, 61.1 percent of the Park's acquired acreage had been sold for development.

7. The records show that $50,000 was received by the University of North Carolina General Administration on September 16, 1975.

8. The National Humanities Center appendix to the 1975 proposal from the Committee of 13 to the Research Triangle Foundation drew on the research of Steven Marcus of Columbia University. See below.

9. According to the undated notes of Kent Mullikin of the National Humanities Center, as early as 1968 fellows at the American Academy of Arts and Sciences Center for Advanced Study in the Behavioral Sciences began discussing the desirability of a similar institution for the humanities. In the fall of 1972, preliminary planning began, and then in early 1974 a formal planning office was opened at Columbia University.

10. On April 30, 1976, in a memorandum to the TUCASI board of trustees, Caldwell wrote that "our full name, 'Triangle Universities Center for Advanced Studies, Inc.' is quite a mouthful and also that our hastily projected acronym, 'TUCASI,' has an awkward character." He proposed using the acronym 'CAS' for the Center for Advanced Studies or 'CASI' to emphasize its incorporation, but the records do not show that this recommendation ever gained attention.

11. As well as the institutions themselves, there were important off-campus activities that demonstrated the ability and desire of the three universities to collaborate. Two such activities sponsored through TUCASI's financial support were the Triangle Universities Libraries Network (TULN)

and the Triangle Universities Licensing Consortium (TULCO). The library network project began in the mid-1970s, and in 1979 a consortium was created to combine the library holding of the three universities in a common computer database (Hammer, Siler, George and Associates 1999). In 1986, TUCASI extended the U. S. Department of Education's original support of this undertaking with $3.5 million (Little 2000a). Also in 1986, TULCO was created as a marketing/licensing organization governed by the three universities to coordinate the licensing of university-owned intellectual property to industry. Until 1993 it was funded by a $1.8 million grant from the Research Triangle Foundation through TUCASI.

12. The North Carolina Research and Education Network (NCREN) is a private telecommunications network connecting eighteen university sites in the state. See Internet site http://www.ncren.org for additional information.

13. The North Carolina Supercomputing Center (NCSC) is discussed in Chapter 10.

CHAPTER 9 *National Humanities Center*

1. See Internet site http://www.nch.rtp.nc.us.

2. The American Academy of Arts and Sciences was founded in 1780 by John Adams, James Bowdoin, John Hancock, and other leaders of the nation at that time to "cultivate every art and science which may tend to advance the interest, honor, dignity, and happiness of a free, independent, and virtuous people" (Internet site http://www.amacad.org).

3. The American Council of Learned Societies was established in 1919 to represent the United States within the International Union of Academies (IUA). The IUA was established to encourage cooperation in the advancement of studies through collaborative research and publications (Internet site http://www.acls.org).

4. The academy and the committee were familiar with the Center for Advanced Study in the Behavioral Sciences at Stanford University and the Institute for Advanced Study at Princeton (Miller 1979), so its planning did not begin from scratch. The National Humanities Center is now a member of a consortium with these two institutes and with three distinguished European centers for advanced study in Berlin, Uppsala, and the Netherlands. Over the years, the center has served as a model for some of the more than 200 humanities centers that have been founded on college and university campuses.

5. Those involved in preparing a proposal to submit for the National Humanities Center were E. Walton Jones, vice president of research and public service in the General Administration of the University of North Carolina, C. Hugh Holman, professor of English and former provost of the University of North Carolina at Chapel Hill, Bill Little, professor of chemistry and vice chancellor for Development and Public Service at the University of

North Carolina at Chapel Hill, Claude McKinney, dean of the School of Design at North Carolina State University, Sam Tove, professor of biochemistry and chairman of the faculty at North Carolina State University, and George Pearsall, professor of engineering and former dean of Engineering at Duke University.

6. Contributions ranged from $7,500 to $225,000. Some of the major contributors were American Telephone and Telegraph, William R. Kenan, Jr., Charitable Trust, Research Triangle Foundation of North Carolina, Z. Smith Reynolds Foundation, and the State of North Carolina.

7. The theme of *A Generosity of Spirit* was that individuals committed themselves to the creating and then to the success of the Park because it was good for the state, in general, and the three sister universities, in particular. One should be struck by Holman's understanding of how the proposed National Institute for the Humanities could have similar wide-ranging benefits.

8. According to Connor (2000), "These scholars have also helped design and lead the Center's vigorous efforts to strengthen teaching in both schools and colleges. Several hundred high school teachers have participated in the Center's summer programs, as have college teachers in the Jesse Ball DuPont summer seminars. An interactive, web based curriculum enrichment service called TeacherServe® has won awards for excellence."

CHAPTER 10 *MCNC*

1. This background material comes from Lindsay (2000) and Little (2000b).
2. See Internet site http://www.governor.state.nc.us.
3. In the late 1970s, public funds had been given to North Carolina State University for a research center in solid state electronics. Governor Hunt realized the benefits associated with eventually centralizing North Carolina State's electronics efforts into the Park (Hart 1998).
4. Internet2 is a consortium of more than 170 universities working with government and industry to accelerate the development and use of the next generation of the Internet. See Internet site http://www.internet2.edu.
5. See Internet site http://www.ncni.org.
6. This section draws from Little (2000b).
7. See Internet site http://www.ncsc.org for a technical description.

CHAPTER 11 *North Carolina Biotechnology Center*

1. While most think of biotechnology as a relatively new application of science, the Sumerians brewed beer from living organisms in the 1750s B.C., and the Chinese used moldy soybean curds as an antibiotic to treat warts in the 500s B.C. And the so-called biotech industry has grown ever since, especially in North Carolina. See Internet site http://www.ncbiotech.org.

2. See Internet site http://www. ncbiotech.org.

3. In 1985, the center moved into rented quarters in the Park with a staff of six. In 1986, $1 million was legislated to plan for a permanent building in the Park. When occupied in 1992 at a cost of $6.55 million, almost equal amounts came from the North Carolina General Assembly, the U. S. Department of Agriculture, and the combination of Ciba-Geigy, the Research Triangle Foundation, and the center itself (Hamner 1998).

4. Hamner has been the president since 1988. The first president of the North Carolina Biotechnology Center was Richard J. Patterson (1984–1986).

5. See Internet site http://www.ncbiotech.org.

6. The center does not do research; rather it fosters research. See Internet site http://www.ncbiotech.org.

CHAPTER 12 *Sigma Xi*

1. For a complete history, see Sokal (1986). This brief background description of the organization draws directly from that reference.

2. The chapter at the University of North Carolina at Chapel Hill was the first Sigma Xi chapter in the Southeast.

3. This chapter was founded by Nobel Laureate George H. Hitchings and Bill Little.

4. This section draws from Ferguson (1998) and Keever (1998).

5. Also on this committee were Mary Nijhout from Duke University and Raymond Fornes of North Carolina State University, along with the three chapter presidents: A. G. Turner from the University of North Carolina at Chapel Hill, Richard A. Palmer from Duke University, and E. J. Kamprath from North Carolina State University (Little 1998).

CHAPTER 13 *National Institute of Statistical Sciences*

1. This report was authored by Ingram Olkin, professor of statistics at Stanford University, and Jerome Sacks, professor of mathematics at Northwestern University and later founding director of the National Institute of Statistical Sciences.

2. See Internet site http://www.niss.org.

3. In July 2000, Alan F. Karr, former associate director of NISS and before that professor of mathematical sciences and associate dean of the School of Engineering at Johns Hopkins University, was named director.

4. See Internet site http://www.niss.org.

CHAPTER 14 *Burroughs Welcome Fund*

1. This section draws from Internet site http://www.bwfund.org.

1. Appendix J contains a list of all organizations listed on the wall of Park Plaza, the commemorative park commissioned as part of the Park's fortieth anniversary celebration. Also, a complete listing of the companies and organizations in the Park is at Internet site http://www.rtp.org.

BIBLIOGRAPHY

All correspondence and news articles cited in the text but not listed here are located in the Research Triangle Foundation archives. Also, unless otherwise stated, all interviews were conducted by the author.

Association of University Related Research Parks. 1998. *Worldwide Research & Science Park Directory 1998*. Nashville, Tenn. BPI Communications.

Aycock, Elizabeth J. 1991–2000. Telephone and personal interviews at Research Triangle Foundation, Research Triangle Park, N.C.

Blatecky, Alan R. 2000. June 27 electronic mail to Albert N. Link.

Bond, Enriqueta C. 2000. October 10 electronic mail to Albert N. Link.

Burke, Steven. 1998. July 9 interview at North Carolina Biotechnology Center, Research Triangle Park, N.C.

Caldwell, John T. 1979. January 16 letter to Archie K. Davis.

———. 1982. "A Summary Review of TUCASI's Development and Activities, 1974–1982." Mimeographed report.

Committee of 13. 1975. "A Proposal to the Research Triangle Foundation." Mimeographed report.

Connor, W. Robert. 1998. October 5 interview at National Humanities Center, Research Triangle Park, N.C.

———. 2000. December 7 letter to Albert N. Link.

Dardess, Margaret B. 1998. November 11 interview by telephone.

Davis, Archie K. 1975. Letters to potential contributors to the National Humanities Center.

———. 1992. March 4 interview at Davis's home, Winston-Salem, N.C.

Daugherty, Richard L. 1998. October 26 interview at North Carolina State University, Raleigh, N.C.

——— 1999–2000. Electronic mail to Albert N. Link.

Ferguson, Evan. 1998. July 28 interview at Sigma Xi, Research Triangle Park, N.C.

Frankel, Charles. 1980. "Research Triangle Park—Leaders," in *North Carolina's Research Triangle*, Chapel Hill: The Chapel Hill Newspaper.

Friday, William C. 1993. March 29 interview at the Kenan Center, University of North Carolina at Chapel Hill, Chapel Hill, N.C.

———2000. October 4 interview by telephone.

Hammer, Siler, George Associates. 1999. "The Research Triangle Park: The First Forty Years." Silver Springs, Md.: Hammer, Siler, George Associates.

Hamner, Charles E. 1998. July 9 interview at North Carolina Biotechnology Center, Research Triangle Park, N.C.

Hart, Frank D. 1998. November 9 interview at Governors Inn, Research Triangle Park, N.C.

Hobbs, Marcus E. 1982. "The Research Triangle of North Carolina: An Example of University, Corporate, and Government Working Together for the Common Good." Paper presented at Florida State University, March 5–6.

Keever, J. Renee. 1998. July 28 interview at Sigma Xi, Research Triangle Park, N.C.

Larrabee, Charles X. 1992. *Many Missions: Research Triangle Institute's First 31 Years*, Research Triangle Park: Research Triangle Institute.

Lindsey, Quentin. 2000. August 18 interview by telephone.

Link, Albert N. 1995. *A Generosity of Spirit: The Early History of the Research Triangle Park*. Research Triangle Park: The Research Triangle Foundation of North Carolina.

Little, William F. 1957. February 20, 1957, letter to George L. Simpson.

———. 1989. "The Research Triangle Park of North Carolina." Paper presented at the Corporation Associates of Pacific Basin Societies, Honolulu, Hawaii, December 19.

———. 1993. October 6 interview at the University of North Carolina at Chapel Hill, Chapel Hill, N.C.

———. 1998–2000a, 2001. Interviews at Research Triangle Foundation, Research Triangle Park, N.C., and by telephone and electronic mail correspondence.

———. 2000b. "Thoughts on TUCASI and Other Organizations." Mimeographed paper.

Malone, Thomas F. 1989. April 20 letter to James O. Roberson.

MCNC. 1985. "Annual Report." Research Triangle Park: Microelectronics Center of North Carolina.

Miller, Nory. 1979. "Monastic Retreat for Secular Scholarship." *AIA Journal*, May: 1–9.

Mullikin, Kent R. 1998. "History of National Humanities Center." Mimeographed page.

Research Triangle Park. 1999. *North Carolina's Research Triangle Park: An Investment in the Future*. Video prepared by the Research Triangle Foundation of North Carolina.

Research Triangle Regional Planning Commission. 1960. Guides for the Research Triangle of North Carolina. Research Triangle Park: Research Triangle Regional Planning Commission.

Roberson, James O. 1989. March 27 memorandum to William F. Little and others.

———. 1999. June 18 electronic mail to Albert N. Link.

———. 2000. November 10 electronic mail to Albert N. Link.

Solomon, Daniel L. 2000. July 19 interview by telephone.

Sigma Xi. 1997. "1997 Annual Report." Research Triangle Park: Sigma Xi.

Simpson, George L. 1988. "Comments on the Research Triangle of North Carolina." Mimeographed article.

Stephens, Louis C., Jr. 2000. October 10 interview by telephone.

Stewart, Pearson H. 1961. "Research Triangle Region Population Estimates 1970–1980." Mimeographed report.

———. 2000. October 4 interview by telephone.

Sokel, Michael M. 1986. "Companions in Zealous Research, 1886–1986. *American Scientist*, October: 486–509.

Teer, Robert D. 2000. August 11 electronic mail to Albert N. Link.

Voss, John. 1996. Quoted from Mullikin (1998).

INDEX

American Association of Textile
  Chemists and Colorists
  ground breaking for, 25, 27f
  on map of 1965, 15, 16f–17f
American Chemical Society
  accreditation by, 128
  meetings of, 133
American Council of Learned Societies
  establishment of, 250n 3
  National Humanities Center planning
  meeting at, 82
American Scientist, 108
American Statistical Association, 109
American Telephone and Telegraph,
  National Humanities Center funding
  from, 251n 6
"An Act to Authorize Counties to Estab-
  lish Research and Production Service
  Districts" (House Bill 926), 24
Ann Arbor, Michigan, potential Sigma Xi
  office relocation to, 104, 105
Anniversary celebrations, fortieth
  (1999), 33–34, 50, 51, 247n 1
Archie K. Davis Awards Luncheon
  (1999), 33
Archie K. Davis Building, 74, 86, 89f
Architectural exhibits and buildings of
  interest, 154–55
Arnold, Matthew, on growth, 9
Art galleries, 60, 153, 202–3
Asian studies, in TUCASI, 66
Association of University Related Research Parks, *Worldwide Research &
  Science Park Directory,* 56–60, 57t–60t
Atlanta, Georgia, potential Sigma Xi
  office relocation to, 104, 105
AURRP (Association of University Related Research Parks), *Worldwide Research & Science Park Directory,* 56–60,
  57t–60t
Aycock, Elizabeth J.
  acknowledgment of, xiii
  advertising Park from 1959 to 1965, 5
  on early years, 7
  on growth of Research Triangle Park, 9
  at National Humanities Center
  ground breaking, 88f

on Research Triangle Institute, 53
Research Triangle Park Committee,
  Inc. and, 3
on success of Research Triangle Park,
  36, 53, 60–61
on Triangle Service Center, 43
on TUCASI, 78

Babbage Institute, 74
Ballentine, Bruce, Little contact with,
  245n 7
BASF, 102
Basketball teams, 156
Battelle, as Triangle Service Center ten-
  ant, 247n 4
Bayer Biological Products, 116
BD Technologies, 117
Beaunit Corporation, 116
  land purchase by, 15
  map of (1965), 15, 16f–17f
Bennett, William J., as National Human-
  ities Center director, 86
Bevan, William, on TUCASI board,
  249n 4
Biogen, 102, 116
Biotechnology. *See* North Carolina
  Biotechnology Center
Blatecky, Alan, on Microelectronics Cen-
  ter, 95–96
Blitzer, Charles, as National Humanities
  Center director, 86
Bloomfield, Morton W., 71, 81–82
  at National Humanities Center
  ground breaking, 87f, 88f
Bolin Creek, 216
Bond, Enriqueta C., on Burroughs Well-
  come Fund, 114
Book clubs, 154
Boorstin, Daniel, at National Humanities
  Center ground breaking, 87f
Bowdoin, James, as American Academy
  of Arts and Sciences founder, 250n 2
Bowman Gray Medical School, 155
Briggs, James E., on Research Triangle
  Regional Planning Commission, 206
Broad, Molly Corbett, on success of Re-
  search Triangle Park, 51, 53

labor force of (1950 and 1959), 190
population of (1950 and 1958), 189
See also Duke University; Durham
Durham Theatre Guild, 153

Easements, purchase of, 229
East Asian Center, 66
Eberhardt, Allen, 52f
Economy
    Research Triangle Park influence on,
        33–34, 37–40, 38f, 39f, 55–56
    status of
        1930 to 1960, 21–22, 21f
        1960, 212
Education
    continuing
        on electronics, 137
        on engineering, 151
        on forestry, 163
        on pharmaceutical science, 122
    leadership in, 60–61
    private, 196
    public, 155, 195
        Burroughs Wellcome Fund contri-
            butions to, 114
        in corridor development scheme,
            224
    university
        in chemistry, 127–34
        in electronics, 135–42
        in engineering, 143–58
        in forestry and forest products,
            159–66
        in non-Western studies, 66
        in pharmaceutical science, 121–25
    See also specific institutions
Electrical engineering, research resources
    for, brochure on, 135–42, 143–58
Electricity services (1958), 192
Electron microscopy center, 68
Electronic News, on semiconductor in-
    dustry, 92
Electronics, research resources for,
    brochure on, 135–42
Elion, Gertrude B., 117, 118f
Elizabeth City, financial support from,
    40

Ella Lyman Cabot Trust, National Hu-
    manities Center grant from, 82
Employment, statistics for, growth meas-
    urement by, 28, 30f, 31
Engineering, research resources for,
        brochure on, 143–58
    electronic, 135–42
*Engineering Resources for Industrial Re-
    search in The Research Triangle of North
    Carolina,* 143–58
Enlow, William, 206
Equipment
    for chemical research, 132
    for engineering research, 147–49
    See also Computers
Ervin, Sam, Jr., on Chemstrand, 246n 7
Evans, E. J., 206

Fadum, R. E., in TUCASI planning,
    248n 3, 249n 5
Fair, Richard, as Microelectronics Center
    vice president, 96
Ferguson, Evan, on Sigma Xi, 108
Football teams, 156
Fordham, Christopher, at Microelectron-
    ics Center dedication, 95
Forest Theater, 153
Forestry and forest products, research
    resources for, brochure on, 159–66
Forestry Sciences Laboratory, on 1965
    map, 15, 16f–17f
Fornes, Raymond, 252n 5
Forrestal Center, Princeton University,
    New Jersey, vs. other research parks,
    58t, 61
Foundation. *See* Research Triangle Foun-
    dation of North Carolina
Frankel, Charles, National Humanities
    Center and
    as director, 86
    at ground breaking, 87f, 88f
    at planning meeting, 82
    site selection, 83
Franklin, John Hope
    at Archie K. Davis Building dedica-
        tion, 89f
    at National Humanities Center, 86